Wall Street Ventures & Adventures Through Forty Years

Richard D. Wyckoff

Traders Press, Inc.
PO Box 6206
Greenville, SC 29606

Serving Traders Since 1975

http://www.traderspress.com

Originally published in 1930
by Richard D. Wyckoff

ISBN: 0-934380-13-9

Traders Press, Inc.
PO Box 6206
Greenville, SC 29606

Serving Traders Since 1975

http://www.traderspress.com

CONTENTS

CONTENTS

CONTENTS

CONTENTS

CONTENTS

ILLUSTRATIONS

ILLUSTRATIONS

Publisher's Foreword

Richard D. Wyckoff, widely known as founder and publisher of the Magazine of Wall Street and author of a legendary stock market trading course, led a Wall Street career which was truly an adventure. In this classic work he brings this adventure alive for us again as he takes us on a nostalgic trip through Wall Street history. Wyckoff personally knew many traders of his time who became legendary, such as Jesse Livermore, James Keene, Jay Gould, Edward Harriman, J P Morgan, and others. In this book, he recalls their trading methods and campaigns. A wise trader realizes how much can be learned from those who have gone before and who have spent years learning how to cope with the vagaries of the marketplace and to operate profitably in an environment that appears chaotic to the average investor. Wyckoff spent much of his life studying the market , and through conversations with many of the successful traders of his time, such as the aforementioned, he developed his own trading methodology which concentrates on price and volume analysis, and which is the basis for his well known trading course. Enjoy your trip back through the annals of market history in this fascinating autobiography by a Wall Street legend.

Edward D. Dobson
President, Traders Press, Inc.
Greenville, SC
July, 2004

Published by Traders Press, Inc.®

7 Secrets Every Commodity Trader Needs to Know (Mound)
A Complete Guide to Trading Profits (Paris)
A Professional Look at S&P Day Trading (Trivette)
A Treasury of Wall Street Wisdom (Editors: Schultz & Coslow)
Ask Mr. EasyLanguage (Tennis)
Beginner's Guide to Computer Assisted Trading (Alexander)
Channels and Cycles: A Tribute to J.M. Hurst (Millard)
Chart Reading for Professional Traders (Jenkins)
Commodity Spreads: Analysis, Selection and Trading Techniques (Smith)
Comparison of Twelve Technical Trading Systems (Lukac, Brorsen, & Irwin)
Complete Stock Market Trading and Forecasting Course (Jenkins)
Cyclic Analysis (J.M. Hurst)
Dynamic Trading (Miner)
Essentials of Trading: It's Not What You Think It's How You Think (Pesavento & Jouflas)
Exceptional Trading: The Mind Game (Roosevelt)
Fibonacci Ratios with Pattern Recognition (Pesavento)
Futures Spread Trading: The Complete Guide (Smith)
Geometry of Markets (Gilmore)
Geometry of Stock Market Profits (Jenkins)
Harmonic Vibrations (Pesavento)
How to Trade in Stocks (Livermore & Smitten)
Hurst Cycles Course (J.M. Hurst)
Investing by the Stars (Weingarten)
Investor Skills Training: Managing Emotions and Risk in the Market (Ronin)
It's Your Option (Zelkin)
Magic of Moving Averages (Lowry)
Market Rap: The Odyssey of a Still-Struggling Commodity Trader (Collins)
Market Beaters (Collins)
Overcoming 7 Deadly Sins of Trading (Roosevelt)
Planetary Harmonics of Speculative Markets (Pesavento)
Point & Figure Charting (Aby)
Point & Figure Charting: Commodity and Stock Trading Techniques (Zieg)
Private Thoughts From a Trader's Diary (Pesavento & MacKay)
Profitable Patterns for Stock Trading (Pesavento)
RoadMap to the Markets (Busby)
RSI: The Complete Guide (Hayden)
Short-Term Trading with Price Patterns (Harris)
Single Stock Futures: The Complete Guide (Greenberg)
Stock Patterns for Day Trading (2 volumes) (Rudd)
Stock Trading Techniques Based on Price Patterns (Harris)
Technically Speaking (Wilkinson)
Technical Trading Systems for Commodities and Stocks (Patel)
The Amazing Life of Jesse Livermore: World's Greatest Stock Trader (Smitten)
The Handbook of Global Securities Operations (O'Connell & Steiniger)
The Opening Price Principle: The Best Kept Secret on Wall Street (Pesavento & MacKay)
The Professional Commodity Trader (Kroll)
The Taylor Trading Technique (Taylor)
*The Trading Rule That Can Make You Rich** (Dobson)
Top Traders Under Fire (Collins)
Trading Secrets of the Inner Circle (Goodwin)
Trading S&P Futures and Options (Lloyd)
Twelve Habitudes of Highly Successful Traders (Roosevelt)
Understanding Bollinger Bands (Dobson)
Understanding Eminis: Trading to Win (Williams)
Understanding Fibonacci Numbers (Dobson)
Viewpoints of a Commodity Trader (Longstreet)
Winning Edge 4 (Toghraie)
Winning Market Systems (Appel)

FOREWORD

In a poorly lighted room a youth sat in deep thought. With bowed head and weary eyes, he filled page after page full of computations, only to push them away from him and stare at the bare walls of his room. About him on the table, on the floor, were papers, pamphlets and volumes of statistics. A bundle of daily market reports jostled his elbow, but his mind was no longer in the little room. The Stock Exchange, Wall Street, railroads, great industries, the stock market, obsessed his mind.

Could he solve the riddle of the stock market? That was the problem. Others had done it. A long line of great operators marched through his thought. Why should he not find the secret of their success?

No Aladdin with his wonderful lamp ever felt more magic in his task. If he could solve his problem, he saw his meager job fading behind him, and capital, his own small capital, growing like a mountain. At six per cent per annum it would double in a dozen years. But if he could make it earn twenty, thirty, fifty per cent! And suppose the multiplied amount grew at the same swift rate!!

But how was all this to be done? He knew little about the gigantic problem. Then he must learn. All his spare time and thought must be concentrated upon his task. No amount of work or study should discourage him. He would overcome every obstacle.

It might take months to make a beginning. He might be years achieving his goal. But what was the effort compared to the game?

FOREWORD

In his little room, far into the night, the youth sat in deep thought. But he knew he was on the right road. Study, effort, patient endeavor, with these he was bound to be successful.

1888 AT THE OPENING

THAT FIRST JOB—A WALL STREET RUNNER—A LITTLE BROKERAGE HOUSE AND ITS CLIENTS

As an infant, I was "expected" about October 1, 1873, but I must have decided, after considering the matter, that this date would be a most unpropitious one on which to be born.

There was a panic in Wall Street.

The great banking house of Jay Cook & Co. had failed. The Stock Exchange was closed. Jay Gould, bear raider and wrecker, was spreading rumors of more and greater calamities.

I probably suspected that my father was long of the stock market, on margin, and that my arrival at this time would only add to the general excitement. So, while my outfit was all ready and my nurse was on the job, I hesitated.

Expecting a Wall Street career, I saw no advantage in making my initial bow, or my opening bawl, when the Stock Exchange was closed! So I deliberately postponed my arrival until November 2. By that time the Stock Exchange had reopened, the panic was over.

* * *

Graduating from a Brooklyn public school when fourteen, I polished off my education with a post-graduate course of one day in high school; then started on a law course at three dollars a week with a firm that needed an office boy.

But the fly in that ointment was a cousin who was making four dollars a week. He didn't appear to know any more than I did. Why should his salary be four and mine only three? I couldn't stand that at all, especially as I had just passed my fifteenth birthday. So I began to hustle for an opening that would yield four or better. I landed one.

It is rather a good idea to start Wall Street operations in short pants, as I did. You are not risking losing so much as the other fellows.

Monday morning, December 10, 1888, found me employed as stock runner by the firm of Hazard & Parker, members of the New York Stock Exchange. Mr. Parker had a big, tall fellow there waiting for me. His name was Neal and he was about the size of a cop. It was his job to break me in.

How it did rain that day! Neal and I trudged around, delivering stock, certifying checks, making deposits and comparisons, until we looked like a pair of well-swum muskrats.

Of course, Neal was doing everything. He explained as we went along. What these paper things were that we kept poking into the little wickets and why the men concealed behind the partitions should pass out checks amounting to thousands of dollars in return for these papers was hard to understand. But this went on until we had a whole flock of checks together, amounting to not far from $100,000. This staggering sum we took to the receiving teller at the Fourth National Bank—he with the curled mustache and the fiercely surprised red hair and eyebrows.

We did this for three days, after which I was held to

be "broken in." I now started to do these marvelous things all by myself, and to feel a real—if small—part of the Wall Street machinery.

How much finer it was to be a runner in Wall Street than an office boy in a law office! But that was not all. Mr. Parker was paying me the munificent salary of twenty dollars a month! That four-dollar cousin was licked!

When the end of the week came and no salary was forthcoming, I couldn't understand it at all. Monday morning I plucked up courage and asked the boss whether they paid "their employees" (I was the only one) by the week or the month.

"You can have it any way you like," replied Mr. Parker. Then taking a pencil and paper he figured: "If you want it by the week it will be four dollars and sixty-one cents for twenty-six weeks and four dollars and sixty-two cents for the other twenty-six."

I had figured roughly that twenty dollars a month made five dollars a week. But I was glad to get the four-sixty-odd.

* * *

The Mills Building, in which Hazard & Parker had their offices, was the Wall Street architectural wonder of its day. It was surrounded by rat-traps of only three or four stories and was overtopped only by such buildings as the Produce Exchange Tower, the Boreel Building, at 111 Broadway, some thirteen stories I'll have you know, and the old eleven-story Equitable Building, from the roof of which I used to be able to gaze all over the city. Henry Clews & Co. and H. P. Goldschmidt & Co. were on the ground floor. On our floor, two flights up, were John Bloodgood & Co., Post & Flagg (then a very small concern), de Neufville & Co., Noble & Mestre, and Joseph Walker & Sons; and on the floor below, I. & S. Wormser, J. & W. Seligman & Co., and Chas. Head & Co.

Across Exchange Place were Whitehouse & Co. on the corner at 25 Broad, and in the same building Chauncey & Gwynne Bros. Hallgarten & Co. was across the street at 28 Broad. Spencer Trask & Co. occupied a floor of the Western Union Building, at No. 16, a narrow brick structure with elevators like squirrel cages.

On the corner of Wall and Broad stood Drexel, Morgan & Co.'s white marble office building. J. B. Colgate & Co. and C. I. Hudson & Co. were at 36 Wall; A. M. Kidder & Co. at No. 18, as also were Buttrick & Elliman; Zimmerman & Foshay were on the corner at No. 11. E. & C. Randolph were in Nassau Street, at No. 7.

Harriman & Co. had offices in the old Equitable Building at 120 Broadway. Dominick & Dickerman were in 74 Broadway, Fellowes Davis & Co. in No. 70, and R. P. Flower in No. 52, across the street. In the old Exchange Court Building at 56 Broadway were H. L. Horton & Co. and Jones, Kennett & Hopkins. Some old barnlike structures on the south side of Exchange Place housed Ladenberg, Thalmann & Co. and Wassermann Bros.

Runners not only had to know the addresses of these firms and of all the others in the Stock Exchange Directory, but also must be familiar with the short cuts, from Broad Street to Broadway, or from Wall to Pine, Exchange to Beaver, etc., etc. We also must know what floor every firm was on, and which way to turn after we got out of the elevator—when there was any.

A visitor to our office, after a slow two-floor elevator ascension, stepped around the corner of the hall into Room Five. He found himself in a three-by-six vestibule

Copyright Brown Brothers

1863. *Gold Exchange Which Adjoined the Stock Exchange*

walled by low walnut partitions, in which were a couple of wickets. Inside there were a high desk about eight feet long, a tall safe, and, between the windows, a ticker. Two rocking-chairs such as you find on summer boarding-house porches, a double desk, a water cooler, a washstand, a few coat hooks completed the furnishings. That's all there was to the outfit except the new office boy, who was supposed to get there at nine-thirty. Unless there was much business —and that was seldom—his hour of escape was four.

Both my employers, Hazard and Parker, had been connected with the pre-Civil War firm of Vermilye & Co.; Hazard as cashier and Parker as government bond man. Parker still bore an atmosphere of Eli Yale's New Haven institution. Both were fine fellows; they had splendid reputations, good connections, some money and a knowledge of the brokerage business.

Parker used to sit in one of the high-backed wooden-and-wicker porch rockers, oscillating it violently when the market was active; when things were dull, he watched the tape with his feet up on the basket, and sang "Little Annie Rooney" or "A Bicycle Built for Two."

He used to trade in a couple of hundred shares at a time for himself. He liked Atchison—both on the long and on the short side. But he traded in other stocks that were selling as high as $100 a share—although there weren't so many of those on the Stock Exchange list.

Hazard spent his day on the floor of the New York Stock Exchange, where his membership was then worth about $20,000. His specialty was trading in "RT," which was then the tape abbreviation for Richmond Terminal, since reorganized into Southern Railway; and also in Nickel Plate, then selling in its 'teens. I always thought he chose these two as his pampered pets because a move of an eighth was a thrill and a quarter point a sensation.

Another specialty of the firm was "washing" Buffalo, Rochester & Pittsburgh. We would sell 100 shares to a certain firm, which would, in a day or two, sell them back to us. This process continued for some years, thus creating most of the transactions that occurred in the "pup," as a low-priced inactive stock is dubbed in Wall Street. Some one must have had a bunch of that stock in a loan somewhere and a desire to see a quotation every Tuesday and Thursday so it would have value as collateral with the banks. I think it was Stock Certificate No. 13 or No. 23, which monotonously used to bob into the office with a sales ticket pinned to it. A little later, out it would go with our sales ticket, and four more pin punctures in the poor old picture, which looked as though it had been riddled with bird shot. However, Vanderbilt, or whoever was responsible for all those "wash sales," seemed satisfied.

Many of the clients of Hazard & Parker were losing money at this time, but the majority could afford it. Investors could easily be distinguished from the speculators. One of the most active of the latter was a tall, lanky individual with a long, thin nose, and a habit of walking with his left shoulder ahead of the other one so that he sidled into our door like a crab. He sloshed around in stocks and managed to lose money rather fluently, being adept at picking the wrong stocks at the right time and the right stocks at the wrong time.

Then there was Mr. G——, who, if still living, must be approaching one hundred. He was a bit parsimonious. His derby hat, originally black, was turning green; its ribbon was bedraggled. His clothes were shabby, dusty, ill-fitting, spotted, and as if about to disintegrate. His eye-glasses were fastened to the buttonhole in his lapel by a piece of Indian twine. His trousers seemed always about to depart from him. He specialized in the highest grade bonds; he ground his teeth together and held his lips so tightly that you could almost imagine him grubbing for pennies to buy each $1,000 unit. He talked about his bonds as though they were his pet babies, and his mouth would then water till he almost drooled. No one knew how many of these gilt-edge securities he had in his safe deposit box.

Another client was Albert G. Jennings, the venerable lace manufacturer from Brooklyn—a fine, snowy-haired old fellow with a pink complexion and a fatherly attitude toward the office force. He used to buy rafts of bonds. Sometimes there was doubt about their paying interest, too. He did not speculate in stocks; that was left to his son, Oliver, a handsome young fellow who liked to plunge. His father said, "Well, he's got to learn by experience."

Then there was Paola La Villa who used to do more talking and less security-buying than any other client. He always knew more about railroad statistics than his audience. But I landed him once on the rate of dividend paid by New York Central at the time and he lost a dinner to me. I had just looked up the rate and knew I was right.

Tall, broad-shouldered Mr. Crittenden, who carried a thicket of beard and a bustling behavior, was another client. Once he had opened an account at Vermilye & Co.'s, with a Reading Third Income Bond, at that time worth $300, and with it he had pyramided and pyramided until at one time the account was worth over $250,000. But he wouldn't take that profit. He wanted a million.

And now he was breezing in and out of our place with only a few low-priced bonds and an odd lot of stock to his name.

These clients amused, interested and instructed me. I've seen many, many thousands like them since, but few have remained more sharply outlined in my memory.

* * *

1889 OLD TIME WALL STREET

ANTIQUATED BUILDINGS—RUSSELL SAGE BOMBED—FIRST STEEL BUILDING—VOLUME OF TRADING—TOY BANKS—JAY GOULD AND HIS TRICKS

THOSE who know only the Wall Street of today have no idea of the vast changes in its physical aspect since 1888. The typical building in those days was only three or four stories in height, brick, brownstone or wood, often cement-covered. The floors and most of the stairways were of wood. All down through Wall, Broad and New streets, Broadway and Exchange Place, to say nothing of Nassau, Pine and William, these low, dingy structures stood with most of the windows marked by signs of bankers and brokers. There were a few slow-moving elevators, but it was much quicker to skip up, two at a time, the worn, hollow, wooden steps, and to clatter down the same way.

Where the Empire Building now stands, at 71 Broadway, the Manhattan Elevated Railway owned what was then known as The Arcade, which ran through to the elevated station. The "L" Railroad Company had its office in this building; as did the Union Trust Company and Russell Sage.[1]

[1] One day an anarchist named Norcross went in to Sage's office with a dynamite bomb in his satchel, and under a threat demanded a million dollars from the aged financier. Not getting it, he dropped the bomb, which blew his own head off, and knocked Uncle Russell into a corner. When I ran around to see what the explosion was, they were carrying the old man across Broadway to the drug store.

An old building at No. 50 in lower Broadway was torn down soon after I went to work in Wall Street. It was replaced by a structure that could be regarded only as queer in comparison with its contemporaries. It seemed to be constructed of steel beams that were naked on the inside. With the exception of the window, door and partition frames, nothing apparently was combustible about it. That was the first steel frame building ever erected anywhere in the world and was the father of all the present-day skyscrapers. In 1914 it was torn down and an Arcade erected in its place. In 1926 the Arcade was replaced by a thirty-five story building.

The size of the stock market at that time and the scope of financial operations are shown by financial reviews published January 1, 1889. The entire list of the year's transactions, set out in tabular form in the New York *Herald,* took up less than one two-inch full column. During the year 1888 the largest volume of transactions in one day was of 573,000 shares, and the smallest, regular session, of 36,000 shares. In one session only $625,000 worth of railroad bonds was dealt in. But during the first day of the blizzard of March, '88, only thirty-two brokers appeared on the floor and only 15,800 shares were dealt in. The next day was only a half session, on account of weather conditions, and 2,075 shares were bought and sold during the two hours.

The *Financial Chronicle* stated that: "In the spring Western railroad officials started to cover their shorts in the stock market and a smart rally ensued." The Little Wizard (Jay Gould) had defaulted on International and Great Northern first mortgage bonds and "this created

---

It looked as if the entire contents of the office had been blown out the window all over the graves in Trinity churchyard.

widespread distrust of American railway securities in Europe," the *Chronicle* went on to say, "and London operators began selling the market. Deacon White, Russell Sage and Washington Conner—all the magnates of the board rooms—presently began to issue bullish pronunciamentoes, but the tariff agitation depressed business; iron broke, crop prospects were not improving, gold was going out, and the Granger roads were obviously in bad form. Naturally stocks were heavy and June opened with markets dull, duller, dullest. Missouri Pacific took a further tumble of $11 per share in one day on the reduction of its dividend to a 4 per cent basis."

The "Wizard's" gang had continued to say of Missouri Pacific "earning 14 per cent and paying 7" right up to the time Gould abruptly cut the dividend. No doubt he wanted to cover his shorts.

Shipments of ore from Lake Superior mines to furnaces in Pennsylvania and New York were 275,000 tons.

Loans and discounts of New York City banks amounted to $356,540,009. Deposits were only $3,000,000 more than this. Surplus reserve of all the New York City banks combined amounted to only $8,500,000.

Total transactions on the New York Stock Exchange were 62,000,000 shares, an average of a little over 200,000 a day, or 700 shares a minute. The ticker was often silent for minutes at a time. Reading, the most active stock, changed hands to the extent of 6,000,000 full shares, averaging 20,000 shares a day. The year's extreme fluctuations on that stock were confined to a range of about 18 points. And this was the market leader!

Chesapeake & Ohio sold at 1 and closed the year at 2. Lake Shore was selling at 85; Louisville & Nashville, 50; Michigan Central, 72; Central of New Jersey, 74; New

York Central, 103; New Haven, 243; Nickel Plate, 13; Norfolk & Western, 15; Northern Pacific, 20; Southern Pacific, 24; Union Pacific, 48; Wabash, 12.

In 1888 the Chemical National Bank, because it had continued specie payments all through the Civil War, was regarded as the strongest New York financial institution. It had a paid-up capital of $300,000 and a surplus of $5,000,000.

The First National was a close second, with $500,000 capital and $5,000,000 surplus.

The Chase National had $500,000 capital and $400,000 surplus; (mark this) undivided profits were $43,805!

The American Exchange National Bank and the National Bank of Commerce had the largest paid-up capital, amounting to $5,000,000 for each, but none had greater surpluses than the Chemical and the First National.

The National City Bank had $1,000,000 capital, $1,000,000 surplus and $1,014,000 undivided profits. That bank and the National Bank of Commerce, with $1,215,000 undivided profits, were the only ones who could boast of as much as a million dollars in that column. Most of the banks had undivided profits of far less than one million; many of less than $100,000. Some had none. Others had neither surplus nor undivided profits.

* * *

Jay Gould's office boy, Gus Thomas, was one of my chums and the captain of my baseball team, and I was particularly interested in the way he handled those who came to see the great but not very scrupulous financier.

Gould's office was in the old Western Union Build-

Photo H. N. Tiemann Company

1863. *Brokers Outside the Gold Exchange*

ing, 195 Broadway, but the corridor door which bore his name opened into an empty closet, because too many people had tried to step in at that door and shoot him. The only way to get to him was through the Missouri Pacific transfer office, which was at the end of the hall in the front part of the building. This office contained a counter about four feet long where runners for brokerage houses handed in certificates of Missouri Pacific stock for transfer into other names. Behind this counter my chum Gus was on duty getting rid of most of the visitors. To one handing in a card Gus would say: "I am very sorry but Mr. Gould is at a meeting of the Missouri Pacific and I can't interrupt him." To the next: "Mr. Gould is in a conference and I think you better call tomorrow." To a third: "Mr. Gould is out of town today."

I asked him how he knew which lie to tell.

"Oh, you have to use your judgment about that," he replied.

On my way to the Wall Street ferry in the afternoon, I would sometimes see Jay Gould in the hall of the Mills Building as I went through the corridor leading to the 35 Wall Street exit. He was a small man, short, hiding behind a tremendous black beard and slinking along close to the marble wainscot like an alley cat, as though he expected some one would kick him as he went along.

"Lucky thing the mob didn't catch Jay Gould on Black Friday, eighteen seventy-three," Mr. Parker used to say from his seat in the rocker. "They were going to hang him to a telegraph pole for what he did that day, and they would have gotten him if Old Uncle Russell Sage hadn't hidden him under a boat down on Long Island and carried his meals there for three days."

1890 LEARNING THE RUDIMENTS

FERRY VOYAGES—GETTING GRUB—
STATISTICAL START—BARING PANIC—
BUCKET SHOPS—CONSOLIDATED EXCHANGE
—MORGAN'S—TOO MUCH CASH

IN THIS year I began to get a better idea of Wall Street routine and a few glimmerings of what it was all about. Every morning I walked five miles from my house in Bedford Avenue, Brooklyn, to the Montague Street ferry, where for two cents one could sail across the river. The voyage required seven minutes and was rather a social affair, the status of the passengers being indicated by the boat they were on. The ten-minutes-to-nine boat, for example, was patronized by the door-opening and furniture-dusting employee. The nine-o'clock carried a few of the higher order, and the 9:10 was laden with cashiers or stock clerks. As for the 9:20—well, that was quite a boat; it careened beneath the weight of the first delegation of bosses. But anyone who could boast of the 9:30 was either the Big Boss himself or the Stock Exchange partner. Much hobnobbing on the decks. "The situation" thoroughly hashed over; tips transmitted, orders collected from some of the early customers.

The Brooklyn Bridge, originally opened to "foot passengers" in 1883, soon boasted of cable cars. So at this time the edge was off the ferry stocks, although no one dreamed of a second bridge, to say nothing of a tunnel under the river.

As runner in a stock broker's office, I took pride not only in the speed with which I made deliveries, certifications, deposits and comparisons, but in remembering the location of every brokerage house. I was thus able to lay out a string of deliveries or comparisons in such a manner as to get me around without doubling on my tracks and in the shortest time possible.

There was no Stock Exchange Clearing House at the time. This was not established until the early 'nineties. All deliveries had to be made by messenger, between 10:00 A.M. and 2:15 P.M. The first three and a half hours of this period were gone about much as they are now; but from one-thirty on, there was a speeding up by the messengers until, for the last fifteen minutes, youths were rushing wild-eyed from one house to another to complete their deliveries before the last fifteen seconds of the delivery hour were ticked off on the old Gold and Stock tickers.

What amazed me was the value of the negotiable bonds and stock certificates entrusted to mere boys, mostly poor and uneducated, on meager salaries of from five to ten dollars a week. Many of these were messenger boys in uniform, hired at 30 cents an hour.

My jump in salary from $3 a week to $4.62 marked the end of the hip-pocket lunches, for my budget could now stand an appropriation of 5 cents a day for the midday meal. After skirmishing about the neighborhood to test the various lunch markets, I soon had six of them listed and ate at them in rotation. Every day I consulted my list, which told me where and what I was going to eat at noon.

There was the old, short, plump, gray-bearded lunch-stand keeper on the northwest corner of Wall and Nassau, diagonally across from J. P. Morgan's. My nickel meal at his little wooden stand consisted of a vanilla cake with white icing, and a glass of milk.

Where Schrafft now glitters on Broadway near Morris Street, there was then an eating emporium in the cellar, down the usual flight of wooden steps with thin iron railings. There my nickel would get me three butter cakes and a deluge of syrup.

On the southwest corner of Pine and Nassau, 'longside the old Continental National Bank, an ancient and sad-eyed pushcart keeper specialized in bananas. Some rather healthy-looking ones sold as high as two for five. But down at the other end he always had some small ones, their skins turned a deep brown, which sold for a cent each; five of these fitted perfectly under my belt at noontime.

Sometimes we were so busy at the office that Mr. Parker would say, "go out and get it." This sacramental phrase meant that lunch was to be eaten in the office, and that the firm paid for it. On such days I blew myself to two sandwiches and a piece of pie at an expense of fifteen cents.

The Big Bosses had a wider choice of eating places. There were no luncheon clubs as now, but Delmonico's ran through from Broad to New Street, and there an ordinary sandwich cost fifteen cents and a chicken sandwich a quarter. On New Street, next to the Stock Exchange, S. M. Robins even then had a reputation for a marvelous hot roast beef sandwich with mustard pickle.

But the big hangout for Stock Exchange members was Fred Eberlin's, down in the cellar at 8 New Street. Fred knew them all, rejoiced over their winnings and sympathized in their losses. Old-timers will recall the interest-

1870. *Lower Part of New York before the Mills Building Was Erected*

The Drexel Building, occupied by Drexel, Morgan & Company is on the left, and the Broad Street section of the Stock Exchange (with flagpole) is in the center. The roof of the New Street section is marked by three ventilators.

ing pictures that adorned Fred's walls and the rare expertness of those officiating behind the bar. Although not too young to appreciate the pictures, it was some years before I was initiated into the mysteries of the rare, potent and delicious mixture which he had baptized the Jack Rose.

One day Mr. Parker said to me: "Richard, if you are going to stay in this business, you ought to be studying up on these railroads—finding out how many miles long they are, where they run, who is managing them, and all about their earnings, and so on. You will find all that information in the *Commercial and Financial Chronicle* and *Poor's Manual.*"

That seemed to be a good idea. I pulled out the latest *Chronicle* supplement. Starting on the spot with Atchison, Topeka and Santa Fé, I began to read up on railroad and industrial earnings, balance sheets and other statistical data, a study which I have continued to a greater or less degree through most of the forty years.

* * *

The Baring panic, which came this year, was important enough to keep shivers down the Wall Street spine while it lasted; but in comparison with those which followed in 1893, 1901 and 1907, it was an opera-bouffe affair. It began with money stringency early in November, when the New York banks in their weekly statement showed a heavy deficiency below the 25 per cent reserve. Call loans ranged as high as 183 per cent per annum, which meant that the use of $10,000 cost the borrower $50 a day. Renewals ranged from 10 to 50 per cent during that week.

It is amusing to compare these with conditions prevailing as I write, when a change from 5 to 6 per cent in the call loan rate is sufficient to bring a decline in stocks.

Uneasiness prevailed not only in New York but in London. This was partly relieved abroad by the fact that the Bank of England was able to obtain a loan of £3,000,000 from the Bank of France! Still rumors of serious financial disasters persisted, and after a continuation of the liquidation that had been going on for several weeks, there came what contemporary financial publications described as "a general break in which prices tumbled with frightful rapidity; the bottom dropped completely out of the market."

Two firms failed—C. M. Whitney & Co. and Decker, Howell & Co. These precipitated other smaller failures. The Decker firm had been active in stock of properties controlled by Henry Villard, chief among which was North American Co. This stock declined in the panic from 34 to 7, but recovered to 11 "on a better understanding of the company's condition."

So much for the toy panic and the comparatively infinitesimal money and stock transactions of those days.

* * *

Ever hear how a certain old, famous hotel in downtown Brooklyn came to be built? The owner in his younger days went up against the bucket shops and after several sad experiences said to himself: "I see the game now, only I started on the wrong side of it." So he opened a bucket shop, made wads of money and built the hotel.

Wall Street was infested with bucket shops in 1889 and for many years afterward. The New York Stock Exchange had always fought these outfits bitterly. One day, driven to the last extremity in its endeavor to shake off the bucket shop, the Stock Exchange suspended the ticker service, even to its own members. We boys replaced the tickers. We had to run back and forth between the offices and the Exchange to get quotations and prices and report what was going on. No one in any of the offices knew prices until his boy arrived. This could not last. Nobody wanted to trade when the ticker wasn't ticking.

Up to the time when the bucket shops were finally deprived of tickers it was possible to go into any of these places, not only in New York but all over the country, and buy or sell any quantity of stock at the price of the next sale, or at the price that was chalked on the quotation board.

Suppose Erie were selling at 40 and you wanted to buy fifty shares in a bucket shop. You would plunk down $100 and say: "I'll take fifty Erie at 40," and if that was the price on the board you would be handed a slip indicating that you had bought fifty Erie at 40 and that you were margined down to 38¼; your $100 represented two points (dollars) margin on fifty shares. One-eighth each way was deducted for "commission"; there was no tax at that time.

If Erie rose in price to 43, you would say to the clerk: "I'll sell fifty Erie at 43," and hand him your slip. He would thereupon pay you your profit of three points, or $150, less ¼ of 1 per cent commission on the round turn, $12.50, a net profit of $137.50, as the result of your shrewd judgment. But if after you bought Erie at 40 it should decline to 38¼, you would thereby automatically be "sold out" and your $100 would be lost. You were simply betting on the quotations, and the bucket shop was betting against you, with one quarter of a point for the kitty.

The bucket shop proprietor did not care much whether you won or lost, so long as you kept on playing; the hungry kitty was fed frequently. Ten trades would cost you two and a half points, or $250 on one hundred shares. But the commission was really the least of it. You were generally a bad guesser.

Your tendency was to grab a profit of two or three points. If the market went against you, however, you might put up another "margin" or two, that is, another two or four points, and you would then be "protected" down to 36¼, or 34¼, as the case might be. Taking small profits thus, and letting your losses run, was simply a reversal of the well-known rule for making money in Wall Street (no guarantee goes with this) that it is best to cut losses short and let profits run.

Clerks, messenger boys, brokers' runners, telephone boys and pages on the floor of the Stock Exchange, and many other small margin traders, did all their operating through the bucket shops. Many who became prominent traders and spectacular plungers got their original stock market education there. With a little money traders got action and got it quickly. No waiting for execution of orders. You just stepped up to the desk and in a few seconds they had your money and you had their slip.

There was one outfit in the basement gin mill somewhere in the No. 50's in New Street where a one-share lot could be traded in on a one-point margin. It was quite customary for four rummies to get together with twenty-five cents each and indulge in microscopic plunges in which, according to rule, they were wiped out if the stock went down three-quarters of a point. Of course there was no limit to the profits they could make on their one-share gambles. A stock might even go up as much as five points, and the syndicate would then cut the rich melon, the members benefiting to the extent of $1.25 each, less, of course, their pro rata commission. But the market did not have to fluctuate much to dip three-quarters of a point, thus wiping them out. And so these calamities were both sad and frequent. Of course, these plungers could always go out and panhandle additional quarters from the passers-by. Usually what the bucketeer didn't get the bartender did.

On the west side of Broadway, corner of Tinpot Alley, now more respectably known as Exchange Alley, a big bucket shop was operated by Haight and Freese (Hate and Freeze). In a large room on a floor above the street, fifty to one hundred "clients" could be seen anxiously eyeing the large silicate quotation board with its strings of chalked figures. An intermittent procession passed up and away from the windows where the transactions were made, otherwise designated by Weber & Fields as "the put-in-and-take-out department." Needless to say, the "put-ins" were heavier than the "take-outs."

Haight & Freese was an enterprising bucket shop. It advertised widely in all the papers, offering to send a cloth-bound book containing statistics of all the stocks listed on the New York Stock Exchange. This book was bright red with gilt lettering. In addition to the statistics, there were copious illustrations of Wall Street, J. P. Morgan's office, and Haight & Freese's office, with its various departments in a state of intense activity. The book was a condensed edition of statistics out of *Poor's Manual* and the *Chronicle.* It was fairly easy for a beginner to understand. Procuring a copy, I began to dope out the best purchases.

* * *

The Consolidated Stock and Petroleum Exchange was on the corner of Broadway and Exchange Place. Originally it included, as members, John D. Rockefeller, H. H. Rogers, and all the big and little oil men. There they dealt in petroleum by the "contract" for so many barrels. Speculation in petroleum at one time far exceeded that in railroad stocks. Hundreds of thousands of barrels were dealt in every day on this Exchange until the time came when Standard Oil saw fit to kill the speculation in order better to control the market. The big trust did this by the simple expedient of placing orders to buy or sell at 50 cents a barrel any quantity of oil that anybody wanted to deal in at the price. Naturally, in a market that wasn't allowed to fluctuate, no speculator could make any money; speculation in oil perished and the Consolidated Exchange was forced to shift to other fields.

In the late 'eighties the business done on that floor was nearly all in lots of ten shares or small multiples of ten. New York Stock Exchange members, with few exceptions, would not deal in less than 100-share lots on margin; this gave the Consolidated its opportunity to cater to the small fry.

The Consolidated did not furnish a primary market in the same sense as the New York Exchange. On a long blackboard extending the full length of its wall on Exchange Place prices were posted at which stocks were selling on the New York Stock Exchange; all trading on the Consolidated was done with one eye on that board. If the price of St. Paul were 56 on the Stock Exchange, there would be trading in ten, twenty or fifty share lots on the Consolidated at a fraction over or under that figure.

The New York Stock Exchange tried its best to deprive the Consolidated of its ticker and quotation service, thus to force it into confining its operations to mining and other unlisted stocks. But the Consolidated successfully fought this attempt to strangle it. Up to the time when its building at Broad and Beaver streets was sold, the ticker service was still running on its floor and in the offices of some of its members.

* * *

While the center of Wall Street activity was the New York Stock Exchange, with its main entrance on Broad Street and a little side entrance at No. 13 Wall (which some people thought unlucky), the real Boss made his headquarters just across the way. On the southeast corner of Wall and Broad streets stood a white marble building; "Drexel, Morgan & Co." was carved above the door.

At that time all the firm's business was done on the one main floor of this marble building. Other brokerage houses occupied the low-ceilinged offices on the Broad Street side, where the sidewalk sloped down toward the Mills Building. A big doorman stood just inside the main entrance on the corner, scrutinizing and directing all callers. A long counter stretched on the left, along the Wall Street windows, and here a growing list of railroad securities, known as Morgan stocks, were transferred, coupons paid and other banking operations accomplished.

Across the floor of white marble blocks notched at each corner with a little black tile, a large room had been partitioned off. At its far end, against the wall next to the Mills Building, behind windows screened with wire, was the Wall Street throne, occupied by John Pierpont Morgan whose personality was so awe-inspiring to me as a youth that I almost shivered as I beheld that towering form, those shaggy eyebrows, and those eyes that seemed to pierce me.

* * *

The business of my employers, Hazard and Parker, was transmitted to the Stock Exchange by a short private telephone. There was a button on the side of the telephone in the office; you pressed it and pressed it, and the bell at the Stock Exchange end would go ding, ding, ding. Doc Hewitt, who officiated also for Vermilye & Co., was at that other end just along the wall on the right as you went in. Our office had no other telephone. We could telephone only to the Stock Exchange. Nobody outside could telephone to us. We had no typewriter, but we had a safe and a letter press. Reports of purchases and sales and all correspondence were written in pen and ink, and copied in a book by the letter press.

Investors and traders came in, one at a time, usually—and very few a day at that; the first would seat himself in the rocking-chair facing the ticker, or on the low radiator if it was not too hot. It took but a few customers to fill the place.

To get one's start in such a small concern had its advantages, however. I had before me in miniature all the processes of the brokerage business. Every operation which was carried through in the larger offices by a dozen clerks was simply an enlarged form of the motions I made.

One day Mr. Parker handed me $25,000 in bills and told me to take "it" to the bank. I tucked the wad in my inside coat pocket and went down the stairs and out into the street, feeling as though all the money were shining through the fabric of my coat. Just outside the Mills Building I met a cop, to whom I said: "Say, I've got a lot of money in my pocket, will you walk up to the Fourth National with me?"

"Oh, there's another fellow up by the Sub-Treasury; get him to go," was his lazy reply.

I shivered my way up past the Sub-Treasury but didn't see the "other fellow." Having made half the journey safely, however, I took a chance on the rest and arrived, to my great relief, at the window of the red-mustached teller, where I unloaded more money, it seemed to me, than I had ever hoped to jump over in my whole life.

* * *

1891 SIGNS OF AN ADVANCE

CASHIER AT SEVENTEEN—FINANCIAL LITERATURE—BROKER'S ADVICE

In the third year of my employment by Hazard & Parker, I ceased to be a runner and became a combination cashier, bookkeeper and office manager. I was seventeen; an inside job was something to be proud of. The office force under me consisted of one tall, lanky, dark-haired college graduate who was now the runner. His salary was $5 a week. Mine was $10.

I received the stock certificates that were delivered to us, drew the checks in payment therefor, and handed these to Mr. Parker for signature. I phoned orders to the Exchange, received the reports, made out purchases and sales notices to customers, kept the purchase-and-sales book, the blotter and the ledger, made monthly statements to clients, and otherwise carried out the clerical work formerly done by Mr. Parker.

During the year, Mr. Parker's health failed, and he decided to give up active business to become a special partner. Thereafter, with Mr. Hazard on the Stock Exchange floor all day, in addition to the previously named duties I was now in charge of the office, was the reception committee, waited on the clients, got them the information they desired and saw that their orders and other requirements were properly looked after. Every morning Mr. Hazard would get out from the safe deposit box whatever securities I needed for the day's deliveries and at night he would put back what we had left over. We had a rubber stamp which read "R. D. Wyckoff or ourselves," and its imprint was stamped after the words "Pay to the order of" on the checks we needed to make the day's payments. Mr. Hazard signed these before going to the Exchange in the morning. Then, when stocks were delivered at the window, I would pay for them by endorsing one of the checks to the firm who made the delivery, my signature on the endorsement making the check O.K. for certification at the bank.

I was continuing my statistical studies with increasing interest. By this time I could state, out of my head, most of the essential facts as to the principal companies whose stocks were listed on the Stock Exchange. I had a smattering of knowledge as to the comparative values of these stocks. It seemed strange to me that some should sell ten or twenty points higher than others, while paying the same rate of dividend. I had then little knowledge of intrinsic values nor of investment merit. I had no idea of the importance of knowing where a stock stood in the various stages toward becoming a seasoned investment. And I was ignorant of manipulation.

All the while I was trying to get a better idea of the relation of the brokerage business, the Stock Exchange and the public. It seemed to me the market was being juggled back and forth by a lot of big operators; the traders on the floor were trying to scalp fractions and points out of the small fluctuations, while the public, with no means at hand for learning what made the wheels go round, simply made intermittent or habitual jabs at the market, much as they would take chances on a horse race or a roulette wheel.

Up to that time one of the few pieces of literature

containing any suggestion as to how money was to be made in the stock market was a small book by Jared Flagg.[1] This had evidently been written to induce people to put money into Flagg's own scheme, which was based on the fact that some stocks are in a strong position and going up, while others are in a weak position and likely to decline. All one had to do, according to Flagg, was to sell small lots of the weak ones every point up and buy similar lots of the strong ones every point down. Whenever any lot showed a profit of one and a quarter points (the quarter to cover commission) it was to be closed out.

Flagg claimed to have made a good deal of money in this manner, but I always suspected that most of his profit came from the public and not from the stock market. At any rate, with such textbooks the public had but a small chance of learning the game.

In the next ten years a meager amount of instructive literature began to ooze out of some of the brokerage houses and bucket shops, much of it of a type containing suggestions such as this:

"When the market closes strong after a very weak day, buy stocks at the next morning's opening prices."

Or, "Dull markets are not good ones for selling. It may be that the dullness precedes activity in an upward direction."

Outsiders were heavy losers in their stock market operations—how heavy I could judge from the varied fortunes of our own Hazard & Parker clients in their speculations.

While Parker was rather reluctant to advise and usually said: "It's your money; you had better decide what

[1] Now out of print.

you want to do," yet now and then he would express an opinion. But Hazard's answer, if asked about the market or any particular stock, would be something like this: "Well, I think the way money is now, and with crops looking pretty good and railroad earnings picking up, there is a chance St. Paul might do better; but of course when you consider this government bond situation and the state of foreign trade, you might be taking chances in going long."

* * *

1892 A CHANGE OF BASE

ON THE STOCK EXCHANGE FLOOR—IN MONTREAL—BEATING THE BUCKET

IN THE spring of the year, Hazard and Parker dissolved their partnership, and I found myself out of a job. Across the hall, on the Exchange Place side of the second floor, Mills Building, the firm of La Montagne, Clarke & Co. was doing a general brokerage business in stocks and grain. I went in and saw Smith, the managing partner, and he told me they could use a telephone boy on the floor of the Stock Exchange at $10 per; upon which I closed with him on the spot.

In the old Exchange (it was torn down in about 1903), telephones lined three walls inside a low rail which separated the telephone boys and messengers from those known as "subscribers." These, for a yearly fee, were allowed to stand outside the rail. On the south wall, but nearest Broad Street, were the telephones of the houses which did an arbitrage business with London and the other European exchanges. They had a pneumatic tube service from the floor to the offices of the cable companies, which were in the basement, or to the Western Union Building next door.

Close to my firm's telephone was the Rock Island "post." "Billy" Henriques, famous for his droll stories, was a specialist there. Other posts were farther away, but although the whole market at that time was small and the period a dull one, I was where I could observe quite a bit of the trading and learn something of the day's work on the floor.

Telephone clerks all around me, as well as the uniformed pages on the floor, were trading in small lots of stocks either in the bucket shops or with some of the houses. Many of the phone boys seemed quite important parts of their firm's machinery; they gave out the orders and at times would favor certain "two-dollar" brokers, from whom they apparently were getting a rake-off. All the boys—and some of them were fairly old boys at that—had their ears out for tips, and would pass them along to certain of their friends. I would often hear a boy say: "That five thousand St. Paul that just went in was for So-and-So." It might have been an order sent through his house for the very purpose of concealing the real purchaser, but through the underground information bureau which was run for the benefit of Tom, Dick and Harry, so long as he was a telephone boy, good things were to be had by all once in a while.

My firm consisted of Edward La Montagne, son of a wine merchant in Beaver Street, well known in society and sporting circles in the big town; Herman Clarke, better known in sporting and theatrical circles; a man named Smith, and E. M. Fulton, Jr. La Montagne was the board member—a handsome, splendidly built fellow with a peculiarly graceful way of stepping around the floor. Clarke was rather a big man, smooth-faced, heavy-jawed, sportily dressed, and did the big talk in the customer's room. Smith was the managing partner and had charge of the machinery of the business. Fulton put in a considerable chunk of capital, most of which he did not succeed in getting back, as I will explain.

The orders would come over the telephone to me.

"Buy 500 Northwest at the market," for example. As soon as I heard the first word indicating that an order was coming on the telephone, my finger would press a white button alongside it, which would release La Montagne's number on the wall. As he worked on the floor he would always keep an eye out for his number, and then would either step in for the order or send a page for it. By the time he or the page arrived, I had the order written out on a Buy or Sell slip and was standing at the rail. However, if he was within sight, I would bellow "E-e-e-yell" (E. L., his initials and his call), and having no adenoids could usually make him hear halfway across the floor. After he had executed the order he sent a page to me with the report, or came back with it himself.

After working at the telephone for some months, it occurred to me that I wasn't getting ahead very fast handling orders and yelling "E-e-e-yell," so I hit Clarke for a better job. He said: "We are opening a branch office in Montreal and we need a bookkeeper up there. I'll give you seventy-five dollars a month if you want to take it."

"I'll take it," I replied, "when do I leave?"

"This is Thursday—go up there Sunday night."

Sunday night found me rumbling over the New York Central and Central Vermont. In the morning I awoke to look out at a strange and barren country with all the signs in French. It seemed a long way from home.

Arriving at Bonaventure Station, Montreal, early in the morning, I took a hack for our office in the Temple Building on St. James Street. Carpenters and painters were still at work finishing the place. In a little while we were doing a fair business. One of our best customers was

Photo H. N. Tiemann Company

1870. *Broadway Looking North from Liberty Street*

Charles R. Hosmer, head of the Canadian Pacific Telegraph lines, an active trader, in 200-share lots usually. I suspect that some of the orders were meant to encourage us in maintaining the office and the wire. He used a two-point stop on all his trades and I hate to think of the many stop orders we executed one-eighth or one-quarter away from the stop price in a market that was deadly dull, and which offered little excuse for such ruthless executions.

One day our manager came into the bookkeeping department and introduced me to a young man named F. J. Lisman, who had charge of the Bond Department in the New York office. I don't know whether this was Lisman's first job of the kind; but rumor had it even then that he breakfasted on *Poor's Manual,* lunched and dined on the *Chronicle,* and was so familiar with the former's green-and gold volume that he rarely used the index.

We had a private wire to New York. The operator in New York had a stock ticker on his table and transmitted to us the price changes as fast as they came on the tape. A bucket shop was around the corner. One day I happened to look in and saw that some sharp moves in one or two active stocks had not been posted on its blackboard. So I began to watch for other occasions like this and found it was the regular practice of the bucket shop to hold back on quick moves so that when a trader came in to buy or sell they could always give him the worst of it. For instance, if General Electric was selling at 110 and took a quick run up to 113, they wouldn't print that on the board. They might make the stock a little active around 110 or give it a quick run up to 111 on fictitious quotations with the idea that some of the traders might sell it short on that bulge. If a trade or two came in on it they would then release the rest of the "run" up to 113 and the fellow who had sold short at 111 would be wiped out. This was standard bucket shop practice.

I saw a chance to benefit by this. If the prices of stocks coming over our wire indicated the real market—right under the wheel of the tape—I could beat the bucket shop by rushing there and buying a stock which I knew had risen, and do this before they posted the higher quotation. Of course, I couldn't be running in and out of the office all the time. But once I was satisfied that this method would work until they got on to me, I arranged with a friend to stand outside our front window. Whenever an opportunity appeared I slipped my friend a piece of paper, telling him what stock to buy and what to pay for it; he would trot to the bucket shop, get the bet down, and grab the profit—for me.

* * *

1893 to 1896 PANIC AND DEPRESSION

THE CRASH IN CORDAGE—RECEIVERSHIPS —OUT OF A JOB—LIVING ON TWENTY-FIVE CENTS A DAY—A TURN FOR THE BETTER—SELLING PAINT—A SOUND BUSINESS PRINCIPLE—THE BRYAN PANIC—BACK IN WALL STREET

IN THE spring of 1893, the firm's special partner, young Fulton, together with his father and associates, became interested in the National Cordage Co., or the "Trust," as everything in the way of an industrial combination then was called. They arranged with James R. Keene to run a pool in the stock. Just what happened on the inside I never quite learned, but the pool blew up and Keene lost all he had except $30,000.[1]

The market began to slump, with General Electric breaking from 114 to 30, and finally collapsed in what was known as the Panic of 1893. My firm was badly hit and word came to Montreal that it was going out of business. The office was closed and I took a ride back to New York.

Of this period the *Commercial and Financial Chronicle* of January 6, 1894, said:

"During 1893 the United States passed through a financial crisis of appalling severity. It was much more than a crisis arising from over-sustained mercantile credits like that of 1857, or from excessive industrial

[1] With this he pyramided on the short side and made $1,500,000.

development like that of 1873; the distress came at the end of the silver inflation period which began in 1878, and it marked the culmination of events in that disastrous era. The crisis terminated with a great historic change in the currency standard of the country by the virtual adoption of gold as the only measure of values when the Silver Purchase Law of 1890 was finally repealed on the first day of November. . . . The course of the year was strewn with the wrecks of great corporations, which had a deadly effect upon prices at the Stock Exchange. On February 20 came the Philadelphia and Reading receivership; on May 4, National Cordage; on July 25, Erie; on August 16, Northern Pacific; on October 13, Union Pacific; on December 23, Atchison, and on the 27th New York and New England."

Financial institutions were failing at an appalling rate. Fifty-five banks went under, together with a number of mortgage loan and trust companies.

More than 27,000 miles of railroad capitalized at nearly two billion dollars went into receivership this year. They were to be followed by 10,000 miles in 1895, 12,000 in 1896, and 40,000 in the three following years, a total of 89,000 miles in six years.

In many cases the bondholders were required to surrender part of their rights, and in nearly all cases the stockholders were heavily assessed. One can imagine the effect of this vast shrinkage in railroad security values and the resulting enormous losses to individuals and institutions. Fortunes invested in railroad stock were swept away.

Atchison common was assessed $10 per share; its stock sold down to 5¾ soon afterward. Baltimore & Ohio was assessed $20 per share, and the stock touched 12⅜

1873. *Broad Street during the Panic*

soon after. Erie, assessed $12 per share, went to 8½. Northern Pacific, assessed $15 per share, sold down to 1½. Reading, assessment 20 per cent a share, was worth 2½ one month after. Richmond Terminal (reorganized as Southern Railway), assessed $10, went to a low price of 2⅞. Union Pacific, assessed $15, reached a low of 2.

* * *

Back in New York from the closed Montreal office I was given two weeks' salary in advance and told I wouldn't be needed any more. And now began a desperate period of three lean years.

I tried to connect with other Wall Street firms; I couldn't even hook up at my old work of stock runner. Willing, anxious to take anything, for two months I could get nothing. Finally I went to work in the office of a man named Snell, who ran a trucking business and built trucks at the corner of Bay and Montgomery streets, in Jersey City. I had to get up at 5:30, take an elevated train down to the Jersey City Annex at the foot of Fulton Street, Brooklyn, catch the 6:30 boat, and arrive at the office at 7:00. During that winter I made the fire, swept the place out, fed the dog, kept the books, hustled around on the work that was under way, but most of the time had to listen to the chatter of a lot of bums who made the office a hang-out. My salary fell back to the old figure of $10 a week, out of which came 60 cents carfare and 60 cents annex fare, leaving me a net of $8.80 on which to subsist.

The fellow who did most of the truck building was a tall, blond German, very thorough at his task. He frequently alluded to his "invention." He was working on it at home; it consisted of "a wagon that would run without a horse." It had a steam engine to make it go, he said, and a seat for two people on top, and an appliance to make it jump over logs or obstructions.

One day he came over to the office with tears in his eyes, and, handing me a newspaper clipping, said sadly: "They've got my invention." The clipping described a horseless carriage which had been run in a park in Paris, and which was being brought over for an exhibition in Central Park, New York.

When, some months before that, my Jersey City boss had heard me say that I thought the day *would* come when they would make wagons run without horses and that if they could do it with a trolley car they could make a wagon run by some similar fashion, he said: "Why, Richard, you're just plumb crazy."

Ready to jump out of my skin from impatience at my situation, I finally landed another job and became a butter-and-egg man. Literally one. I was a bookkeeper for a commission broker on Greenwich Street who dealt in butter and eggs. His methods, in his dealing with farmers, were so questionable, however, that one day I objected and was promptly fired.

Then I saw an advertisement of Armour & Company, asking for a salesman to sell butterine. I tried to sell butterine and wore out my shoes with little success.

My next "opportunity" came from an advertisement in the New York *Herald:* "Salesman! Better than a salary of $20 a week." So I blew into a place at the corner of Beekman and Gold, down about five wooden steps from the sidewalk, and in the back of an express office found a big raw-boned individual occupying desk room and surrounded by three or four applicants. His name was

E. R. Bathrick, he was from Ohio,[2] and he had concocted a floor oil, which had the remarkable quality of keeping down dust. We were instructed to sally forth with this product and extract orders from a waiting world. I seized a handful of circulars that looked like programs of a dime museum, and out I went. I made $1.50 that day; but couldn't collect until the goods were delivered.

The morning of my twenty-first birthday found me with a working capital of two cents. I borrowed three cents, took the car to New York, and collected a little of my "commish."

Soon I began to work up quite a trade in Mr. Bathrick's floor oil. In Murray and Barclay streets were concerns like L. Strauss & Sons, Bawo & Dotter, with china and glassware on display; and they welcomed this stuff which reduced the amount of dust on their stock. Before long, I sold Bawo & Dotter a couple of barrels, each of which brought me a $20 commission.

Then ambition seized me to become the "manager of a branch office." I chose Chicago as my field and on a bitter day in January started west on the Lehigh Valley in a tourist car.

Within a few days, in the Windy City, I had found a boarding place and an office; I had bought a desk, got my stock from the freight yard, and was sitting down to figure where I stood. I had paid a month's rent, $15, for the office, and $6 for a week's room and board (good board, too); my working capital now consisted of $30. I had financed my trip west, all except the oil, which was billed to me by Bathrick.

Then I began to advertise for myself. "Salesmen! Better than a salary of $20 per week." Soon a flock of

[2] Bathrick afterward became a Senator in Ohio.

disreputables, some without overcoats—and it was cold—came in seeking these promising jobs. Repeating what I had heard Bathrick say about the oil, and adding some arguments of my own, I sent out this nondescript force laden with enthusiasm and circulars. Then, feeling a little lonely, I sat on my stool in front of a roll-top desk and behind the door on which was printed "Manager," and tried keeping up my courage with my last dollars going, a thousand miles from home or friend, and no place to borrow.

February and March were the toughest months I ever experienced. Cash resources so lowered before spring that I gave up my comfortable room and slept on the office floor with crumpled newspapers for a mattress, a bagful of newspapers for a pillow, and my overcoat as blanket. Allowance for meals was reduced to hardpan. Down on South Clark Street I could dive into a cellar for an egg, buckwheat cake and coffee breakfast at ten cents. I skipped lunch. About two miles up North Welles Street a Swedish Restaurant served a fifteen-cent dinner from a platter that was passed around to all hands. Thus on a food budget of $1.75 a week—with no other expenses—I was able to get by until spring came and business picked up. That was the last of my hardest times. Never since then have I worried about making a living.

I actually made money in the next six months, and although my mother had predicted I should walk back from Chicago after freezing in a cold hall room, I came back to New York in a Pullman.

Here I found Wall Street conditions still bad. The gold supply in the Treasury of the United States had reached such a point that at one time there was less than one day's supply. The Morgan-Belmont Syndicate had to come to the rescue. It was a question whether the United States could continue to make specie payments of its obligations as the gold in the Treasury stayed close to the vanishing point. Business throughout the country was paralyzed.

I now ventured into sale of fire extinguishers, and undertook advertising, solicitation, etc., none of which panned. In the first half of this year, I traveled New York and the New England States selling ready-mixed paints. This occupation, while bringing no munificent rewards, gave me one of the most valuable lessons in my life. In Putnam, Conn., I was trying to sell my line to an old man who ran a general store on the main street. He listened carefully to my story, and when I was all through, said: "Young man, if you want people to do business with you, you've got to make it to their advantage. You come along here and ask me to throw out this other line of paints I've been carrying all these years and take yours on. What inducement can you offer, so it will pay me to do this?" I admitted I couldn't offer any inducement but would like the order.

The old man kept his old paints, and I went on my way with mine, but also with a bit of advice the value of which I cannot estimate.

Through a hundred and sixty towns in Connecticut, through practically every town in Rhode Island and Massachusetts and a number in eastern New York, I went in that period of mixed-paint selling. In Rhode Island and Massachusetts factories by the score and employees by the hundreds of thousands were idle because of the business depression. It seemed as if all the inhabitants of some towns were idly walking the streets. Manufacturers were sending delegations to Washington asking President Cleveland what he was going to do about the prostration of trade.[3]

All of this time I was hankering for Wall Street and every day I scanned the Help Wanted columns of the New York *Herald.* At last I saw a small advertisement: "Stock brokerage house wants purchase-and-sales clerk, $15 per week. P. M. & Co., P.O. Box 296." Calling at the post office I asked a clerk if he wouldn't tell me who was that P. M. & Co. "I just *have* to have that job," I pleaded. He looked it up; P. M. & Co. was Price, McCormick & Co. In five minutes I was interviewing Theodore H. Price, managing partner of that firm, as the first of the applicants. The others had to send in their letters by mail. I told Price I could fill the requirements; understood every operation in a brokerage office, and could keep any or all of the books. He called in his elderly stock clerk. "Herbert, here is a young man who thinks he can run our purchase-and-sales department." Herbert looked me over and asked how long it was since my last position in Wall Street. "Three years," I admitted.

"Oh, you won't do at all," he said grandly, "we've got to have a man who is right up to date."

"If you'll put me on the job and I don't satisfy you within two weeks, you can fire me without paying me a cent," I said.

"Better give him a trial, Herbert," said Mr. Price.

[3] In the free silver political campaign which culminated in the Bryan panic of August, 1896, Atchison touched 8¼, Chesapeake & Ohio 11, Louisville & Nashville 37, Nickel Plate 9, Northern Pacific 12¼, Union Pacific 3½, Wabash 4½, Baltimore & Ohio 10½, Burlington 53, Missouri Pacific 15, Norfolk & Western 12½, Texas Pacific 5, General Electric 20, Canadian Pacific 52, New York Central 88, St. Louis & San Francisco 4, St. Louis & Southwestern 2⅞, Southern Pacific 14, Southern Railway 6½, National Lead 16.

I followed Herbert back into the long, narrow accounting department on the ground floor of the old building which then stood at 72 Broadway, and started to work entering purchases and sales from the slips that came over from the Stock Exchange and making out clearing house slips and comparisons—while a little bull market of joy bubbled in my heart.

I was back in Wall Street!

The firm was known as a "wire" house, having telegraph lines to Boston, Philadelphia, Pittsburgh, Chicago and other Western cities. Some of their correspondents were Bright, Sears & Co. and Leland, Towle & Co., in Boston; Winthrop, Smith & Co., in Philadelphia, and R. H. McMullen in Pittsburgh; A. O. Slaughter & Co., Logan & Bryan, Kennett, Harris & Co., Bartlett, Frazier & Co., and others in Chicago and elsewhere. A large commission business was done in stocks, cotton and grain, and most of it came over the private wires.

After I had become familiar with my new work I began to look about to get a measure of the competition I might expect from other employees. Henry A. Taylor, the cashier, in charge of the securities and finances, was a nice chap, but seemed to require frequent liquid stimulants. Herbert, the stock clerk, was a highly nervous old fellow who made three or four circles with his pen before he could write the first letter of a word. He handled the incoming and outgoing stocks and bonds, issued the checks, and turned the securities over to Taylor, who used some as collateral and put the balance in the safe deposit. Back-to-back with me was the double-length bookkeeper's desk where the auditor, Richardson, and his assistant posted the ledger from the day's blotter, the latter calling off the entries while the former did the posting. Richardson also handled the expense items and petty cash.

A few weeks' experience convinced me that there were opportunities here, and I began to play a game of checkers with a better job as my objective.

A couple of months later Bryan and free silver had been beaten, McKinley elected; Wall Street was encouraged, and business was picking up.

Richardson, our auditor, thought he could do better elsewhere, so along in December put in his resignation. I asked him if he wouldn't recommend me for his position, which he did, and I was given the auditor's desk with $100 a month.

My predecessors had had great difficulty in striking their ledger balance. Having listened to their singsong when they were calling off and posting, I had concluded that many errors were due to their own carelessness. Sometimes they would struggle for days to find a difference in the trial balance, only to learn later that the blotter from which they posted had been out of balance.

In the public school I had attended when a boy—No. 11, Brooklyn—Principal Leroy F. Lewis was strong for teaching by visualization. He would write a rather long word on the board and tell all of us boys to look at it intently for a minute, so as to make a picture of it in our minds; he would then rub out the word and ask the boys to spell it. Almost everyone would do this correctly. I now applied his idea to posting the ledger. I made sure my blotter was balanced; then before posting an item, I simply looked at it as it appeared on the blotter, and after I had posted it in the ledger used my eyes to compare the two entries. This method worked so well that with several pages of entries going through the books

1873. *Jay Gould*

every day, I frequently was able to bring my monthly trial balance out to the penny at the very first shot. I soon told Price I didn't need the assistant, and from that time did the work of two men.

Thus ended my long three years' struggle during the Hard Times.

* * *

1897 BROADENING ACTIVITIES

EXPANDING BUSINESS—EATING STATISTICS —ONE-SHARE TRADES—PRICE'S FIRM —DIAMOND JIM BRADY

WHILE there was a reaction in the market after the McKinley bulge, there was a tremendous reawakening and resumption of activity in commerce, industry, transportation and banking in the following year. Newspapers told of new companies being organized, factories resuming work, employees being taken on. The business of Price, McCormick & Co. began rapidly to increase. New wire connections were made with out-of-town firms, branch offices were started, more people employed.

The firm opened a bond department in charge of Anthony A. Lisman, a brother of F. J. Lisman. Anthony was stout, blond and so near sighted he had to put his nose down to the paper when reading. Very smart and shrewd. A money-maker. He began trading in bonds and unlisted stocks. The card index system was not used generally at that time, and he kept in a sort of ledger a list of people who wanted to buy and sell different securities over the counter. He obtained a book containing the classified holdings of insurance companies and financial institutions, and he would wish aloud that it be indexed. "Having no assistant," he'd say, "probably I'll have to do this myself." I finally volunteered. This kept me at the office two or three nights a week for quite a while, and the other clerks thought me foolish. But I was thus learning another branch of the business.

Lisman was a jolly chap and was always joking and kidding the other men, so one day we thought we'd have a little fun with him. One of the clerks went into the telephone booth and asked the operator to connect him with Lisman's phone.

Clerk: This Mr. Lisman?
Lisman: Yes.
Clerk: You're dealing in these unlisted securities. Will you please quote Grant's Tomb Preferred?
Lisman: What kind of a stock is that?
Clerk: Why, don't you know it? It's a four per cent preferred, guaranteed by the Riverside Drive Company.
Lisman: Oh, yes, that stock is par bid offered at damn fool!

I resumed my studies of securities and financial statistics. I read the financial pages of the newspapers, the *Chronicle* from cover to cover, *Poor's Manual* for reference, and books on banking, railroad operation, and railroad accounting. One of my textbooks was the *Anatomy of a Railroad Report* by Thomas F. Woodlock, then one of three owners of Dow, Jones & Co., publishers of the *Wall Street Journal.* It taught me how to analyze a report from the standpoint of one who not only aimed at ascertaining earnings and financial condition, but also whether earnings were legitimate, based upon ton-mile cost and other standards of railroad operating efficiency.

Woodlock's little book showed how the receivership of Atchison, Topeka & Santa Fé, which had occurred in recent years, was forecasted by its operating figures and balance sheets for years previous to the collapse. I have read since many other and far more elaborate volumes on this vitally interesting subject, but none that handled the subject more simply and clearly.

Years afterward, Woodlock, who is now a member of the Interstate Commerce Commission, told me that I could have the copyright of the *Anatomy* for a box of cigars. I told him what an important part it had played in my studies.

For the next several years, I scarcely read anything that did not relate to Wall Street and the stock and bond markets. Much of this reading and studying was done on trolleys going back and forth. A good share of my evenings was devoted to working on the intrinsic value, earning power and financial position of the leading corporations whose securities were dealt in on the Stock Exchange.

The *Commercial and Financial Chronicle* was my Bible. At the end of every half year I would have the weekly issues bound up into a big, fat volume weighing several pounds. One day Mr. Price came in and saw one of these tomes wrapped up in paper lying on my desk. "What's this, Wyckoff?" he asked, placing a pudgy hand on top of it.

"That's a bound volume of the *Chronicle.* I'm not going to work behind a desk all my life."

"That's right, Wyckoff, that's right," he said.

A long series of imaginary paper transactions preceded my first real investment in a listed stock. This was one share of St. Louis & San Francisco common, selling at 4. I began to put all my savings into a list of equal amounts of diversified stocks, of which I figured that, although some might go wrong, the majority would make good.

Copyright Brown Brothers

Late '70's. *Looking up Wall Street*

I based my investments on pure statistical position and prospects. It was not until some years later that I began to study the technical aspects of the market and to recognize the importance of manipulation. Also of the smaller swings of the market and the tidal swings, indicated by the march of prices from the depths of a panic to the apex of a bull market and back again.

Panics were far more frequent in those days; I had witnessed three already in eight years: the Baring panic of 1890, the industrial and financial panic of 1893, and the Bryan panic of 1896. It was typical for the market to advance from the low point for about two years, and in the following year crash down to the low levels again. Some of the causes for this were a badly organized banking situation; agitation for unsound currency; over-extended railroad construction; unintegrated industrial organizations, most of them not represented on the New York Stock Exchange and having no broad market. Carnegie was still saying: "The steel business is either a prince or a pauper," for when times were good the mills could not handle the business offered, but when depressions came, as they did every few years, there were price wars and idle factories and thousands out of work. All this resulted, of course, in instability, for when conditions were bad the earnings and purchasing power of millions of people were affected, and every line of business suffered.

* * *

Theodore H. Price was the organizer and active head of Price, McCormick & Co. Everything focused around his personality, and the firm expanded rapidly as a result of his forceful and progressive methods. McCormick was not active in the business but evidently had put in a lot of capital.

The customers' room was in charge of old man Morris, a tall, broad-shouldered, gray-haired fellow; a fine, genial, upstanding character, whose watchword was: "Energy is all right as far as it goes, but what counts is *sustained* energy."

The firm was quite a factor in the cotton future and spot markets and did no small amount of grain business. This it distributed among its Chicago wire connections, thus reciprocating for their stock business. It always had a trading position in cotton and did a good deal of spot business through H. H. Johnson, a Cotton Exchange member. Price was an excellent judge of the cotton market and swung much business from big cotton traders like Pat Calhoun of Pittsburgh. He became an important operator at various times in later years.

One of our customers in both stocks and cotton was Diamond Jim Brady, who came in frequently and took away with him $25,000 or $50,000 in high-grade bonds or gilt-edge stocks. Diamond Jim was evidently making money in his own business which was railroad supplies. He was famous for the diamonds of staggering size and brilliancy which adorned his fat fingers, his stiff white shirt fronts, and his necktie. He gave lavish entertainments and had many lady friends. So many that, to look after them, he employed a young secretary, who also frequented our office.

The diamonds Jim wore would be in harmony with the day's activities. One day his cravat would bear a diamond locomotive and the studs would be railroad cars. Another day it would be a diamond horse that galloped on his tie, while horseshoe studs were in his shirt.

Bill Gallagher, who joined our organization as Lisman's assistant about that time, would go to Diamond Jim's office to deliver securities. Brady would pay for them, put them in his safe, then would open another compartment and take out a black velvet bag. "Want to see something pretty?" he would say. He would then go to the window where the sun was pouring in; pulling the shade down to within an inch or two of the bottom, he would empty out into one hand the bag full of white and brilliant diamonds. In the rays of sunlight which shot in under the shade, he would pour the precious stones from one hand to the other, just to see them sparkle and to watch the rainbow colors reflected from their facets to the walls and the ceiling.

Diamond Jim was also a famous epicurean, as was indicated by the size of his paunch. He would consume a whole punch-bowl full of lettuce hearts, covered with French dressing, at one sitting.

Brady was largely influential in organizing the Pressed Steel Car Company, in which he made quite a heap of money, and in other big deals.

* * *

1898 STEADILY ADVANCING

BRANCH OFFICES—BARGAIN IN UNION PACIFIC—BIRTH OF THE CURB—ORIGIN OF THE STOCK EXCHANGE—HORSE COLLARS—FIRST CAPITAL—GETTING ALONG—BURNED OUT

PRICE, McCORMICK & Co. continued to expand. Branch offices were opened in various cities through which our wires ran, and, during the season, at resorts like Newport and Old Point Comfort. Our monthly private wire rental ran into five figures. We had a large wire room where all these telegraph lines terminated, and excellent facilities for quick execution of the orders which came pouring in over the wires when the market was at all active.

Our business in the customers' room was only a small portion of the total. Comparatively little came in from individuals, either by wire or mail, and I often wondered why those two ends had not been developed. The reason was that nobody in the place understood how to go after such trade.

Operations of the clients in our customers' room were a good deal like those I had seen while with Hazard & Parker. Few of these clients seemed to know much about the market and Mr. Morris and his assistants could do little more than express their opinions and give the service required. Everyone seemed to concentrate on handling the business. Little or no attention was paid to the statistical side—unearthing opportunities or trading in a scientific way. In fact, this seemed to be the rule throughout the Street. For every one who considered the statistical side of securities, there were twenty trading on tips.

* * *

Union Pacific had just been reorganized and the common stock had been assessed $15 per share. Its price "3rd assessment paid" was around $17 per share. Holders who paid these assessments were given preferred stock to the amount of the assessment, and this preferred "when issued" was selling in the 40's.

I wrote a memorandum to Price. It called attention to the remarkable opportunity seemingly afforded to present purchasers of this stock, and pointed to the probability that eventually the preferred, received in exchange for the assessment, would sell at par; thus the holder would get the equivalent of his assessment back, leaving his common stock costing him $2 a share. The Boss thought well of the suggestion, and had duplicates made of it. It brought in a number of orders to buy the stock. This bit of financial writing, published in this small way, was the forerunner of over twenty million pieces issued from my office during the following two decades.

* * *

A. A. Lisman's work in the Unlisted Security Department confined him to the office but he used to send Bill Gallagher around the Street to see what the other dealers wanted to buy or sell and to work up trade outside of the telephone business, which he himself handled.

Bill made frequent rounds of a number of houses like Tobey & Kirk, Frederic H. Hatch, Gus Maas, H. I. Judson & Co.—a mere handful of people, who, eventually, in order to save so much running, formed the habit of meeting each other at certain hours under the big archway at the entrance of the Mills Building, 15 Broad Street. Their number increased gradually. Dealers who wanted to know what was going on either came to the archway or sent clerks there. This was the beginning of the New York Curb Market, which is now the second largest stock exchange in this country. The New York Stock Exchange had had its origin in much the same way.[1]

[1] In *The Story of a Street,* by Frederick Hill (Harper & Bros.), the following appears: "Wall Street's destiny had been determined at that little dinner at Jefferson's house, where Hamilton had sold New York's political birthright to assure the assumption of the State debts, for most of the public stock (virtually the same as modern government bonds) which the Treasury issued to finance its plan, was marketed through the auctioneering establishments located at the eastern end of the still fashionable thoroughfare. Indeed, the first 'Stock Exchange' known to the city opened at No. 22 Wall Street about the first of March, 1792, was a direct effort on the part of the auctioneers to control this business, and it is a curious fact that two of the men associated in this enterprise, McEvers and Pintard, represented families closely identified with Wall Street's previous history. No marked alteration had yet occurred in the appearance of the Street, but under one of the few shade trees (a buttonwood which stood in front of Nos. 68-70 Wall Street) which had escaped destruction during the Revolution, there now gathered daily a small group of men who acted as brokers in the purchase and sale of the public stock, and their presence gradually effected a change in the character of the quiet residential neighborhood. Moreover, it was soon apparent that these men had determined to maintain the foothold they had acquired, for they were quick to resent the combination of auctioneers which threatened to drive them from the field, and lost no time in declaring war against the allied firms. At a meeting held in Corre's Hotel on March 21, 1792, they resolved to have no dealings with the monopolists, and on March 27th of the same year they subscribed to a written memorandum agreeing upon a definite commission and undertaking to give each other preference in all brokerage transactions."

Such was the origin of the New York Stock Exchange, but there was no immediate attempt to effect a permanent organization, and for some years the trading conducted under the old buttonwood tree was almost entirely confined to the marketing of the public stock.

We soon began to hear much of the Curb, and within a year, forty or fifty dealers and brokers were making a regular market on the Broad Street Sidewalk. Later the entrance of the building and the sidewalk in front of it became too crowded and the market was moved out into the middle of the street. At one time it worked up toward the front of the Stock Exchange; then it moved along Broad Street just below Exchange Place. It there reached its greatest proportions as an outside market. Finally it was incorporated as the New York Curb Market and was housed in its present building with entrances on Trinity Place and Greenwich Street, north of Rector. As one of the founder members, I paid $1,500 for my membership.

* * *

A friend who had heart trouble and who had been advised by his doctor to keep out in the air as much as possible, bought a horse and a two-wheeled carriage. He would take me out for a drive down Ocean Parkway now and then.

Driving thus one day he began to tell me of an invention by a friend of his—a new horse collar. Instead of being stuffed with straw, the collar was lined with a pneumatic tube and was pumped up with air like a bicycle tire. Friends in Philadelphia had suggested that he form a company; they would make him money out of it. I asked him if he wanted to make money out of the manufacture of horse collars or out of the sale of the stock to the public. He said he hadn't gone far enough to decide this, and the Philadelphia crowd would probably make the decision eventually. He didn't know a thing about incorporating or stocks, and, in fact, very little about horse collars, which is, after all, a rather circumscribed business.

I gave him a few simple pointers on the financial details common to all such enterprises. I said that if they really were going to make horse collars, they first should obtain working capital, then get hold of a factory, and then begin to make the horse collars.

One day a note from him said: "My Philadelphia crowd have decided to go ahead making horse collars and they have a factory in Philadelphia. They've also incorporated the company with one million one-dollar shares. You have given me some valuable suggestions and I have decided to send you the enclosed three hundred shares in your name. The stock is going to be listed on the Philadelphia Stock Exchange before long."

As all my "holdings" were still of or near the one-share caliber, and as I was still on a moderate salary, this looked like quite a lot of stock to me. Having no idea as to when and at what price the initial trading in the stock would be, I sent this message over our private wire to J. W. Sparks, one of our Philadelphia correspondents: "There will shortly be listed on your Exchange a stock named 'Pneumatic Horse Collar.' The minute it peeps, quote it."

Some days later a message was shot to my desk through the pneumatic tube: "Pneumatic Horse Collar 3½ bid." I wrote on the same message: "Sell 300 at the market," and in a few minutes, for the first time in my life, I had $1,000!

The Philadelphia Horse Collar Syndicate was greatly disturbed that somebody should come in and poke their bid with even such a trifling quantity as three hundred shares; the next day one of their representatives came in to see me and asked me to have a heart and to hold off from further sales. He was eloquent on the company's glowing prospects. The Philadelphia Fire Department, it seemed, had adopted the collar; the stock would shortly be selling at $5 a share. I didn't tell them that 300 shares was all I'd ever had. In fact, I told him nothing, just listened. He said that all the other holders were tied up in a pool and couldn't sell.

After he went out I started on a still hunt and, even if the holders were tied up in a pool, succeeded in ferreting out a thousand or fifteen hundred shares which I bought privately. Immediately, I sold these in Philadelphia, netting a profit of $1,500 more. None of the other numerous deals I have made since, some involving profits of a few hundred thousands, have held the interest of the acquisition of this $2,500—my first capital.

* * *

Price's organizing and executive qualities, combined with his tremendous physical and mental energy, gave him great capacity for work. He was inclined to spread out rapidly, even if in so doing the expansion was somewhat unhealthy. With a bull market on and new wire connections and branch offices, we began to do entirely too much business for the firm's capital. A new special partner was admitted into the firm in the person of George Crocker, one of the sons of the famous early California millionaire. Crocker was a rather undersized man with a mild voice and of the type of serious-minded rich men's sons. His name and the prestige of the family were an asset to the firm. He came in with $200,000 special capital and commanded considerable business. This enabled Price to take care of the firm's development.

I was personally benefiting by better positions and frequent increases in salary. Supervision of the six or seven branch offices was one of my new tasks. Another was the installation of cost accounting by a method of my own which alloted expenses directly to the branch office, correspondent, or department where they belonged, while wire rent and other common expenses were prorated. Thus, by working nights in addition to my regular duties I was able to give Price a statement which showed him just where he was making money, just where he was losing money and where he could find the leaks.

* * *

One morning I came down to the office and found that our building at 72 Broadway had burned during the night. The fire engines were still at work, but Price had already rented a vacant basement on the New Street end of the Manhattan Life Building (where Cabassud's Restaurant was to open later). By nine o'clock in the morning he had telegraph operators working on temporary tables and carpenters putting up planks for the bookkeepers. The fire was out but water was still being shot into the ruins. The "old man" seemed to enjoy the experience as he did everything which meant an opportunity to use energy and brains.

With Broadway and New streets filled with fire engines and jammed with a howling mob, it was my task to go up the rear fire escape, escorted by the Fire Chief, to open the safe and get the books so that we might proceed with business. Water was pouring down through the hole burned in the ceiling; some parts had caved in, but we reached the safes. The noise of water pouring down on all sides was like that of a cataract. The Chief had on his helmet, waterproof coat and rubber boots; I wore a derby, an overcoat and low shoes. It was so dark we had to use a lantern to see between fallen ceilings, timbers and wreckage-covered desks. As we approached the big safe, the Chief said to me: "Now be ready to jump any minute; if you hear a noise upstairs it's a safe coming through." The last word was hardly out of his mouth when we heard a terrific crash in one of the upper stories and made a dive for the New Street window. Whatever was coming through did not reach our floor, however, so we tiptoed back and while a stream of water poured down the back of my neck I twirled the knob and opened the safe. I then made a line of the bookkeepers from the safe to the window, where the floor would hold them, and along this chain passed out the books.

The building was beyond repair; in a few days we moved from our emergency quarters to the ground floor in 44 Broadway, running through to New Street.

While there, we experienced the toughest siege of long hours, hard work and nervous strain I ever went through. The market was growing by leaps and bounds. Everybody was speculating, the volume of stock trading was making new high records. New companies were being formed, their securities dealt in—first on the Curb and then on the Stock Exchange. Great industrial combinations were being put together, with heavy dealings in their syndicate allotments and their securities "when issued."

* * *

1899 ON THE GROUND FLOOR

BULL MARKET—OVEREXPANSION—DIFFICULT FINANCING—INSURANCE DEALS—AMALGAMATED COPPER FLOATED—MCKINLEY AS A SPECULATOR—A TIP FROM GOULD—THE SUGAR CONGRESS

I WOULD get to the office at nine o'clock in the morning. My lunch consisted of a couple of sandwiches and a cup of coffee, eaten while at work, and six or seven o'clock would come before I and the others in my department went out for a square meal at the old Stevens House across the street. We had been on our feet most of the day working under such terrific pressure that we were all fagged out; we felt justified in spending an hour or more over our evening meal. Then back we would go and work until eleven, twelve or one o'clock. For a period of several months my average time of home-coming to my house in Flatbush was between twelve and two o'clock. It was an hour away by trolley; I slept both ways most of the time. At nine I was on the job again.

We simply couldn't keep pace with the growth of the business. Employees who understood stock market bookkeeping were hard to find. One day, after I had succeeded in getting three or four new men, Price came in. "Wyckoff, you've got too many men around here; fire about five of them," he said. "Mr. Price, we need eight more," I replied. I knew what I was talking about; I could see faithful stand-bys like John Platt and Harry Alexander fairly drop from exhaustion. I would see Alexander on his high stool, his head gradually sagging and his ears turning blue with the congestion of blood in his head from continuous mental effort over endless masses of figures.

We would at times work until three or four o'clock in the morning, then go to Dolan's on Park Row for beef and beans, then to the Astor House for a few hours' sleep, to show up at the office again at nine. Sometimes Price came down to the office after the theater and went to Dolan's with us. The other partners occasionally dropped in, at from eleven to twelve o'clock. They knew they could always find us there.

This overwork could have but one result. I reached a point where I had to go away for a while purely in self-defense. My memory faded perceptibly and did not fully return for nearly two years.

Because of the shortage in help, the long hours, the exhaustion of the men, many errors occurred in the stock department, and in securities that were in and out of the transfer offices, to say nothing of errors in bookkeeping. Not only were our books out of balance, but some certificates were lost and it took months to get our affairs back to normal again. At one time, for several weeks, I worked from seven P.M. to seven A.M. and slept in the daytime.

The business had expanded to such a point that our resources were strained, in spite of the additional capital supplied by Crocker. We were carrying a lot of securities which were not good banking collateral, and when the time of day came for getting together the collateral for the loans, much scratching was needed to make good the bank balance. At such times Price would say: "Wyckoff, take these securities up to the Western National and see what you can do with Mr. Snyder." I would peer at the list of stocks and bonds on the envelope, and then look at him, and he would look back at me as much as to say: "I don't believe you can do it, but try anyhow." I would go to the Western National Bank, plunk down in the chair alongside the cashier's desk:

"Now, Mr. Snyder, here is some stuff that I know isn't regular, but we need $100,000 on this until morning."

He, too, would scan this dubious collection of chromos, and say:

"You've got a nerve to come up to me with a bunch of stuff like that."

"Well, Mr. Snyder," I'd say, "I can't go back without the check; you know that's what I came for, and I promise you I'll pay it off in the morning."

"You can have it this time, but don't you ever bring me a collection like that again," he would conclude, with the air of a man about to have a tooth pulled. When I would return to the office with the check, Price would breathe a sigh of relief.

There were breaks in the market at times which, in the course of a few hours, would force us to call on our customers and correspondents—mostly on private wires, in distant cities—for something like $2,000,000 in margins.[1] There was a day when we didn't make our bank balance good until seven o'clock in the evening, what with the crowded wires, public and private, and the necessity of out-of-town houses, who must get their

[1] That would be a small amount now.

money in before they could instruct their banks to remit to us.

One day Price figured that by rearranging all his loans he could release a bit of collateral. Instead of doing this gradually without disturbing anything, he stayed down at the office one night and, with the assistance of the cashier, massed all the securities into one consolidated list from which he made up a list of new loans which he believed would give the desired relief.

On the following morning we paid off $15,000,000 worth of loans as rapidly as we knew how, and collected all the securities in one room, with a representative of the bank sitting by, at Price's request, to see that we were doing what we had undertaken. As fast as the securities came in, my assistants and I sorted them into alphabetical piles. Then each alphabetical pile was sorted again into groups of like securities. When all this had been done, we made up the new loans. Two or three men were busy picking out the securities I called for to make up the lists; as soon as a loan envelope was filled up, out a boy would go to get the check for it. The afternoon was gone when the job was done. What a day! But fortunately, out of the welter, some collateral was actually released.

Our business grew larger than ever. Mr. Crocker bought the building at 74 Broadway, next door to our old location, and Price had it entirely remodeled and all fitted up for our office, with the exception of the top floor (the 4th or 5th) where Price organized the Luncheon Club.

The ground floor was laid out for a private customers' room, in charge of Franklin A. Plummer, on the Broadway front. The Bond and Unlisted Securities Department was just back of that, in charge of Gallagher; then came the wire room with pneumatic tubes connecting all the important desks in that and other rooms; behind was a board room for customers, in charge of Mr. Howell, afterward a partner in Kelley, Howell & Co.

Price's office was on the second floor in front, together with other private offices and a big accounting department of which I was in charge, with 30 men. We had something like 125 employees in the whole organization by that time, counting those in the branch offices. The firm was recognized as one of the largest houses in the Street.

* * *

By this time the majority of the railroad receiverships that had occurred during the previous years had been cleaned up. With the completion of these reorganizations, the heavy sacrifices and assessments imposed upon security holders were in a fair way to be recovered. In most cases new preferred stock was given for the amount of the assessments paid, and there were further indications that, with the growth and development of the country and the rehabilitation of the railroad systems, these preferred stocks promised to possess sufficient earning power to warrant their selling at their par values, which in most cases was $100 per share.

* * *

I felt certain by now that I would break down at this business, even though I did win increases of salary and more important positions. I decided to leave Price, McCormick & Co. and to go into business for myself. When I told them this, they assured me that I was mak-

Photo Tiemann Company

1880. *Grand Central Depot*

ing a mistake. Soon after the new year Price called me in and announced that I would be given a small interest in the business if I would stay, and also power of attorney to sign checks jointly with H. H. Johnson. It looked like recognition and I said I would remain, although still nursing this bug about going into business for myself.

This was only two years and four months after I had joined them at $15 a week. I was just past twenty-five.

The business had been more prosperous than ever during the past year. I kept the private ledger and knew that the net profits had amounted to about a million dollars, a lot of money in those days.

The firm was undertaking new operations in new fields. For instance, they were buying up small insurance companies which had book values in excess of the market prices of their stocks. The insurance risks would be transferred to other companies, and the assets, consisting chiefly of cash and securities, would then be liquidated with considerable profit. One of the companies thus bought was the Firemen's Fire Insurance Co. of Boston. As I was going out of the New Street door one day, Price met me and said:

"I'll be wanting you to go to Boston soon. When can you be ready?"

"I'm ready now," I answered.

"All right," he said. "Meet me at the Touraine Hotel, in Boston, at eight o'clock tomorrow morning."

At "eight o'clock tomorrow morning" I knocked at the door of his room in the Touraine in Boston. After breakfast we went to the insurance company's office; I had a list of the company's securities, and we went directly to the safe deposit box and compared the list with the securities stacked there. The company was finally liquidated at a very fair profit.

The firm attempted to gain control of the Hanover Fire Insurance Co. of New York. I was making a record of the proxies that had been secured from the company's stockholders and chanced to remark to Price that my grandfather had organized that company and was its first president.

"You haven't any objection to doing this work on that ground, have you?" Price asked.

"Certainly not," I said. "I'd like to see you do the trick; looks as if there would be a big profit in it."

But the Hanover management made a hard fight and the attempt was given up.

* * *

The year 1899 marked the birth of many important industrial combinations such as Allis-Chalmers, Amalgamated Copper, American Beet Sugar, American Car & Foundry, American Hide & Leather, American Smelting & Refining, American Woolen, Republic Iron & Steel, United Fruit and United States Cast Iron Pipe & Foundry. These companies represented consolidations of numerous scattered units in their respective fields.

The details of the consolidation which resulted in Amalgamated Copper are interesting. Thomas W. Lawson, financial mountebank, habitat Boston, was the confessed instigator of this operation.

Lawson for many years had been an active figure on the Boston Stock Exchange, where most of the coppers found an active and ready market. For a long time he had endeavored to interest William Rockefeller and H. H. Rogers, the Standard Oil people, in the possibilities of a big copper combine. Anticipating success in this, he accumulated a considerable line of Butte & Boston, Boston & Montana, and other leading Boston coppers as the probable nucleus of the new combination.

After some months of investigation in typical Standard Oil fashion, they expressed their willingness to proceed, with the understanding that Rockefeller and Rogers were to furnish the capital, and be given three-quarters of the profit with one-quarter for Lawson.

After allowing Lawson to continue the accumulation of Boston coppers, which he expected to be included in the first section of the new combination, Rogers suddenly announced that he and Rockefeller had bought control of the biggest copper property in the world, the Anaconda, and that the Lawson properties were to be included in the second section of the deal. Lawson found himself holding the bag with no place to empty it.

Anaconda had been bought from Marcus Daly, J. B. Haggin, and Lloyd Tevis for $24,000,000; other properties, such as the Washoe and the Parrott mines, for $15,000,000, a total of $39,000,000.

Amalgamated Copper Co. was thereupon organized with 750,000 shares of $100 each, and the stock offered to the public by means of newspaper advertisements and circulars.

A $75,000,000 stock offering, while a comparatively small affair nowadays, was, in the closing year of the nineteenth century, the greatest in Wall Street's history. Sponsored by the Standard Oil and National City Bank powers, over the signatures of Rogers, Rockefeller and Stillman, and with Lawson in charge of the preliminary publicity, the offering received a public subscription of $132,000,000.

The stock immediately sold at a premium and ranged above par for a considerable time. Rogers and his associates, who had given the public only a small percentage of the amount applied for, endeavored to distribute the additional stock at more than $100 per share, and not succeeding, called in James R. Keene, who managed to unload, at below par, the block turned over to him.

Paying $39,000,000 for the original properties and selling them to the public for $75,000,000, the Rogers-Rockefeller-Lawson promoters might have cleaned up $36,000,000 on the very day the subscription books closed. How much they did realize, after allotting $26,000,000 of the stock to the public and retaining $49,000,000 of it for themselves, is not known; but it is clear that they got back two-thirds of their purchase money while retaining nearly two-thirds of the capital stock.

Lawson claimed that his share in the flotation profits was $9,000,000; that he was first offered $2,500,000 in settlement; then when he raised a row he "accepted $5,000,000," most of which he lost in an alleged attempt to support the market for Amalgamated on which the rest of the party were endeavoring to unload.

I was on the Curb when, for the first time, the stock broke below par. Edgar Williamson, of W. H. Berger & Co., apparently had the inside scale order to buy every eighth or quarter down. The Curb Market at that time was in front of the Mills Building, and it seemed as though the whole world were trying to sell Amalgamated Copper. Such a howling mob piled onto Edgar with their offerings that he was gradually backed up in a north-easterly direction across from the Mills Building to the old Stock Exchange Building. There he turned and backed to the southwest until he came to the corner of

Broad Street and Exchange Place on the opposite side of the Street, buying all the while, five hundred or one thousand shares at each fractional drop as was his order, while a crowd of raving maniacs pursued him, intent upon filling him up with their stock.

The low point in 1899 was well under par, from whence it rose to 130 in 1901. The panic of May 9 in that year saw it down to 60½. In the panic of 1903 the low point was 33⅝, around which figure Lawson always claimed that the stock which had been distributed to the public at three times that price was reaccumulated by the original distributors.

This peculiar procedure has never been entirely confined to those having their headquarters at 26 Broadway.

During the Spanish War loan, we bought a large number of allotments from those who had subscribed for the new United States Government 3% bonds. These allotments were selling at several points above par, but the bonds sold still higher so that we made a substantial profit by arbitraging—selling the "when issued" bonds against the allotments. In the meantime much of our working capital, already scarce enough, was tied up. Finally there was nothing else to do but get these funds released in some way. I went to Francis L. Hine, then cashier of the First National Bank, to see if I could arrange a loan with him secured by our allotments. I told Mr. Hine that if he would let us have $100,000 on the allotments, I would immediately go to Washington, jam the bonds through the Treasury Department, and pay off the loan within a few days; whereas ordinarily it was taking weeks to get the bonds through. I succeeded in this but the incident pointed again to the risks we were running in attempting to finance such a big and growing business on limited capital.

Price's branch office in Washington was in the old Hotel Chamberlain, since demolished. It was under the management of Arthur E. Bateman, formerly a member of the New York Stock Exchange, and once a partner in the firm of Greene & Bateman—one of Jay Gould's brokers.

Bateman used to describe his early start in the brokerage business in Washington with a capital of $5,000 and only one customer. The customer was not well; Bateman feared he might die, so every night he would go by the house to see if there was a light in the window. The customer recovered.

Later Bateman secured, among other clients, William McKinley, afterward President of the United States, and then a member of the lower House. He came into Bateman's office one morning, bought fifty shares of Erie, and put up a $500 margin, and left word that he did not wish to be bothered by telephone messages, that he meant to pay no attention whatsoever to the stock's fluctuations. Ten minutes later the telephone rang. It was Mr. McKinley speaking. "How is Erie now?" he asked of Bateman.

Bateman afterwards moved to New York and became one of Jay Gould's brokers. One morning he made his customary call on Gould. The big operator was pulling excitedly at the tape with one hand and pounding on the corner of the ticker with the other; he looked more or less like a maniac. He was growling to himself: "I'll teach them to sell that Union Pacific short! I'll teach them to sell that Union Pacific short!"

Bateman said, "Good morning, Mr. Gould, I see you are very busy, and I won't bother you now," backed out

Copyright Brown Brothers

1881. *Wall Street*

The buildings on the left are now replaced by the New York Stock Exchange. The one on the right corner was the first of three buildings that have stood there since 1881.

the door, bolted downstairs, across Broadway, down through the old iron-railed steps of No. 72, came into the New Street entrance of the Stock Exchange like a bomb, and rushing into the Union Pacific crowd, he bought everything in sight.

He turned over a big profit within a few hours, and when he saw Gould again, the latter said: "What was your hurry this morning, Bateman? If you had waited a few moments, I might have given you an order."

On the floor above Price's Washington office there was an interesting room. It had been the scene of one of the most flagrant pieces of political-stock market operation this country has ever witnessed. In two corners of the room were shelves which had held stock tickers. Back in the 'nineties the Congress, in session, was debating whether to take the tariff off sugar or leave it on. Violent fluctuations were taking place in the stock of the American Sugar Refining Co., then in the control of Havemeyer. Everybody in Washington knew what was going on, but few were in a position to prove it.

In this room two Senators were speculating in Sugar Refining stock for themselves and for those members of the Senate and the House who were "in." For weeks the course of probable legislation oscillated as the two senatorial operators went long or went short of sugar. The tariff was going to be left on; no, the tariff was going to be taken off: meanwhile the gang was making millions. Sergeants-at-arms sent out to locate the precious pair could not find them. Much of this business was going through the Washington branch office of Moore & Schley, of which Elverton R. Chapman was the resident partner. It was because of his refusal to disclose the identity of the principals in certain numbered accounts that Mr. Chapman later was sent to jail for contempt of court. Whether the Senators deserved such loyalty is a question. But Mr. Chapman won by it the respect of everyone in Wall Street.

* * *

1900 FLOATING MYSELF

FIRST STOCK EXCHANGE FIRM— GEO. J. GOULD'S MISSOURI PACIFIC MANIPULATION

I FINALLY determined to pull out and go into business for myself. I had already played my cards so as to be transferred into the Unlisted Security Department. There I traded in securities over the counter and by telephone, executed orders in the out-of-door Curb Market, and was engaged in activities which were an excellent preparation for starting on my own account.

Toward the end of the year I sent in my resignation, leased an office on the Broadway front of the seventh floor of the Empire Building, at 71 Broadway, bought office furniture and equipment from John Wanamaker on credit, engaged a clerk and a boy, and at the end of the year moved in.

I started on the day after New Year's with a few ten-share accounts and began dealing in unlisted stocks and bonds. Soon, executing orders on the Curb and specializing in inactive securities, I began to make money.

Within six weeks, Price phoned that he would like to see me. Hadn't I had enough of being in business for myself, he wanted to know, and wouldn't I like to come back? I had assumed an overhead of $7,000 a year on little capital but I told him I was going to keep on flying my own kite.

Later in the year I signed a partnership agreement with

Bernard J. Harrison and Frederic H. Smith, Jr., a millionaire, known as "Short-tailed Smith," this nickname being applied to him while in the business of manufacturing men's shirts. His reputed practice was to cut the shirt tails fairly short in order to save the fabric. He also had a weird habit of laundering his celluloid collar in the office washbowl.

Smith intended to have his son, Fred, join the firm later, but in the meantime wanted us to have a fourth partner, having interested Mr. Gaddis, of the well-known firm of Wilkinson, Gaddis & Co., of Newark. We thought that was too many for such a young firm.

It was finally agreed that Charles C. Hoge, a former schoolmate of mine, and a friend of Smith's, should put in part of the special capital and become a silent partner. The papers were signed in October, 1900, during the Bryan-McKinley campaign and it was agreed that the papers would be destroyed if McKinley were not elected.

The Bryan forces being completely routed, the firm of Harrison & Wyckoff began business on the day after election in November, and did a gross business of $114,000 in the next fourteen months.

* * *

My partner Harrison had done quite a little floor brokerage business while he was alone; now that we had facilities and capital for clearing trades for other brokers, much of that trade came our way. We were friendly with the firm of George P. Butler & Bro., who were handling Missouri Pacific and other Gould stocks for George J. Gould. Butler used our firm among others to conceal some of their operations. We thus earned com-

Photo H. N. Tiemann Company

1884. *Broad Street about the Time the Mills Building Was Erected*

missions on fairly large blocks of stocks which we bought, or sold short, as per their orders.

I could always tell when Missouri Pacific was being accumulated or distributed by the part we would be playing at the time; when we were picking up a few thousand shares at a time over several days, then Gould was getting ready for an upward move. If Missouri Pacific suddenly rushed up ten or fifteen points and Harrison was sent into the Missouri Pacific crowd on the floor to bid loudly for ten thousand shares in one lot, then the Butlers were selling through other brokers whatever volume the market would absorb, and the move was over. Harrison's bid would invariably be at the top eighth or within a fraction of it.

The trouble with the Gould forces was that they never varied their method. Manipulation calls for the deceiving of the public into doing the opposite of what the operator is doing; and after a game like the above has been worked a number of times in a relatively short period, the floor traders, the big operators and even the public learn to recognize the symptoms announcing the turning points and play the same way as the manipulator. So after a while the Butler brothers didn't get the Gould business any more and we didn't get the Butler orders.

The firm of Ellingwood & Cunningham were good friends of ours. We did a lot of "give-up" and clearance business for them—five and ten thousand share lots of the active stocks. Many of these happened to be in the Morgan stocks and it was whispered about the Street that the new firm of Harrison & Wyckoff was a Morgan house. Of course, that didn't do us any harm.

We had quite a lot of other manipulative business. Occasionally Harry Content, who was evidently handling

Amalgamated Copper for the Standard Oil party, seemed to have instructions to keep this stock, say, between 90 and 93. When the price would decline to the lower figure, we would receive buying orders from him for round lots, and when it would advance to 93 or thereabouts, we would become heavy sellers.

* * *

1901 INSIDE INFORMATION

JOHN W. GATES' BEAR RAID—FORMATION OF U. S. STEEL—A CLEAN-UP IN BURLINGTON—NORTHERN PACIFIC CORNER—THE INSIDE OF THE PANIC—SCHWAB BUYS SOME PENNSYLVANIA—THE AMERICAN CAN DEAL

A CLOSE friend and a good client of mine was William O. Jones, Assistant Cashier of the Chase National Bank. We rode into town together every morning, and often home together after business hours. Traveling thus together, we would discuss the day's events and the market prospects. He had good sources of information. Every morning he dropped in to see Dow and Woodlock, of Dow, Jones & Co., and now and then James J. Hill, president of the Great Northern Railway, and other important financiers would come into the bank to see Mr. Cannon, the president. Hill called my friend, the assistant cashier, "Jonesy" and would often give him bits of information which Jones promptly noted in shorthand on a small scratch-pad which he always carried in his vest pocket. This dope in turn came to me, and what I derived from it was of no small value to my clientele.

One morning, as we sat side by side in the train, Jones said: "I was up at the Waldorf last night and met John W. Gates with some of his crowd. While we were talking about the market, Gates said to some one who had just joined the party: 'We're going to close our steel mills tomorrow morning.'

"Somebody said, 'What's the matter? Business falling off?'

"Gates answered, 'No, we're short of the stock.' "

John W. Gates was the organizer and dictator of the American Steel & Wire Company, a combination of competing mills which he had brought together, and which became a unit, later, in the U. S. Steel consolidation.

The next day announcement was made that the mills had closed down. The stock broke from in the 60s to the 40s and 30s.

Gates then covered his shorts, making a big clean-up; then he took a long position.

The mills went to work again; the stock rose again. The closing of the mills had been nothing but a stock market maneuver.

* * *

The formation of United States Steel Corporation is a notable chapter in Wall Street history.

In 1899 Judge William H. Moore had successfully floated the American Tin Plate Co. and the National Biscuit Co. From these operations he had emerged with holdings of some $10,000,000 in American Tin Plate stock. He then organized the American Steel Hoop Co. and the National Steel Co., and made thereon $10,000,000 more.

In company with Frick and Phipps, he conceived the idea of buying out Carnegie's interest in the Carnegie Steel Co. He gave Carnegie $1,170,000 for a 90-day option on his controlling interest, the price of this being set at $158,000,000. The deal was taken to J. P. Morgan for financing but it required the use of $60,000,000 cash, which was a large amount in those days. "J. P.," for a number of reasons, refused to undertake it.

In the midst of the negotiations, which occurred during a bull market, the sudden death of ex-Governor Roswell P. Flower, acknowledged bull leader, produced a temporary panic. Money became scarce; courage still scarcer. Frick and Phipps tried to secure an extension of their option, but Carnegie wouldn't allow them a single day, and pocketed the option money.

Finding himself in control of this situation, Carnegie announced that in further negotiations the price of his interest in Carnegie Steel would be $300,000,000. He tried to sell out to his partners at this price, but they were unable to meet the terms. Carnegie then decided that his interest would be worth as much as $400,000,000 within two or three years and, in order to make other large interests realize his strategical position, started on an immense expansion of Carnegie operations: the transportation of ore by his own railroad and steamship subsidiaries; the erection of new mills to compete with the National Tube Co., American Steel & Wire, other competitors. He seemed bent upon driving these out of business.

Moore, Morgan and Rockefeller realized the bombshell Carnegie had thrown into their camp. Rockefeller had an important interest in the new Federal Steel Co., controlled the Lake Superior Iron Mines, and had previously sounded out Carnegie unsuccessfully with a view to buying him out. These interests, combined in self-defense, now saw that in order to save their own hides and the entire steel situation they must agree to Carnegie's terms.

Charles M. Schwab and John W. Gates began working

on both the Morgan and the Carnegie ends of the proposed combination. Meanwhile Carnegie was going right ahead with his new steel plant, as well as railroad and steamship lines to carry his ore and a new railroad from Pittsburgh to the Atlantic seaboard. Schwab finally succeeded in inducing Carnegie to accept the following securities for his holdings and those of his partners: $304,-000,000 in 5 per cent bonds of the proposed consolidated company; $98,000,000 in preferred stock and $90,-000,000 in common stock, a total of $492,000,000 par value in securities—a greater sum than the value of the whole American wheat crop of 1900; and greater than the combined dividends of all American railroads for the four years ending in 1900.

As soon as the creation of the giant corporation had been decided on, the stocks of all the proposed subsidiaries commenced to advance. Morgan announced that a $200,000,000 syndicate would underwrite the deal, and a "when issued" market was established on the Curb for the new common and preferred stock of the new United States Steel Corporation.

Our firm made quite a lot of money arbitraging. We would buy the preferred and common stocks of the subsidiaries and sell the equivalent in new shares, often at a profit of several points, especially in the preferred stocks of old companies that were comparatively inactive and neglected.

The underwriters' syndicate, which received its profit mostly in the form of U. S. Steel common, engaged James R. Keene to make a big market and distribute this stock to the public. The newspapers became filled with bullish interviews from Carnegie, Schwab, Frick, and other leading steel men and bankers. The possibilities in this colos-

Photo H. N. Tiemann Company

1885. *Looking up Broadway at Rector Street*

sal organization and its properties were extravagantly appraised.

First sales of the "when issued" stock occurred February 26, 1901: 39 for the common, 84 for the preferred. By March 28 the stocks were listed on the Exchange and sold around 44 and 94, respectively. Transactions ran from 100,000 to 275,000 shares a day in both common and preferred.

On April 30 the transactions on the Stock Exchange rose to 3,000,000 shares[1] for the first time in history. Nearly one-fourth of the sales were of U. S. Steel common and preferred. The day's closing showed Steel at 53⅞ and the preferred at 101.

Nine days later came the Northern Pacific corner and panic, in which Steel common dropped to 24 and the preferred to 69. On the afternoon of the panic the stock recovered to 42 and 89½, and the next day to 45 and 93¾.

Two-thirds of the American iron and steel trade had been welded together into this corporation; industrial war had been prevented and common and preferred Steel was recorded in the names of 40,000 stockholders. These soon increased to 80,000. As George W. Perkins, of J. P. Morgan & Co., said at the time: "The people of the United States have bought the steel business of the country."

Jim Keene's fee for handling this distributive operation was a million dollars cash and a percentage of the syndicate profits. These profits were reported as amounting to about $40,000,000, or 20 per cent on the syndicate's com-

[1] The first two-million-share day was January 7, 1901. Under the influence of this great increase in trading, Stock Exchange seats rose from $35,000 in 1900 to $71,000 about the time U. S. Steel was a month old—May, 1901.

mitments, of which only one-eighth, or $25,000,000, was paid in.

* * *

One of the best bits of information that ever came through Jones was when J. P. Morgan and James J. Hill bought control of the Chicago, Burlington & Quincy Railroad. This purchase preceded an attempt to secure the dominating interest in the Chicago, Milwaukee & St. Paul. It was well known that the Morgan-Hill interests wanted a connection which would make Chicago rather than St. Paul the eastern terminus of their system, and that they looked upon the St. Paul road as the most desirable to this end.

My friend, Wilbur F. Herbert, was sitting in his office at 20 Broad Street one day, looking out of a window which gave an excellent view of the directors' room of the St. Paul, and of a meeting being held there, when suddenly he became the witness of a very animated scene. J. Pierpont Morgan had come to his feet; he was standing, arguing, waving his arms, shaking his fists. "He wants the St. Paul and he can't get it," my friend Herbert thought. Then he saw "J. P.," evidently foiled in his purpose, storming out of the room in a towering rage. The news slips announced that the St. Paul directors had refused to make any deal.

Only a short time later Jones asked me to stop in at the Chase National Bank on my way home and there he gave me facts and data which indicated that Morgan, having failed to acquire the St. Paul, had begun to buy control of the Chicago, Burlington & Quincy in the open market in order to accomplish what he had failed to do with the St. Paul.

Burlington was then selling at about 135. The original

source of the information was J. P. Morgan's office and Jones' data was unquestionable. Jones bought a lot of Burlington; I loaded my customers up with it. The stock rose steadily on heavy and increasing transactions.

We knew from the same source that James R. Keene also had the information; his buying wasn't hurting a bit. By the time the stock got into the 160s those on the inside denied that there was anything in the story. Many people knew what was going on but were afraid to buy in the face of the advance that had already occurred. Knowing, as we did, that there might be as many more points profit in it as had already been made, we held on, and bought more. Finally, when insiders "admitted" that they had control, the stock was around 195. We then cleaned up.

It is curious how skeptical men are toward real information from the inside. They are stung so often by what sounds real that they have no courage when the real thing comes along. Already there had been a sixty-point rise in the stock, and the market was being shown the truth of the information more and more every day, yet some people who got in early had taken five or ten points profit when they should have pyramided, and those who had held on for twenty points or more began to get dizzy and fearful. It is often said in Wall Street that "inside information will break anyone." Inside misinformation is what the saying means.

In those days I used to go to great lengths to find out what important people were doing. Not having many good connections, but making the most of those, I could have surprised many a large operator by giving him a memorandum of what he had done in the market during the day. For example, Charles M. Schwab was a tremendous buyer of Pennsylvania Railroad stock through a house on one of the lower floors of the Empire Building. I used to get a daily report of the number of shares he had bought on balance and my clients were long of Pennsylvania. I watched Schwab buy it up into the 160s and then suddenly stop.

I've never known whether this was a stock market move in behalf of Mr. Carnegie or whether Mr. Schwab was employed by other interests to do the buying and see whether control could thus be obtained.

* * *

In the previous summer of 1900 rumors of great damage to the crops along the Northen Pacific had resulted in a decline of the stock to around 46. With the stock below 60 and on the way up heavy accumulation now began to take place, although for no reason apparent at the time. Undoubtedly some of the largest operators were taking on a big line.

Then, through my friend Jones, I learned of important and continuous buying of Northern Pacific preferred. These purchases were distributed among various brokerage houses, but were traced to Kuhn, Loeb & Co. as the principals. At their office all of this stock would be finally delivered. Northern Pacific preferred was then selling below par, and as its dividends were limited to 4 per cent, there seemed to be no great advantage to anyone in buying large quantities of it at rising prices; there were other more attractive preferred stocks.

While the formation of United States Steel Corporation had stimulated speculation in every branch of the Stock Exchange list, the feature early in May was strength in railroad shares. Northern Pacific was one of the leaders.

On Monday, May 6, Chicago, Burlington & Quincy was selling at 198. Great Northern preferred was 188. Chicago, Milwaukee & St. Paul common, 185. Chicago & Northwestern, 206. Northern Pacific was strong on an increasing volume of trading, touching 110.

On Tuesday, the seventh, there was a boiling railroad stock market. Canadian Pacific was up 13 points—a great advance for those days. All the big rails and the little railroad pups were strong. But the transactions in Northern Pacific common overshadowed everything, amounting to over 400,000 shares, with the stock making 133—an advance of 23 points from the previous day's high. There was a rumor that the preferred stock was to be retired; all sorts of stories sought to give the cause of the big transactions.

The market had a queer look. I didn't know what was going on but I could sense an approaching squall, and having made money for most of my clients on the bull side of the market, I now concluded it was time for everybody to take their profits and get long of cash. All that day and the next I was telephoning and wiring clients to get out and stand pat.

The morning of Wednesday, the eighth, was marked by what looked like heavy distribution in railroad and other stocks. But Northern Pacific was up to 149¾. Later in the day the rest of the market was clearly under liquidation and Northern Pacific still up; it was evidently cornered. Those who were short or had stock coming from abroad, or out of town, and who had to borrow the certificates, paid $700 for the use of one hundred shares of Northern Pacific overnight.

Came Thursday, May 9. The air was charged with excitement before the opening. No one knew what was going on under the surface of the Northern Pacific volcano. The chairman's mallet struck. Everything except Northern Pacific opened far down, and in the following hour, the nearest to hell I ever saw in Wall Street, the bottom seemed to drop out of everything.

Northern Pacific was jumping up fifty and a hundred points at a time until it sold at $700 a share regular way and $1,000 a share for cash.

Those who were short bid $2,500, then $5,000, and finally, at one time, $6,600 premium was bid for the use of one hundred shares of Northern Pacific overnight.

Typical examples of the decline in standard stocks on that day follow:

Stock	*Highest*	*Lowest*	*Last*
Amalgamated Copper	116	90	106
Atchison	78¼	43	66¾
Baltimore & Ohio	102	84	94
Chesapeake & Ohio	47	29	41½
St. Paul	165½	134	141
Rock Island	158	125	146
Delaware & Hudson	165	105	150
Louisville & Nashville	103¼	76	95½
Manhattan Elevated	120	88	109
Missouri Pacific	103	72	93
Northern Pacific	700 (reg.) 1000 (cash)	170	325
Southern Pacific	49	29	45⅛
Union Pacific	113	76	90
U. S. Steel	47	24	40¼

This decline was the swiftest and most disastrous in the history of the New York Stock Exchange up to that time. A glance at the above figures—and this shrinkage occurred within the space of an hour—will enable one to realize that at these low figures not only were margins exhausted but many clients so deeply in debt to their brokers that the majority of the brokerage houses could not possibly have met their obligations if the market had stayed down at the low point. These were the days of ten-point margins. Disaster would have overwhelmed Wall Street had it not been for the rapid recovery that set in immediately after eleven o'clock. Within the next few hours the stocks that had been the weakest had recovered the greater part of their losses.

As the result of my warnings before the panic, most of my clients held now nothing but money; but in the gorgeous opportunity presented by the panic they failed to buy much at the bottom. In that hour of pandemonium the tape was so far behind that only through the report of executions and through telephone communications from the floor did we know anywhere near at what prices stocks were selling. But that was not the only reason. Most of my clients were scared to death. Two things must be possessed by people who buy stocks: money and courage. With the money and without the courage they all stood dazed and paralyzed. When the worst was over they were like men who had seen a cyclone pass; they didn't feel much like flying kites. After a while, however, they began to get back a little of their nerve and by twelve o'clock were scooping some of the remaining bargains. For the rest of the day I was busy placing their buying orders, and at the close they held substantial paper profits. These were subsequently greatly increased.

At nine that evening I went out to lunch.

The panic demonstrated a number of interesting points about the stock market, the public and the brokerage business. First of all, it showed that no one can ever tell what is going to happen to the market nor how badly it will be affected by a single bit of news or a calamity such as this. Then it proved that, while real values are of most importance in the long run, much allowance must be made for the unknown and the incalculable. Not even the insiders who were running this fight for control of Northern Pacific realized, when they began, what harm it might do to millions of people who were operating in the market. But the conclusion I got out of it was this: That the action of the market itself was the best clue as to what it might do. The tape had said: Danger! That meant: Get out!

* * *

The inside story of the panic was this: The acquisition of control of the Chicago, Burlington & Quincy by Hill and Morgan had been a grievous disappointment to Harriman, head of the Union Pacific. The Burlington had its eastern terminus in Chicago, covered a vast field in the Granger states, and connected Chicago with the eastern terminus of the Union Pacific. It had a great network of branches and feeders in Kansas, Nebraska and Colorado and collected vast quantities of freight originating in or destined for Union Pacific territory. The Burlington was nearly 8,000 miles in length, well constructed and managed—one of the most profitable systems in the west.

Harriman and Kuhn, Loeb & Co. had been working for control of the Burlington for some years without success. Harriman, Jacob H. Schiff, James Stillman and George J. Gould formed a pool in the spring of 1900 for the purpose of acquiring up to 200,000 shares of Burlington, of which 1,105,000 shares were outstanding. But after buying steadily for several weeks, the pool had secured only about 80,000 shares, and the supply of stock had become so thin that further attempts were abandoned. The great body of small shareholders refused to part with their holdings, and speculators who knew what was going on caused a rise in the stock from about 130 to 140.

Then Harriman discovered that Hill and Morgan were negotiating for control of the Burlington. He asked to be given a one-third interest in the purchase. This offer being refused, he is reported to have said: "Very well, that is a hostile act and you must take the consequences."

It was then I learned that Northern Pacific preferred was being bought under cover and delivered to Kuhn, Loeb & Co.

By seizing control of the Northern Pacific, Harriman would thus get his paws on his love, the Burlington, in which the Northern Pacific had just acquired half interest. The joint ownership of the Burlington could then be vested in the Great Northern and the Union Pacific with the latter in the stronger, if not the dominant, position.

By April 15 the Harriman coterie had accumulated 150,000 shares of common and 100,000 shares of preferred. The Hill-Morgan party was so unsuspecting that three lots aggregating 60,000 shares of Northern Pacific common were sold by them for one of their friends.

When Hill finally became concerned over the rapid advance and heavy transactions in Northern Pacific, he came to New York, called on Schiff and was told by the latter that Kuhn, Loeb & Co. were buying the stock on order from the Union Pacific. Hill then cabled J. Pierpont Morgan in Italy for authority to buy at least 150,000 shares.

Up to Friday, May 3, Kuhn, Loeb & Co. had bought 370,000 shares of the common and 420,000 shares of the preferred. The amount they held of the common was within 30,000 or 40,000 shares of the quantity needed to secure control, in that stock. Harriman feared that Hill would retire Northern Pacific preferred in the following January, thus euchring him out of control. On Saturday, May 4, ill at home, he called up one of the Kuhn, Loeb & Co. partners and gave him an order to buy 40,000 shares of Northern Pacific common at the market.

That order was never executed. Mr. Schiff gave instructions that it was not to be executed and that he, Schiff, would take the responsibility.

When, on Monday, Harriman recovered sufficiently to go downtown and find out how matters stood, he learned for the first time that this vital 40,000 shares had not been purchased.

Northern Pacific continued to advance on enormous trading due to Morgan's instructions from London to purchase 150,000 shares at the market. The Morgan buying put the stock to 110 that day and to 133 on Tuesday; then, next day, to 149¾, or about 40 points in two days. These purchases gave the Morgan-Hill interests something like 30,000 shares more of the common than they needed, and positively settled the question of control, as the preferred stock, it proved, was to be retired the following January.

Reports current at the time stated that Harriman had overlooked the possibility of the preferred being retired, but this was not the fact. The whole situation hinged on that 40,000 shares of common which he ordered bought and which Mr. Schiff failed to buy because he thought it unnecessary.[2]

The Harriman party stopped buying on Friday, May

[2] Many of these facts were as stated by Mr. Harriman personally, and by his biographer, George Kennan.

3, and the Morgan buying was completed by Tuesday, May 7. It was not until Thursday, May 9, that the Northern Pacific panic occurred.

The rapid advance in Northern Pacific had led a great many speculators to sell it short. To the public it appeared that the common stock was selling many points above what it was worth. Investors here and in foreign countries had sold a great deal of stock for which the certificates had not yet been delivered in Wall Street. The combined Morgan and Harriman buying had left the market bare of actual stock, and when on Wednesday, May 8, Northern Pacific made its sensational advance to around 150, many brokerage houses were obliged to face enormous losses on the short contracts of clients who could not make good.

Finally Mr. Schiff, with Harriman's approval, proposed to J. P. Morgan & Co. that the shorts be permitted to settle with both firms at $150 per share for Northern Pacific common. This being agreed upon, the panic was ended.

* * *

Here is an example of the way things were done in those days of industrial consolidation. One of our clients owned a tin can factory in the South. When Dan Reed and his associates consolidated this with can companies throughout the country, our client was given preferred and common stock for his property. The preferred was supposed to represent actual assets and the common a bonus. Our man figured that as the preferred he held represented the actual value of his plant, the rest represented the actual value of all the other plants. And as the slogan of all the promoters and consolidators at that time was more economical management, larger earnings and dividends, he decided to hold the preferred and sell out the common, which he considered velvet.

But he did not figure quite correctly, and he did not sell quickly enough. The market for the preferred had been near 80 and the common was above 30, but now both were sliding down rapidly. Other people were apparently agreeing with his forecast. Some were selling their preferred; more were selling their common. Whichever stock went down, it affected the other. And the more he reduced his selling prices the lower the market broke. Only with difficulty did he finally get out in the 20s. Later that year Can sold at 10.

What was happening at the time, I learned through an old friend who was the order clerk in a brokerage firm, where Dan Reed and the Moore brothers did a large business. This firm had orders to "fill up" with Can, common or preferred, every buyer that appeared in the crowd. They were selling for whatever they could get, without offering the stock down.

The promoters not only unloaded all of their promotion stock as the market would take it, but when they had accomplished this, kept on selling short, riding the market down. I figured they would cover their short commitments when the company indicated that its position had improved. Also, they would buy in proportion to what they hoped it could earn. The process of weeding out weak plants, rehabilitating good ones, adding new plants and building up the working capital in this case took over ten years, during which the stock spent most of the time in the single figures.

* * *

The bull market which began with McKinley's election in 1896 had continued right along past McKinley's second election in 1900 and big things had been doing in the market. The numerous industrial combinations of the past few years had resulted in a period of tremendous speculation. Earning power and future prospects had been capitalized at a rate out of all proportion to the earning power of many of these combinations; reams of promoters' and bankers' shares were being issued. Millionaires were springing up like mushrooms, not only in New York but in other industrial centers—Pittsburgh and Chicago—and many of them were big operators in the stock market.

The new industrials of 1901 had big markets, were subject to wide swings and, therefore, furnished plenty of action for pools and plungers.

Another important movement was in the railroad properties. It was based on the so-called community-of-interest idea, popular with railroad financiers. Small railroad properties were being consolidated into larger systems, and some of these in turn were being hooked together. Old, run-down properties were rejuvenated. Systems that had come through the reorganizations of the 'nineties were using their restored credit to borrow enormous sums and to reconstruct their transportation plants. In railroad operation the watchwords were: Better roadbeds, heavier rails, stronger bridges, more powerful locomotives, bigger freight cars; so that the maximum number of tons of freight per trainload might be attained, the cost per ton per mile reduced, and net earnings and dividends increased.

Naturally all these operations, combined with the riotous public speculation, had a tremendous effect upon the stock market. Violent and widespread moves in many leading stocks were so common they attracted little attention.

* * *

1902 GOING AFTER THE PUBLIC

BUSINESS GETTING IN A NEW WAY—THE STOCK EXCHANGE OBJECTS—MARKET LETTERS—MANIPULATIVE FORCES

As a stock broker, my mind worked hard on three problems. The first was, how could I make money for my clients so that I could build up their accounts, retain their patronage, and make my own business successful? Statistics were my second concern: the study of statements, balance sheets of corporations listed on the New York Stock Exchange, so that I might become expert in judging values. Thirdly, I was bent on learning all about the operations of those who were big factors in the market—how they made their money, the details of their manipulative and pool operations.

Our firm was always on the lookout for real information on coming market moves. I was writing and mailing a daily letter on market conditions in which, also, I worked out the value of securities so as to bring them to the attention of our clients. My practice was to summarize the principal elements in the market situation on the day, and to point out one or two of the most attractive opportunities. We drew a good business from this letter. I constantly strove to perfect both the judgment of the writer and the character of the information. An assistant scouted the Street for news of what was going on among the real people and to get clews which might develop into good leads. All this was checked up from every angle.

We were forecasting the action of market and selecting securities with a fair amount of success. This encouraged me to push on along this line.

* * *

It was the practice at that time, as now, for commission houses to employ customers' men to bring in business. There were few attempts to get business by advertising and mail orders. Such newspaper advertisements as appeared were confined to reproductions of cards. "John Smith & Co., Stock Brokers, 20 Wall Street," for instance.

I had for a long time been interested in advertising and believed it could bring business into Wall Street from strangers all over the country.

Having decided to make the attempt, I asked in an assistant to collect for me, out of newspapers and magazines, typical advertisements of houses doing business by mail. I was after the principle upon which they advertised, and built up their mail order campaigns. For some days my man interviewed manufacturers of books, soap, food products, patent medicines, etc. I analyzed the results of these investigations and soon learned to apply the result to the stock brokerage business.

No legitimate firm in Wall Street had attempted anything of this kind. The bucketeers had mostly confined themselves to advertising market letters, and a "come-on" sort of correspondence designed less to secure commission business than to extract capital from easy victims.

I started an advertising and follow-up campaign which began with a small booklet about the brokerage business. Inserting, on the first page of the *Wall Street Journal,* an

1885. *The New York Stock Exchange*

advertisement which offered this booklet, I began to receive inquiries by mail. I followed these up with personal letters, and business came. Clients thus won were likely to belong to the firm; they would not easily be controlled or taken away by my own or other firms' customers' men.

The new department soon had fifteen employees. We were getting new clients right along, a good sprinkling of them with fair-sized accounts, and I was encouraged to get up a new booklet, better printed matter, more efficient follow-up letters.

One response came from de Clerq & Van Essen, a banking firm in Amsterdam, Holland. It was an inquiry about Southern Pacific. I gave the desired information in several typewritten pages. Within a couple of weeks we received a cabled order from this firm, instructing us to buy 4,000 shares of stock at the market and stating that their bank would pay us $40,000 for their account. This proved what could be done by mail.

I was still making a point of going after business personally. One day a friend gave me a list of names of parties in and around Roanoke, Va., who were interested in the market. I took the first train for Roanoke, landed there at three o'clock in the morning, got a few hours' sleep and at nine o'clock was starting my calls. A number of good clients resulted from this trip, and also some other interesting by-products. One of these was acquaintance with the leading officials of the Norfolk and Western Railway. It is surprising how easy it is to obtain real information on the condition and prospects of a big railroad property, its earnings and dividend outlook, if one goes to those who know the most about it.

I had already a favorable idea of the road's future from the way the property was being built up. After talking with its officers and traveling over part of the road, I now became a sort of permanent bull on Norfolk. The stock was then in the lower 20s; I made money for my clients by putting them into it.

The other by-product of my Roanoke trip was an inside view of a big bucket shop. Its New York headquarters were owned by a New York man, who afterward became well known as an owner of racing stables, oil properties and public utilities—a multi-millionaire. The shop in Roanoke was a correspondent. The owner showed me his sheets and explained to me at great length what a cinch it was for those fellows in New York because the bucket shop traders were always ready to sell at a few points' profit; but when a stock went against them they held on, putting up whatever margin was necessary. They cut their *profits* short and let their *losses* run.

Another trip about that time was to Bath, in Maine, where I met the leading members of the Hyde family. They had recently sold out their shipbuilding plant to the Morgan-Schwab Steel and Shipbuilding combination. The Hydes had received a lot of cash in payment for their properties. I accompanied an uncle of theirs, a Mr. Hayden, who was representing them, to receive the final payment which was in the form of bonds. We went to the Equitable Trust and took over a block of bonds in three big security bags—all that he, I, and a negro porter could carry. I was after an order to sell some of these bonds and buy other investment securities. I succeeded in this.

* * *

How large a business would have been built up by advertising and mail, I have no way of telling; certain influences came in at this point to take the "pep" out of the

Copyright Brown Brothers

1888. *New Street, Corner of Exchange Place, during the Blizzard*

new department. I had lists of names to which I sent my circulars, and although I did not know this, some of the names were of clients of other houses. The partner in an old-fashioned firm on Wall Street went weeping to the Stock Exchange, complaining that we were circularizing his clients. The president of the Exchange, Rudolph Keppler, requested me to call. At his office I listened to mossback talk on the advisability of advertising with business cards instead of circulars which some people thought somewhat flamboyant. I argued with him for half an hour in an effort to get any little leeway that could be considered as perhaps 10 per cent enterprising, while keeping within the Stock Exchange requirements, which meant the requirements of his committee and himself. But I couldn't make any headway at all. "Young man," he said, "if you will sit up nights and think of ways to keep *within* the rules instead of trying to argue with me as to how you can *overstep* them, you will be working more in the spirit which makes New York Stock Exchange seats worth forty thousand dollars."

Meanwhile, my partners, especially the Smith contingent, which now included the son as well as the father, were kicking about the expense of the new department. If I had been let alone we could have bought the Empire Building before the United States Steel Corporation had a chance to do it.

In other ways I was becoming dissatisfied. My office partner, young Smith, had that unfortunate habit of jumping customers in and out of stocks so as to get the commissions. Every time a client's trade showed a couple of points to the good, Smith called the man up, suggested selling, and buying some other stock. He simply couldn't stand seeing a small profit run into a big one.

That kind has to have the "commish." Naturally, people taking small profits and letting losses run hadn't half a chance to make money. The clients' interests were becoming secondary. It was an extremely shortsighted policy. Feeling hemmed in on all sides by narrow, unprogressive people and regulations, I made up my mind I would move.

* * *

Understanding of the action of the stock market demanded a form of reasoning entirely different from that applied to statistics and allied subjects. Forces were at work, influencing prices, which had no relation to real values. Many stocks were put up and hammered down by pools and by individuals for reasons of their own—not because the value of these stocks was any more or any less. Understanding values was one thing; but the subject of manipulation, of the forces that artificially altered the course of prices through the various swings of the market, especially fascinated me.

Being on the lookout for panics and bargain days, I reached the conclusion that these came out of overextension of business, out of money situations, or they might have political or other causes. A panic was a psychological condition—a state of mind into which the public was stampeded, usually by sudden and unexpected events, or by a combination of influences which led to great uncertainty and ended in fright.[1]

It appeared important that anyone operating in the market be on the watch for conditions that might lead to a panic. During a panic the market was at bottom, and usually there followed a year or two of advancing prices.

[1] This was clearly illustrated in the panic of 1929.

While it was all right to be bullish much of the time, one must be guided by the record of the past, be ready to jump out when danger signals appeared, and then get long of cash in anticipation of coming bargains.

* * *

1903 A BEAR MARKET

A NEW FIRM—RESULTS OF ADVERTISING—SHRINKAGE IN PRICES—STEEL AT 10—MORGAN'S OPINION—BUCKET SHOP PRACTICES

RESTRICTIONS in advertising and circularizing imposed by the Stock Exchange, combined with the non-progressiveness of some of my partners, continued to be a source of annoyance to me. I felt that if I were left free to advertise and get business by mail I could rapidly build up a business without the handicap of "business getters." I could see no end to the development of a large clientele all over the country. I studied everything in the line of advertising and follow-up information in all lines of business.

An intimate friend, Daniel T. Mallett, was publisher of the *Hardware Dealers' Magazine;* he had been successful in developing his business by mail. We talked the matter over and finally decided that I should withdraw from the firm of Harrison & Wyckoff and form a partnership with him. And since the New York Stock Exchange would not let me develop my business in my own way, we determined that Mallett should buy a membership on the Consolidated Stock Exchange, which imposed no such restrictions.

Many of my friends thought it a great mistake to step down from a Stock Exchange partnership to a Consolidated partnership. But when I was busy trying to put salt on the tail of an idea which I considered a bird it didn't matter to me what people said. My respect for the Consolidated Exchange was small. I had known much of its history: what kind of people were using it as a blind for certain operations, but it served my purpose. I notified my partners that I would withdraw, much to their expressed regret and in spite of their inducements for me to stay. They knew I would take a large portion of the clientele with me; the move did not please them at all.

Early in 1903, the firm of Mallett & Wyckoff was formed with offices at 10 Wall Street. Mallett did not take an active part. Immediately putting my plans into action, I began advertising in rather a striking style—with unusual type, illustrations, eye-catchers, condensed into small and economical space. In this I called the firm: "Mallett & Wyckoff, the Stock Brokers of Ten Wall Street."

My mailing list consisted of several thousand names of people who, I had reason to believe, were interested in trading and investing. At Mallett's suggestion we got up a small pamphlet in magazine style, called *Practical Investing,* as a house organ. This was mailed to everybody on the list once a month. Now and then we sent out additional printed matter containing ideas, suggestions and information which, according to my studies, were psychologically attractive.

Most of the clientele of my former firm followed me to 10 Wall Street. I had handled their business, had made a good deal of money for many of them, and they had confidence in me. My studies had made me extremely bearish on the situation, and although some clients would not trade on the short side, I had a large number who did, and who made money. Within a few months the advertising and circularizing began to show results, and at times we would open as many as six new accounts a day. Within half a year, our firm stood fourth among the firms dealing on the Consolidated Exchange.

Checking up on the results after a while, we found that four hundred new clients had been gained at a cost of $5,000, or $12.50 for each. And some of these were five hundred and thousand share fellows. Which went to prove the soundness of the theory that stock brokers need not depend on customers' men to produce business.

* * *

The great promotion and flotation period of the preceding years had ended with bankers, syndicates, pools and individuals loaded up with securities that had not been distributed. The public had bought its head off but had not been able to absorb all there was in the bankers' portfolios.

The total capitalization of new companies had amounted to $8,000,000,000. Some had gone wrong. Morgan & Schwab's attempted consolidation of shipbuilding and steel companies had become wreckage. Confidence waned and died. Shares were liquidated through fear or necessity. The whole stock market was undergoing a terrific slump.

Earnings of U. S. Steel for one quarter had amounted to only $2,000,000; 20,000 of the corporation's workmen were out of employment.

The decision in the Northern Securities case, by the United States Supreme Court, brought on a pessimistic attitude in the great financiers interested in railway consolidations. The downward movement was accelerated; liquidation of undigested securities continued; many syndicates closed out at a loss. Capitalists who were rich in certificates but heavily committed and short of cash were forced to let go wherever they could find a market. They were like sailors dumped into the sea and engaged in drowning each other; for, as in all bear markets, whenever weakness showed in one quarter, it would cause weakness in another, and that in another, so on down the line, until there were comparatively few securities pressed for sale.

The bear market continued for about a year. The Dow-Jones averages recorded a break in the average price of twenty railroad stocks from the high record of 192 in 1902 to 89 in 1903; and in the twelve industrials from 67 to 42, indicating a shrinkage of about one-half and one-third, respectively.

Some of the low prices reached by leading industrial stocks in this 1903 panic were: Allis-Chalmers, 7; American Can, 2⅜; Amalgamated Copper, 33⅝; American Car & Foundry, 17¼; American Linseed, 5; American Locomotive, 10½; American Smelting & Refining, 36¾; International Paper, 9; National Biscuit, 32; National Lead, 10½; Republic Iron & Steel, 5⅝; United States Cast Iron Pipe, 6.

* * *

As a natural consequence of its prominence and market leadership, United States Steel common stock had been the subject of one of the public's greatest speculative orgies. For a long period transactions had been 5 to 10 per cent of the total dealings on the New York Stock Exchange. More than once, blocks of 100,000 shares had been bought and sold in single transactions. The Steel

Corporation's affairs were not only in the public eye but on the tip of the tongue of everyone interested in the market, in the United States, in Canada, in the financial centers of Europe.

When, therefore, the market for Steel Common began to weaken and its power to earn its dividends (then 4 per cent on the common and 7 per cent on the preferred) began to be doubted, the decline might as well have been the Chicago fire or the San Francisco earthquake so far as Wall Street followers were concerned. The very heart had been cut out of the market.

Pennsylvania dropped from 157⅝ to 110¾; New York Central from 156 to 112⅝; Chicago and Northwestern from 224½ to 153, and Union Pacific from 104⅝ to 65¾, but none of these carried the weight of influence to the same extent as Steel. The big corporation's securities continued to drop month after month, thus greatly intensifying the depression.

Morgan, when maligned for this decline in Steel stocks, said: "I was the company's midwife, not its wet nurse."

When, in 1903, the price of the preferred stock had declined to 49¾ and the common was selling at $10 per share, I saw a letter which he had written in his own hand at the time Steel preferred was selling at par:

"In reply to your inquiry," the letter said, "I believe that United States Steel Preferred at $100 per share is a sound investment."

And here was now the stock selling at $50! However, he had not said in the letter that the stock would not decline. Probably after creating this organization he did not know just what would happen to it. He had brought it into being; the rest was not his responsibility. But, evidently, he was confident of its ultimate satisfactory development.

* * *

As United States Steel was on its way down, the bucket shops and other get-rich-quick concerns conducted a campaign typified by the operations of a concern located at 25 Broad Street, holding no membership of any exchange. This firm advertised in big newspaper space: "If you are a holder of United States Steel, now is the time for you to buy more and thus reduce the average cost of your holdings. Deposit your certificate with us as collateral and we will buy you, at the present low price, an additional amount equal to your present holdings."

As United States Steel slid from the 30s and down toward 20, with the 4 per cent dividend not yet discontinued, although there were many rumors that it would be, such firms advertised that this stock was now "paying" 20 per cent on the investment. But the big IF here was the dividend. Would it be continued? The state of the steel industry said it would not; the price of the stock yelled NO. In spite of this, many people were misled by hope (in Wall Street speculation a liability, not an asset) and deposited their certificates of common stock with concerns like the above. Thus they found themselves long of 200 shares on margin, for every 100 they originally held.

The bucket shop I have mentioned and others of its kind did a raft of business on this plan; their advertisements and their suggestions as to averaging also led many clients of Stock Exchange houses to do likewise with their own brokers. The effect of this sort of buying through the bucket shops was not to increase the demand from that quarter; it increased the supply, because the bucket shops instead of buying the additional shares to average, merely took the owners' certificates and sold them out.

* * *

1904 UP FROM THE LOWS

BUYING STEEL AT THE BOTTOM—INSIDE BUYING—HOLDING THEM DOWN—FRICK'S DEAL IN STEEL—CHANGE IN TREND—PICKING THE BEST ONES

WITH Steel preferred at 50 and the common at 10, my partner and I took pads and pencils and began to do some figuring. At those low figures all of the common stock had a market value of only $50,830,000, and all of the preferred then outstanding of about $180,000,000—$230,000,000 altogether, compared with a par value of $868,000,000.

We estimated that the decline in the stock market had wiped out much of the overcapitalization and that even though the preferred dividend were passed as rumor had it, the time was coming when the earning power would improve and payment of dividends be resumed.

The position of the Steel Corporation was unique. Taking the value of the sinking fund bonds, together with the preferred and common stock at the prevailing prices, the shrinkage amounted to about $450,000 in market valuation. The company, since organization, had put back into the property $200,000,000 in improvements, new plants and equipment. Its manufacturing costs had been greatly reduced and new economies were constantly being put in effect.

During the first year or two of its history it had earned the 4 per cent dividend on the common several times over.

In the new period of prosperity which must inevitably come, it should be able to earn large dividends and make liberal payments to its stockholders. The corporation's big working capital, combined with its great earning power, should enable it to extend its operations without resorting to new security issues. Earnings in future years should be large.

Facts and probability said that the common stock should be bought for keeps. For when the dividend of 4 per cent would be resumed, the net interest on stock bought at $10 per share, the price now, would be at the rate of 40 per cent per annum.

We went into action right away. Mallett took on quite a jag of the preferred and some common. I bought some common as low as 8⅝, within one quarter of a point of the lowest it has ever sold in the history of the corporation. When my certificates came in, I looked them over and said to myself: "Here is something to put away for my grandchildren."

But, I am sorry to say, I did not keep them that long. My grandchildren never saw them. Yet if I had waited for the World War, when the corporation was paying $17 per share per annum, I would have been making 200 per cent per annum on my investment.

Not long after we had bought, Steel began to creep up. There had been great activity in the preferred within the range of 50 to 60. Vast accumulation was apparently under way. John D. Rockefeller ordered a private telegraph wire run into his house at Tarrytown; the old man was soaking away bundles of Steel preferred in his safe deposit box—large as a bedroom—in one of the downtown vaults. The Morgans were buying heavily; they

Copyright Brown Brothers

1888. *Floor of the Old New York Stock Exchange*

were telling their closest friends to get aboard again. The stock rose steadily.

Much of the inside buying took the form of an equal amount of preferred and common; that is, for each 10,000 shares of preferred, these large interests would buy 10,000 shares of common. At a price of 50 and 10, respectively, their investment was $60,000 per 1,000 shares of each, of which the preferred was paying 7 per cent. The net return on that combined investment was over 11 per cent. Later, when Steel common resumed its 4 per cent rate, the income from the two stocks was $11,000 per annum on the $60,000 investment, or over 18 per cent.

The general market, however, did not commence its upward march until June, 1904. There had been a period of a few months in which stocks had been held down within a narrow range, and the market was lifeless. This was the well-known period of convalescence which generally follows a sick market. Any tendency to advance was promptly knocked on the head because the inside manipulators' game was to keep prices still down while they accumulated. The result was a narrow whipsaw market in which traders, long or short, could not make any money.

These conditions make the public very bearish, for it is a well-known principle in manipulation that more people can be tired out and made disgusted with their holdings, and thus induced to sell, on such a stagnant market than can be shaken out or scared out by a decline. In a steadily or swiftly declining market, many traders and investors will hold on, feed in margins and stick to their holdings in anticipation of a rally on which they can sell. Very often the rally does not come, or if it does, it does not go far enough. If it does go far enough, they will get bullish again, and hang on at the very time when they should be getting out.

My bearishness of the past two years had become temperamental; I couldn't see a thing that looked favorable. The event that finally woke me was the heavy oversubscription by the public of an offering of bonds by the City of New York.

The next day I went down to a little bungalow on the meadows behind Manhattan Beach, broke away from my friends there, jumped into a rowboat, pulled into a quiet creek where there were plenty of cat-tails, and said to myself: "If Moses first saw the light in the bulrushes, perhaps I may, too."

Lying in the bottom of the boat, staring at the sky and thinking hard, I gradually worked myself into an unprejudiced state of mind. I then sat up and jotted down the favorable and unfavorable factors in the situation. I discovered that there was a big balance on the bull side. It was perfectly clear to me that the market must immediately respond to the warning gun set off by the City bond issue.

* * *

The next thing to do was to select the stocks which offered the greatest possibility of an advance in what I regarded as the coming bull market. Here was an opportunity to make a shoestring grow into a pair of top boots.

Selecting railroad stocks was a comparatively easy job, for railroad reports were well standardized. What I was after was not the rate of the dividend nor the percentage of the earnings on the common stock, but the relation of this earning power to the market price of the stock. One company, the shares of which might be selling at $100,

Copyright Brown Brothers

1890. *Russell Sage at His Ticker*

might be earning $10 a share, but they would not be as cheap as those of another company earning $7 a share but selling at $50. After going over all the railroad stocks the earnings of which were shown, I made up a list in the order of their desirability, and found some of the leaders in this order: St. Louis & San Francisco 2nd Pfd., earning on market price 28 per cent; Missouri, Kansas & Texas Pfd., earning 23 per cent on market price; Reading, earning 18 per cent; Union Pacific, 14⅝ per cent; Erie 1st Pfd., 14⅜ per cent; Norfolk & Western, 12½ per cent; and so on down the line until I came to Wabash Bs earning about 1½ per cent on par value, or 2½ per cent on the market price of 60.

After boiling them all down and eliminating, I issued a brief market letter. In this, it will be noted, the buying point in United States Steel common was put down as around $10 per share, and I mentioned it because, whether they admitted it or not, many held it at 40 or 50. The letter follows:

June, 1904.

Dear Friend:

I've been a bear for two years, but I'm a bear no longer.

The return of investment capital to Wall Street, the splendid crop outlook, and the growth of confidence in the election of a "safe" President, are unquestionably forerunners of a bull market.

And it will be here before you realize it, so don't procrastinate.

Here are the best things to buy:

READING, because it's earning 8½% on the common and will probably pay a dividend in the fall. Three-quarters of this stock is "out of the market," and the balance is being steadily accumulated. Besides, it's only a few points from the lowest in three years.

UNION PACIFIC COMMON, earning four times its dividend, to say nothing of its equity in Southern Pacific. It is far cheaper than St. Paul, N. Y. Central or Pennsylvania, and in good times will pay an increased dividend. What's more, it's a market leader, and something you can hand down to the children, so far as income is concerned.

ATCHISON, earning 10% and paying 4%. The cheapest of the active standard stocks. No reason why it should be eight points below Baltimore & Ohio and sixteen points below Union Pacific.

FRISCO 2nd, the lowest 4% dividend payer on the railroad list. Nets nearly 9% on the investment, sells at 46, earning over thrice the dividend, and still showing increases. Close to lowest in some years.

STEEL 5s, should go to 85 on the least revival in the trade. By the way, *better average up on Steel Common around* 10.

MISSOURI, KANSAS & TEXAS PREFERRED, earning over 8%. The big cotton crop should bring a dividend on this stock. The common, too, is dirt cheap (16½). Lowest in recent years 14 5/8.

The big men are accumulating stocks. Better follow suit. You can't buy at the lowest eighth—neither can they.

GET BULLISH.

I had turned from bear to bull just in time. No sooner had I issued this market letter than the market began to climb. It was as though I had got on the last car of the last train just before it pulled out of the station.

The market advanced for two years. Within this period Reading, which had begun dividend payments on a 4 per cent basis, sold at 164. Union Pacific increased its dividend rate to $10 per share, and in a tremendous 60-point advance, within a very short time, surged up to 195¼. Both Atchison and St. Louis & San Francisco 2nd Pfd. nearly doubled in price. Missouri, Kansas & Texas common rose during that period to 40⅝ and U. S. Steel common to 50½.

* * *

Here is an example of what it means to know the inner workings of a corporation: When Andrew Carnegie sold out the Carnegie Steel Co. to J. P. Morgan and his associates, H. C. Frick was one of his partners. Frick's fortune was estimated at $50,000,000 and nine-tenths of it was in U. S. Steel securities.

Frick was a director in U. S. Steel, although he did not attend meetings of the Board. He knew the Steel business and he knew what was going on in the company's affairs, being one of Mr. Morgan's closest advisers in Steel Corporation matters.

In 1902, with the outlook still promising to the outsider, Mr. Frick became convinced that earnings would decline later; with Steel common in the 40s, and preferred in the upper 90s, he carefully sold over 200,000 shares of each stock. Two years later the common was selling below 9 and the preferred around 50, and upon being asked by J. Pierpont Morgan what he would advise in relation to the company's affairs (then in a critical position) Mr. Frick recommended a stopping of dividends on the common stock, a reduction of dividends on the preferred, and a complete reorganization of the operating force. All of these things were done.

When the depression had about run its course, Mr. Frick then repurchased 100,000 shares of preferred and 50,000 of common at the low prices. Had he not known what was coming, that is, had he been an outsider, he might have carried his original holdings of over 400,000 shares down to the low levels, where his paper loss would have been $16,000,000. That would have left him with little money for bargain day.

* * *

The firm of Mallett & Wyckoff made money. Within a year it had the reputation of being an active and growing house. It was more than ordinarily successful in guiding its clients, but I was not satisfied as to this.

Advising clients of a stock brokerage house is one of the most difficult tasks anyone can undertake. The work of a stock broker divides itself into two sections: first, he must properly organize and conduct his business. He must find ample capital, efficient partners and employees; he must get business that will yield a profit on the undertaking. Common sense and business brains can do that. The second part of the broker's work is advisory. This is separate and distinct from the other. A broker's time is so occupied with the routine of the business that he is rarely able to devote sufficient time to the study and analysis of the stock market.

Few people—stock brokers or others—are mentally equipped for the difficult work of forecasting price movements on the Stock Exchange and selecting the stocks that will yield more profits than losses to those who make commitments. Almost anyone with some years of experience in Wall Street can be correct in his judgment from time to time; but the problem is to be correct *most* of the time.

Having learned to get business by mail, I was ambitious to make a great success of the advisory part of the work. If I should gain the reputation of having better judgment than the average broker, I could then secure and hold a large and growing clientele.

I was thirty years old now; had accumulated some capital, but I had been overworked for many years. I decided to lessen my responsibilities and find more time for my study of the stock market. So along in 1904, I dissolved partnership with Mallett and hooked up with the firm of Ashwell & Company, members of the New York Stock Exchange. I brought my clientele over with me and began to devote five or six hours a day to looking after it.

My friends would say: "What a lot of changes you make in business!" My answer would be: "A rolling stone is worth two in the bush."

* * *

Old man Ashwell was a character. He had been in South Africa in his early days. On his office wall he exhibited photographs of some of the largest diamonds that had come from the Kimberley Diamond Mines, and claimed to be one of the discovering party. One Sunday, he said, when they were trekking through, they had stopped for a day's rest; two of the party, a young couple, were strolling in the neighborhood of the camp, and sat down on a fallen log. While sitting there, the young lady poked the ground with a stick and loosened a queer-looking stone, which, when examined, was found to be a diamond, and this led to the discovery of what became the Kimberley Mines. Some time later Ashwell secured an option on these properties for $5,000,000. He came to New York, approached many people who were able to swing the deal, but they all thought it was too far from Broadway.

Ashwell was a good friend of James R. Keene, whose office was in the same building. Many a good bit of information came out of Ashwell's daily calls upon the eminent speculator.

My new business brought me in about $18,000 a year, which was all right so far as making a living was concerned. But my main concern still was to get at the inside of the Wall Street works. Nothing was too much trouble if it would help me accomplish this.

* * *

1905 STUDYING THE BIG FELLOWS

HARRIMAN'S NORTHERN SECURITIES PROFITS—WASSERMAN'S READING OPERATIONS—A BULL LEADER—KESSLER TRIES TO CORNER READING—DICK CANFIELD SELLS OUT—MORGAN BREAKS THE POOL—ORDERS FROM J. P. M.—CONTROL OF TENNESSEE COAL—A FLOOR TRADER'S METHOD—ELBERT HUBBARD'S ADVICE—WALL STREET PSYCHOLOGY—BROKER'S PROBLEMS—PRACTICE IN TRADING

THE Northern Securities Co. held control of both Great Northern and Northern Pacific. In 1904 the United States Supreme Court declared the merger illegal. Union Pacific, in lieu of its Northern Securities stock, received 250,000 shares of Great Northern and 320,000 shares of Northern Pacific common. These were worth approximately $100,000,000 at the prevailing market prices.

While this was going on, a tremendous advance in Northern Securities ran the price up into the 180s. I remember an order which I executed on the Curb in this stock for an important client, on the strength of information I had obtained from a Morgan source. When this client found himself with twenty points profit he became more eagerly bullish than ever and gave me an order to buy more. The stock was scarce. While I waited in the

Curb crowd for some offerings to come in so that I wouldn't have to bid up, a certain broker whom I knew to be doing a large business for the Union Pacific crowd, said to me: "What are you buying this stuff for at this price?"

"I'm not trading in it for myself; I've got an order from a customer," I answered.

"Tell your man not to buy, but to sell; I've been selling it on a scale all the way up for Harriman."

This was good information; official records later showed that Harriman had sold out part of Union Pacific's interest in Northern Securities stock. Later, when the merger had been dissolved, he sold the remaining Great Northern and Northern Pacific, and realized a profit of $58,000,000 in cash for the Union Pacific.

He used this sum with $73,000,000 more to buy big lines of Illinois Central, Atchison preferred, Baltimore & Ohio preferred, New York Central and other stocks, which were still reposing in the treasury of the Union Pacific in 1928.

One day, with New York Central in the neighborhood of 135, he bought 40,000 shares all in one swoop, putting up his own check for $4,000,000 as part payment and having full payment made by the Union Pacific when the stock was received. But this was only about one-quarter of the total of the New York Central that he bought for Union Pacific.

* * *

At that time the firm of Wasserman Bros. was prominent in what I suspected to be the manipulation of Reading. In order to find out what was going on in that office, I got my friend Mallett to open a speculative account there.

Wasserman Bros. seemed to have better information on Reading than on anything else, and this information seemed to be better than that possessed by any other house. I knew the firm had a number of big clients, but who these were I did not know. I decided to find out.

After Mallett had become acquainted, I asked him to tell Edward Wasserman that he knew a man with quite a clientele who wished to talk over the possibility of connecting himself with the firm. Wasserman said that he would like to see me; and I had a talk with him. With the result that I moved my hat from Ashwell's over to Wasserman Bros. I had accepted a fixed salary of $1,000 a month. This was a sacrifice of $6,000 a year, but I felt it would be worth $6,000 a year to learn what I wanted to learn.

The Wassermans had been prominent in past years as one of the brokers used by John W. Gates. They had customers like Richard Canfield, the well-known gambler; George A. Kessler, New York agent for White Seal Champagne; some of the Seligmans; and M. A. Bernheimer, of the family of brewers.

Both Edward Wasserman and his brother Jesse were members of the New York Stock Exchange, and the latter spent all of his time on the floor during market hours. Their office occupied the entire front half of the second floor in 42 Broadway, now occupied by Hornblower & Weeks, whose offices were then in the rear of the same floor.

Soon, I began to nose around to see what I could learn. The firm had the reputation of being a Morgan house because they were more active in Reading than in any other stock. Frequently the news ticker would contain items to the effect that Wasserman Bros. had bought 25,000 or

50,000 Reading. They always seemed to be on the buying side of that stock. Further acquaintance disclosed the fact that Edward Wasserman was more or less obsessed with the bullish possibilities of Reading. It did not take me long to find out how all this had started.

The preceding year, Edward Wasserman had gone on a trip abroad. His first stop was London. There he met J. P. Morgan, who told him the Reading Company was "through spending money on the property; now the stockholders were going to be rewarded." "Eddie" immediately bought himself a big line of Reading by cable, and jumped on the next steamer going home.

Arriving in New York, he went to Dick Canfield's gambling house on 44th Street, next to Delmonico's, and told the noted gambler about it. Canfield immediately gave him an order to buy 25,000 shares of Reading, and later 25,000 more. Wasserman then went to Kessler, and Kessler gave him a big order. He loaded up his other clients, then disclosed the information to large floor traders like Jakey Field and Billy Oliver, who immediately went long of Reading.

Wasserman's methods, when he got one or more of these big orders—and usually he tried to bunch them—was to go into the Reading crowd and make his purchases in a loud and sensational manner, giving the effect that he was sent in to corral all the capital stock. Whether he actually did buy all the round lots of Reading that were credited to him I cannot state. But so long as the news tickers, news slips and newspapers gave him the publicity he was well satisfied.

Reading, under this impetus, began to climb into the 50s, 60s and 70s.

The First National Bank, representing the Morgan

interests, had always held controlling interest in this property, which they had reorganized and built up. The company had been assessed $20 a share in the 'nineties and for a time, after these assessments had been paid, the stock had sold at less than the amount of the assessment, which afforded a rare chance for inside accumulation. It was not to be supposed that the Morgan party, after putting back into the property all surplus earnings for a period of ten years, had failed to complete their purchases at the low levels, prior to the day when old man Morgan had released the decision that they were going to "give the stockholders something." And there did not appear to be any inside stock for sale, judging from the ease with which Reading now mounted to new highs.

As the stock began to approach 100, the big floor traders that Wasserman had brought in, and the general public, began to think this was too high. Large lines of shorts were put out. Wasserman kept close tab on the demand for Reading in the stock loan crowd. Whenever he saw the short interest extended, he told clients that Reading was going to have another big move, got a lot of orders, and going into the crowd, loudly executed them. The shorts would then fear they were going to lose their pants; they covered quickly. Their buying would help Eddie's game, and when they bid it up high enough, he let them have some of the stock.

Although the Street was under the impression that Wasserman was buying most of this stock for Morgan, I could never make sure that he bought one share for the house on the corner. If he did, everybody took great pains to conceal the fact. This was not Morgan's way of doing, anyway. This great financier had a private office of his own uptown, from which his stock market campaigns were conducted; and while he did frequently use Reading to punish the shorts and stiffen the market, his bidding up was not done by Wasserman.

While the latter always claimed that he never had a pool in Reading—and I believe this was true—some of his moves looked like pool manipulation. One strong reason for the Street's pool theory was Eddie's habit of bidding for round lots of stock. He would go into the Reading crowd with an order to buy 10,000 or 20,000 shares, which might have been all or partly for himself, or made up of a number of orders from clients, and after executing these orders as carefully as the market would permit, he would end up in one grand spectacular bid for 25,000 shares.

He really had no such order and the bid was solely for effect. (The rules of the Stock Exchange have since been revised so that a broker bidding for a round lot must accept all or any part of the amount bid for. But the rules at the time permitted one to bid for a round lot without having to accept less.) Making his big bid, Wasserman knew pretty well that no one would fill it.

The bullish effect on the traders in the Reading crowd and in the brokerage offices would be greatly emphasized by the news items which appeared on the slips and news tickers and, later, in the newspapers: "Wasserman pool bids for 25,000 share lots of Reading and gets none." These items led many outside buyers to go into Reading and often Wasserman and his clients realized an almost immediate profit.

Another favorite trick of Eddie's was to bet somebody $1,000 that Reading would sell at $200 before the end of the year. He had no trouble getting these bets on the news tickers, for he was friendly with newspaper men and those in control of publicity. The amount risked by the bet was a mere trifle compared to the market effect. Everyone thought that Eddie had more and better information on Reading than anyone else; that J. P. Morgan whispered into his ear. The New York *American* would run cartoons on Wasserman and Reading; these greatly tickled the expanding vanity of our friend. He would get the original drawings of these cartoons; framed and hung on his walls, they gave proof of his greatness as a market manipulator and financier.[1]

Reading worked up to around 110. Hereabout Canfield took a profit of several hundred thousand dollars on 25,000 shares of his stock.

It was also about at this level that George A. Kessler and some of his friends conceived the idea of cornering Reading. They began to make large purchases of the stock. Some of these orders were given to Wasserman; he executed them in his best style, with a great blowing of trumpet, but he told me he was skeptical as to the ability of the pool to corner the stock.

Reading climbed another 10 or 20 points, and the excitement increased.

Followers of the Kessler party worked like Trojans trying to induce everyone to buy Reading. It "was going to $200, to $300—no telling how high! They were going to corner it!" They seemed to have stolen Eddie Wasserman's thunder and multiplied it several times.

When the stock had reached 135, Wasserman asked me to call up Canfield at his gambling house in Saratoga, to tell him where Reading was, and ask him if he wanted

[1] I recently saw one of these cartoons in Ye Old Chop House, 118 Cedar Street, New York. It showed Morgan, Gates, Schiff, Hill and Wasserman building the market.

to do anything. Canfield promptly gave me an order to sell his remaining 25,000 shares. The order was executed in the neighborhood of 136 and his profit on the two lots was approximately $2,000,000.

Kessler and his crowd went on bulling until Reading hit 164. Then suddenly it looked as though Morgan, the First National Bank, H. C. Frick and all the other big boys had simply opened the floodgates to let those ambitious chaps have all the Reading they wanted.

Reading took a quick flop of fifty points. The pool went home badly spanked and thoroughly discouraged. The real insiders undoubtedly bought back at the low levels what they had sold, for a heavy buying movement around 112 now rallied the stock.

With Reading under 120, Eddie got very bullish again. He bought a lot of the stock himself and started in to collect orders from his big clients and such pool members as had not been cleaned out in the break. But one day a telephone message came from a secretary at "the corner" to the effect that "Mr. Morgan would like to see Mr. Wasserman." Had God Almighty summoned Eddie to the throne he could not have been more respectful. He was like a bad boy who has been running wild and whose dad has promised him a licking.

First he tiptoed around the office and informed everyone, in a mysterious whisper: "Mr. Morgan wants to see me." Then he went to his wardrobe and took down the high silk hat which he kept for such occasions. And after he was all shined, brushed and polished, he started over to Headquarters.

He was back in fifteen minutes, greatly subdued. In the same mysterious whispers he told us all that we were to keep very quiet about Reading from now on. Mr. Morgan did not want any more excitement in the stock.

Morgan's reason was clear. During Wasserman's bullish campaign from the 40s up to the 160s, he had let it ride. But now, having dumped about all the Reading in the world into the Kessler pool, he naturally wanted to buy it back below 120.

Without any bull leader the stock went through that well-known period of rest and quiet, near the bottom of its down swing.

* * *

George A. Kessler's agency for White Seal Champagne netted him 50 cents on every bottle sold in the United States, or some $500,000 a year. This enabled him to play in stocks with some of the big boys.

He came one day to Wasserman's office, and instead of sitting down at the little low ticker as usual, went in behind the order desk and watched the tall ticker there. I saw him talking to the order clerk frequently, but did not know what was going on until he had been there about an hour and a half. He then came out, saying to Wasserman: "Well, Eddie, I have just bought the last twenty thousand shares of Tennessee Coal and Iron necessary to give our crowd control of the company. And if any of you fellows will buy it now at a hundred and twenty-five and put it over for a year, you will get two hundred and fifty for it."

"Oh!" said Major Armstrong, "your buying has already put it up several points. We don't want anything we've got to hang on to for a year. Give us something for a quick turn."

Kessler only smiled at that and a few minutes later

left the office. (Some months later, T. C. & I. sold well above 160.)

The next day Wasserman handed me a fat bundle of stock certificates. "Here's that twenty thousand Tennessee Coal that Kessler bought yesterday," he said. "Will you take it to Moore & Schley and get a check?"

I put the certificates in a portfolio, walked up Broadway to No. 80, passed the bundle into the delivery window in Moore & Schley's office, and received in return a check for something over $2,000,000, which their bank promptly certified for me.

Moore & Schley were the bankers for the pool. It was the tremendous load of Tennessee Coal & Iron they were carrying for the pool in several New York banks that was to play such a large part in the failure of some of these institutions two years later, in the panic of 1907. At that time, with the panic at its worst, it became evident that unless these banks were relieved of their Tennessee Coal loans, more big bank failures would follow, and many brokerage house failures.

The Steel Corporation was willing to take over all of this Tennessee Coal and give in exchange therefor its 5 per cent sinking fund bonds, which would be good collateral. This was at the height of the Trust-Busting days, but J. P. Morgan and E. H. Gary went to Washington, explained the situation to President Roosevelt and asked whether, if this were done, the Steel Corporation would be subjected to further prosecution by the government on the ground that it was establishing a monopoly. The President—whether he was exceeding his authority the Attorney-General was the best judge—promised that no action would be taken by the government if the situation were thus relieved. The transaction was immediately ef-

Photo H. N. Tiemann Company

1892. *Looking up Broadway from Liberty Street*

fected: the Tennessee Coal in the banks was all exchanged for U. S. Steel bonds, and the pool found itself again in a liquid condition.

* * *

A very amusing person, this Edward Wasserman. He was quite a big trader. When he was long of the market, and it was going up, he bellowed like a bull all over the place. Each succeeding advance on the price of his stock was announced in stentorian tones. But when the market crashed and he was either long, or out of it, he would pussy-foot up and down the big office, behind the curved window[1] where the ticker was located, and ask everyone in a thoroughly scared stage whisper: "Do you think there's going to be a panic?"

One day when he was short of about 10,000 shares of Steel, he, his brother Jesse, his friend, M. A. Bernheimer, and I were sitting around the ticker. The day was hot; Eddie went into the shower he had had installed in his private office. While he was taking his bath some one called to him that Steel had just broken a few points. Without a strip of clothing, waving a Turkish towel in one hand, Eddie pranced right into the customer's room. "How is it now?" he yelled. "Anything on the news ticker?"

"Go back, you damned fool," cried his brother Jesse, "all Broadway can see you!"

* * *

At noon he would order lunch from Rohrer's Restaurant in the basement and whoever happened to be in the office at the time would be invited. He selected queer combinations of food. One day, after Eddie had ordered,

[1] Now part of Hornblower & Weeks' front office.

Dick Canfield came in, and was invited. The waiter served the main course—pigs' feet and sauerkraut. On a side table he set the dessert—plum pudding.

"Pigs' feet, sauerkraut and plum pudding!" Canfield exclaimed. "For God's sake, Eddie, let a gentleman order the luncheon after this!"

* * *

Many of Wasserman's campaigns were started out of thin air. One day when the tape was barely moving, he said to the clients in the office: "Let's make up a little pool in Southern Railway and start a move in it. I'll buy a thousand if you will."

Eddie went over on the floor and bought a few thousand shares all at one price. "It came easily," he said. Then he called up friends and told them there was going to be a move in Southern Railway. When all these trades appeared on the tape in such an absolutely dead market, it did look as though something had started. Here was a chance for some of the thousands of people sitting around hundreds of tickers all over the country to get a little action. Outside buying orders began to come into the crowd; in a few minutes Southern Railway was up a point and a half. Eddie and his friends quickly took their profits.

The evening papers said Morgan had been buying Southern Railway.

* * *

Being curious as to the details of the floor trader's point of view, I had a talk about that time with Isaac N. Spiegelberg, who made his headquarters in our office. He had no clients; he simply stood at one of the posts on the floor all day and bought and sold for his own account. I learned that his yearly earnings had averaged in the hundred thousands for some years.

Spiegelberg told me that he had started doing a regular brokerage business on the floor and that he would have been "at it yet" had he not, one day, executed an order in the wrong stock. Instead of cutting his loss short as soon as he discovered his mistake, he had let it run and finally had got into a bad hole. He had decided that there was too much risk in proportion to the small class of business, so he decided to become a floor trader, and leaving out the first few years of apprenticeship, he had made money at this ever since.

His method was to select one of the most active stocks and stay in that crowd day after day, familiarizing himself with the peculiarities of its movements and getting an insight into the manipulation of it. Constant observation showed him that his success or failure depended largely on his ability to follow the immediate trend, and to turn quickly if he was wrong. But he explained that the most important thing in floor trading is to cut your losses short and go with the stock as long as it travels your way. The most accurate guide, he claimed, was the tendency and the technical position of the market.

I asked him whether he ever took a position in the market (that is, took on a line of stocks for a few weeks or months). He answered: "Occasionally I take a position, but whenever it bothers me in my trading I close it out. At one time I got long of Reading before it fell into a slump and when my loss ran into $25,000 I let it go because I found I couldn't judge the other stock in which I was also trading, if I had to be running over to the Reading post all the time."

Losses such as this did not bother him much. I once

heard Wasserman ask him after the day's close how he had come out. He said: "Oh! I got fooling with this Smelters, found myself on the wrong side, took my loss, and finally got a position at the bottom; then I bought some more on the way up, and began to get a profit. But I was too impatient. I sold it out, and then it went up four or five points more."

"How much did you make?" Eddie inquired.

"Only about ninety-seven hundred," Ike replied ruefully, "if I hadn't been in such a hurry I would have had a good day."

* * *

Carsten Boe, who often visited Wasserman to find out what campaign the latter might be planning, got out a market letter. This letter at one time had been quite successful, but unfortunately, after all his bull campaigns, Boe had once turned bearish—and had lost most of his subscribers. They were willing to pay him for advice when it was bullish; they dropped him like a hot potato when he turned bear.

"I vill never pe pearish again," he would wail.

* * *

Jimmy Rascovar, of the New York News Bureau, and J. Arthur Joseph were frequent callers at the office. Wasserman was the acknowledged bull leader in Reading; he often undertook other campaigns. Those with noses for news found it well to keep those noses close to him.

Arthur Joseph, Wall Street's most famous raconteur, and probably the oldest man in the Wall Street news business, held the remarkable record of having reached his office at three o'clock in the morning every day since 1882. Joseph's custom was to secure all the early editions of the newspapers, get his cables from London, and phone his New York clients the prices of our stocks in London and any important overnight developments.

* * *

One day a man came into the office and handed out a card which read: Roger W. Babson. He was his own salesman. His "line" was a directory of stock brokers and bond houses which he was publishing at $5 a copy, and a composite list of securities wanted and offered by the various houses.

* * *

Along about this time I realized that for the work I was doing and planning I needed a greater facility of expression. Having left school early and concentrated on financial statistics and stock market lore, I had not taken up other branches of learning. I felt that an added ability of expression would aid me in many ways.

Two years before, being then thirty, I had seriously considered giving up business to spend some of the money that it had earned me on a college course. I had abandoned the idea because I could not find in the curricula anything that could be put to immediate and practical use. No college, it seemed, could teach me what I wanted most to know: the inner workings of the stock market, how to operate for myself, and how to guide my clients so that they might profit.

I wrote to Elbert Hubbard of East Aurora, and asked for his advice. He answered:

November 14th, 1905

Dear Mr. Wyckoff:

Your kind favor received. This matter of expression is all comparative any way. As a general proposition I would say that the habit of writing out your thoughts as a daily theme is a good plan.

So write one love letter a day, and in the course of two years you will find yourself a literary stylist.

With all kind wishes, ever,

Your sincere,

ELBERT HUBBARD

Following this suggestion, I began to write every day on the topics and incidents that had interested me during the day. I had understood that Hubbard recommended that I put my heart in the work, and that is what I did, writing perhaps fifty thousand words longhand in a few months. This gave me practice and helped me. And, as it developed later, I was unconsciously preparing for a future big job.

* * *

I had now spent the greater part of seventeen years in Wall Street—as a boy, clerk, silent partner and managing partner in Stock Exchange houses. But with all I had seen, studied and observed, I had yet no well-defined plan or method for money-making in the stock market, either for my clients or for myself. Like every other trader and investor, I had had profits and suffered losses; what few notes I have of my early trading indicate that my strongest asset was my determination to keep losses down.

Never risking more than a small part of my capital, I did not lose any big money in the market, even though the term "big" be used in proportion to the capital employed. My commitments were seldom over 500 or 1,000 shares. Just as much could be learned from dealing in hundred-share lots as from larger amounts, and my records were kept with a view to showing progress made

Photo H. N. Tiemann Company

1895. *Arcade Building. Corner Broadway and Rector Street. Where Jay Gould Had His Offices and Where Russell Sage Was Dynamited*

toward having more net points profit than points loss. By comparing the results of different trading periods I could judge whether or not I was advancing.

Like most stock brokers and customers' men, I had found it difficult to concentrate upon the problem of forecasting the market, difficult to do any material amount of deep research. I was faced with the constant example of wrong methods used by clients and resulting in losses. They would insist on overtrading. They would want to use $1,000 to margin two or three hundred shares, whereas with their inexperience and limited capital they should have been trading only in twenty-five or fifty shares.

Clients persisted in buying only when the market was strong; and seldom on reactions, and without any regard for general or technical conditions. Also they would sell out on the weak spots, reversing the rule of the Rothschilds who bought "sheep" and sold "deer."

Many formed the expensive habit of jumping in and out of the market so actively that commissions would eat them up—they paid too much money into the kitty. This was good for my commission account, but killed them off.

One small trader opened an account with $1,000 and bought and sold so frequently that although he was a fair judge of the market and often guessed right, he finally was down to trading in ten shares and was then wiped out. Analyzing the record of his transactions, I found that he had paid $3,000 in commissions while in the process of losing his $1,000. In other words, he had paid in commissions his $1,000 capital and $2,000 he had made in the market.

Most of those who dealt in our office, in spite of all I could do, would take small profits but would let their losses run until they were broke, tied up or crippled. They seemed to apply the rules that they used in their own businesses, rather than those demanded by the peculiar and technical requirements of successful stock market speculation.

* * *

At Wasserman's I was having a better chance. I had more time to give to analysis of the market; I could concentrate on this subject with less interference; there were private offices equipped with tickers where I could study the action of prices without interruption for half an hour or so at a time. Studying my records I found that I was obtaining improving results.

I wanted to find out whether it was possible to develop a judgment that was reliable in the *majority* of cases, never for a moment entertaining the idea that I could be right all the time.

My greatest problem was to eliminate emotion—to learn to trade with a poised mind, without fear or hope. Whenever a stock went in my favor or against me, and I found myself still unbiased in my "feelings," I was much encouraged. What I wanted was to acquire a trained judgment, combined with the experience that comes only from constant practice.

1906 A SHIFT IN TREND

KEENE RAIDS METROPOLITAN—LONDON OFFICE—STARTING IN THE BOND BUSINESS—THE UNION PACIFIC COUP

ONE of the interesting incidents that occurred while I was at Wasserman's was Mr. Keene's raid on Metropolitan Securities. This stock, by which control of the traction situation in New York City was held, had been pegged for a long time at 50; it would fluctuate between 50 and 53 and the pool never allowed it to break below 50. Therefore, whenever it approached 50, traders and specialists would buy it, and whenever it went to 53 or 54 they would sell it short.

One afternoon a sudden activity broke out in the stock. Large lots of it began to come out on the tape at reduced prices.

At about a quarter of three Dave Lamar, known as "The Wolf of Wall Street," came into the office, sat down at the ticker, and began telling us that Mr. Keene was going to "smash that Metropolitan Securities" this time. He and his friends were giving the pool a bellyful, and tomorrow morning it would open away down.

Eddie Wasserman, and others there, decided to help the game along and sold some round lots. Lamar's relationship with Keene was well known. What he was telling us in our office he had told, and would tell, others. Mr. Keene, having sold his own lines short before the joyful news was spread, was taking this method of getting all the help he could. What with Keene's generalship and Lamar's advertising of what Keene was going to do to the stock, the pool had about all they wanted by three o'clock that afternoon. And the next morning, as there was no knowing how much selling was still coming from the same source, the stock opened below 50 and then cracked down another dozen points into the 30s, realizing profits for all hands.

This was an impressive lesson in the law of supply and demand: Supply, *actual* the day before, and *threatened* on the following day, discouraged August Belmont and his associates, who were on the supporting side, and put another feather in the cap of the man to whom the newspapers used to refer as "a prominent operator"—Mr. Keene.

* * *

The firm opened a branch office in London, in charge of Blakeley Hall, a friend of Dick Canfield. The office, at No. 2 Cockspur Street, needed a lot of fixing, and I was sent over there to help get him started. A short time after I arrived, Hall and the firm began an argument by cable, and as Hall threatened to quit unless his demands were met, I could make no further progress and took the next steamer back home, having been absent seventeen days.

Wasserman offered me the management of the London office but I declined it, and not long after that decided to resign. I had learned what I wanted to learn here, and it had become my habit to avoid ruts.

When I told Eddie of my decision he said: "Why do you want to quit? I like you. You can stay here twenty-five years!"

I told him this was kind of him, but that I was rather

Photo H. N. Ticmann Company

1898. *Bowling Green*

fed up on the brokerage business and wanted to get into bonds and unlisted securities for myself.

I went down Exchange Place and engaged a small room at No. 43. Then around to the Bank of the Manhattan Company to see its president, Stephen L. Baker, who knew me through my silent partnership in Price, McCormick & Co. and the thousands of checks I had signed on his bank. Mr. Wasserman had also given me a splendid letter to him.

I told Mr. Baker I was going to start a bond business under the name of Wyckoff & Co., that I would be alone in the enterprise, that my initial deposit would be $20,000. Also that I would clear my own transactions, and for that purpose would like to have him over-certify my checks to the amount of $100,000. This he granted me.

I started doing business, and soon was making much more money than at Wasserman's, mostly in bonds and unlisted securities, without attempting to work up an investment clientele.

* * *

Early in 1906, a conference (so I was told by one who said he had attended it) of the Harriman-Standard Oil party had been held at the house of John D. Rockefeller at Lakewood, N. J. Measures were determined upon with the aim of inducing the public to buy in a volume which would create a market on which these large operators could successfully unload.

Union Pacific was then selling above 150. The plan was to put it on a 10 per cent basis and at the same time establish Southern Pacific as a 5 per cent stock. This, it was expected, would have the desired effect.

Union Pacific was therefore backed down to 139, and heavy accumulation took place. Then one morning, some time after the opening, one or two members of the New York Stock Exchange, happening to glance on the bulletin board on the floor, saw to their amazement that Union Pacific stood announced there as a 10 per cent stock and Southern Pacific as a 5 per cent. Union Pacific jumped to the 190s in a few days and Southern Pacific from the lower 60s into the 90s almost as quickly. This Union Pacific deal produced the climax of the 1906 bull market in which the average price of twenty rails reached 168, a figure not again touched for many years. Following this tremendous rise, in which Harriman made $15,000,000 on his speculative line of Union Pacific alone, the dominating stock market operators, and many of the leading financiers, banks and banking institutions who read the handwriting on the wall, were able to clean house.

* * *

1907 THE MONEY PANIC

CASH ABOVE PAR—A SICK MARKET—MORGAN SAVES THE SITUATION—WORKING FOR KEENE—HIS TRADING PERSONALITY—KEENE'S RAID ON HARRIMAN—SOUTHERN PACIFIC POOL WHIPPED—FOUNDING THE MAGAZINE

AT THE beginning of this year the outlook was ominous. Liquid capital, absorbed by the tremendous financial operations, promotions, and consolidations of the past years had shrunk everywhere—in America and the world over. Jacob H. Schiff, of Kuhn, Loeb & Co., had already sounded a warning. Failure to revise the banking laws and provide a more elastic currency, he had said, would eventually precipitate the worst panic this country had ever seen.

Foreign wars, the Baltimore fire, the San Francisco earthquake and fire, had absorbed $2,000,000,000 of liquid capital, tying up four times that amount of credit.

Through certain channels of information I ascertained that many large estates which held tremendous holdings of railroad securities had split up the certificates running into tens and hundreds of thousands of shares and were liquidating.

Banks were steadily calling in loans. Time money was hard to get. Business was bad. So was the stock market. No one knew just what was going to happen and all those who dealt in stocks—investors, bankers and brokers —were uneasy.

The great shrinkage in security values and the almost total loss of confidence in the financial world resulting from President Roosevelt's campaign against the capitalists who had attempted to consolidate the great transportation systems, was followed by a period of state and federal attacks upon corporations. Financiers crawled into their shells.

Large railroad systems, in process of extension and development, found it difficult to obtain money, even at high rates. Strong companies like New York Central and Pennsylvania were forced to resort to short-term notes. Weaker systems found it almost impossible to finance themselves at all. The railroad outlook was such as to scare both railroad men and investors in their bonds and shares.

Early in the year Mr. Morgan had called upon President Roosevelt at Washington to warn him of the dangers of the situation; suggested he have a meeting of all the leading railroad heads with the President. But Roosevelt was determined to proceed on his aggressive course regardless of the effect upon finance, transportation and business. He did not seem to care what damage was done through the country so long as he should succeed in putting "certain malefactors of great wealth" where he wanted them.

The first section of the panic, following this conference, came in March. Roosevelt blamed Wall Street, and Wall Street blamed Roosevelt.

During the summer another break in the stock market carried prices to new lows. The $29,000,000 fine against the Standard Oil Company was announced. The United States Attorney General was giving interviews to newspaper men. He thought of himself as a hunter. He spoke of "a big covey of game of which he proposed to land a bird or two." The President was issuing statements to the effect that Wall Street was attempting to discredit his administration.

Along in October banks in New York City and elsewhere began to fail; this was followed by runs upon all kinds of financial institutions throughout the land. Cash commanded a premium of 4 to 5 per cent; that is, you could take a thousand dollars in bills to any bank in New York and get in return a check for $1,040 or $1,050. With varying fluctuations this condition kept on for the last three months of the year.

At one time in November the Clearing House banks showed a deficiency of over $54,000,000 in their normal reserve requirements. The Knickerbocker Trust Company paid out $8,000,000 in deposits and then failed. The Trust Company of America, paying off only a few depositors an hour, was emptied of $23,000,000 before the run stopped. Long lines of depositors stood, all day and all night, at the paying tellers' windows of many banks in New York City. Wall Street was jammed from curb to curb with an excited mob.

Finally, there was no money at all for members of the New York Stock Exchange who wanted to borrow. J. P. Morgan stepped in to save the situation. Forming a money pool, he authorized the loaning of $27,000,000 to brokers on the floor of the Exchange. This turned the tide, but it was a long while before money, banking and stock market conditions became normal again.

The action of Union Pacific during that time was typical of what was happening in the market. After reaching its high point of 195⅜ in September, 1906, this stock had declined nearly 20 points in October, and had rallied into December. Then followed a series of further slumps in January and February, 1907, until after March 14, the low point of the first half of the panic, the stock was down to 120, or 75 points under its record high.

Rallies and slumps succeeded each other—10, 20 or 30 points—up into May. Another slump and a rise took up the month of June and part of July; and in August the stock was back nearly to 120.

It was a sick market with the nausea not completed. I should judge that along about then Union Pacific, still a $10 per annum dividend payer, was reaccumulated to the limit of the resources of the Harriman party, for when later, on October 24, the panic had reached its worst and Union Pacific at its low was par, Harriman was walking the floor in Morgan's office muttering: "Union Pacific at a hundred dollars per share and nobody with a dollar to buy it!"

* * *

One day I received word that James R. Keene would like to see me at the Waldorf that evening.

Visitors who called when he was in consultation in the parlor were shown into his bedroom. Nothing in the suite indicated that the occupant was the leading stock market operator and a multimillionaire. There were a few ordinary hotel pictures on the walls. The furniture was the usual Waldorf furniture. A photograph of himself was on his chiffonier. There was no other photograph: he was evidently his own best friend.

The business was this. Keene, through his son-in-law, Mr. Taylor, had become interested in an electrical typesetting machine known as the Graphotype. He had begun by lending some money to the company and had ended by owning it. Meanwhile, the machine had been developed to high efficiency and was now ready for manufacture. He wanted me to secure subscriptions to an underwriting syndicate for an offering that was to be brought out in the Curb Market. He offered me a cash commission of 5 per cent on the amount raised and a bonus in common stock.

We went over the Graphotype deal at length and finally reached a definite understanding. The public stenographer was called from downstairs and a contract was drawn up and signed by us both.

In undertaking to raise this money I first approached the people with whom Mr. Keene was supposed to be friendly, or at least on good business terms, and was rather surprised by the reception I received. People like George W. Perkins of J. P. Morgan & Company, Thomas Fortune Ryan, August Belmont did not seem to be interested in the least. They seemed to think the proposition a rather unusual one for Mr. Keene, who had been identified with such great operations in the stock market as the distribution of Amalgamated Copper and U. S. Steel. He had never promoted a stock of his own, and here he was working to bring out on the Curb an enterprise capitalized at only a million or two. Belmont had his secretary telephone Keene, as the latter afterward told me, to see whether this was really his enterprise, and a lot of the others simply wouldn't go in at all. Perkins told me it was too small for J. P. Morgan & Co. Perhaps they suspected that Keene might unload on the syndicate the package he had been carrying, in which he had several hundred thousand dollars.

I did succeed, however, in getting quite a batch of syndicate subscriptions from Charles W. Morse and others. But just as I was beginning to round these up, the panic broke with full force and practically paralyzed everything in the Street. Mr. Keene extended for thirty days the time in which I had to raise this money, and noted this at the bottom of the contract, in his own handwriting.

One of those on whom I had called was a big floor trader. "Tell Mr. Keene," he said, "that I have lost a fortune in the panic and can't go into anything." [1]

This Graphotype matter took me into Mr. Keene's office frequently. It was on the fifth floor of the Johnson Building, 30 Broad Street, the entrance being at the west end of the corridor. There was no name on the door; from the outside the office looked vacant. A tap brought the clerk, Jimmie, who opened the door a few inches, took the card and left me standing in the hall. If Mr. Keene was ready to see me, Jimmie would lead the way into a small lobby at the end of which was a solid oak door.

Inside, a large office, lighted by several windows, occupied the corner of the building. Screens rose up to the middle sash; when the old man was very busy the shades would be pulled down to the screens. For across narrow New Street, and across the still narrower Exchange Place, people in brokerage offices of Exchange Court and No. 67 had an excellent view of Wall Street's leading operator at his ticker.

The walls of Keene's office were covered with paintings and prints, chiefly of race horses like Domino, Dob-

[1] Some people who have the idea that trading in stocks is always a bed of roses for the big fellows who are supposed to *know how* should note this fact: The only difference between large and small traders is in the size of their operations. No one has a monopoly of stock market knowledge nor can anyone do the trick one hundred per cent of the time. Wall Street history was full of those who, high in the scale of leading operators, had lost all or most of their fortunes, although in the majority of cases recovering them.

1900's. *The Marble Palace in Which the King Was Enthroned*

bins and Sysonby, famous members of the Keene string. In the corner was a roll-top desk and close to it a small, flat one. A divan and a table were on the other side. Three or four more or less comfortable chairs completed the furnishings.

Between the two broad windows on the New Street side, the stock ticker stood on a tall pedestal. In an adjoining room were telephone booths with private lines to his brokers, while the telephone near his ticker evidently ran to the principal house with which he did business.

Keene was an elderly gentleman with a pointed gray beard, a horsy expression, and the sharpest pair of eyes I have ever seen. His air was that of a Southern gentleman, and his handshake was limp. The front of his head was somewhat bald and the gray of his hair like the gray of his beard. His voice was pitched high. He gave the impression of a man close to sixty.

It was Mr. Keene's habit to start the conversation by asking your opinion of the market—as if there were anyone in Wall Street who knew as much about it as he did. The obvious answer was to ask the old man what he thought about it. And while he was not in the habit of giving tips, he seemed to be frank as to whether he was bullish or bearish. One of my calls was just after the big smash in stocks, when the market was at a low point and the situation appeared hopeless. Yet he did not hesitate to say: "I think the market will do better. It looks to me as though it was sold out." And the market did do better.

I used to stand facing him, my left elbow on his ticker while talking to him. He would hold the tape in his left hand and his eye-glasses in his right as he listened to me, then on went the glasses astride his nose as he bent close to the tape in a scrutiny of the length that had passed meanwhile. I might be talking at the moment his eye began to pick up the tape again, but until he finished he was a person in a trance. If, reading the tape, he observed something that stimulated his mental machinery, I might go on talking indefinitely; he wouldn't get a word of it.

His deliberation process would include trips up and down the office, during which his hands would be closed and his forearms slightly upraised as though he were swinging himself along by their weight. He seemed to walk invariably the same number of steps, each exactly measured. He appeared to absorb a certain length of tape, and to devote to its analysis a specified interval, measured by paces. Sometimes he returned to the ribbon for another examination, followed by more pacing. Often he would step to the telephone, and in a guarded tone, would demand: "Who's buying all that Reading?" "What's going on in Union Pacific?" "Did you get the rest of that B. R. T.?" Then back to the tape, more examination, more pacing, and a completion of the mental digestion. All this may have required two or three minutes, but then he could always answer my question as if nothing had happened between and it had been just propounded.

I would finish my business with him and start to go, but occasionally he would say: "Sit down for a moment." In case he had something else on his mind and could not prolong the conversation, he made it known by an instant change in his manner, remarking that he had some one else waiting to see him or that he was busy now about his horses. I knew that these horses were mostly Reading, Union Pacific and Brooklyn Rapid Transit and that he well knew how to ride them.

Although in his trading activities Mr. Keene had often

dominated the market and often bent it to his will, he admitted in his later years that he could not influence prices as in olden times. The market had outgrown him. There was too much stock now; he could not make much of an impression with the lines he was able to swing. There were too many operators and floor traders dealing in 10,000 to 50,000 shares a day. As new issues were listed and the market broadened by greater public participation, his power was fading. But he was still at the game when an extremely old man; when most of those of his age and wealth had settled down to be quiet, sedate, retired grandfathers.

"Why do you want another million?" some one asked in these later years.

"Why does a dog chase another rabbit when he has just caught one?" he parried.

* * *

After Mr. Keene had extended my time for organizing the Graphotype Syndicate, financial conditions became worse instead of better. He decided to wait.

I sent him a bill for my cash commissions. With all my admiration for his ability as a stock market operator, I didn't think much of the excuses he now gave for not paying these commissions. His signature was on my contract; I had done my part of the work, but he acted as though he had gone broke. He "didn't owe it to me." Growing tired, I wrote I would sue him. In response, he had his lawyer give me a long harangue over the telephone. It seemed it wasn't Mr. Keene's fault that he couldn't go ahead. I replied that it wasn't my fault either but that on my side I *would* go ahead. The attorney finally offered to advise Keene to pay, if I would "knock off a hundred dollars for cash." I told the attorney that probably he had the hundred coming to him for the argument he had put up—bad as it was—and agreed to the settlement.

When I went to Keene's office the old man handed me a receipt for the amount of money due me, less the hundred, and asked me to sign it. I signed. But when he reached out his hand for the receipt, I put it behind my back: "I'll give you that receipt when I get my check, Mr. Keene," I said.

He gave me an injured glance, went to his accounting department, and came back with the check, which I took with one hand while I slipped him the receipt with the other. However, he didn't hold that against me.

He once said to me: "The best time to buy stocks is when they are all going down together, and the best time to sell is when the whole body of stocks is strong."

While this rule would not be infallible for such markets as were to prevail twenty years later, it was highly applicable then.

In one of my talks with Mr. Keene I learned that he had seen a communication of mine to another Wall Street man in which I referred to him as a prominent manipulator. The term seemed to incense him. He blustered about his office, grumbling and swearing under his breath; then he burst out with: "Who do you think I am —Lawson?"

It was difficult to understand this fine distinction which he apparently drew in his own favor, for although his methods were different from Lawson's, he certainly was a Wall Street manipulator, as I know the term. Take, for example, his Southern Pacific pool.

The Union Pacific controlled Southern Pacific. Harriman had been diverting Southern Pacific earnings into improvements rather than dividends. Keene saw an opportunity to turn this to advantage. Acquiring a quantity of stock for his own account, he organized a pool, to buy from 200,000 to 400,000 shares of Southern Pacific stock, and force Harriman to begin the payment of dividends.

Harriman first learned of this contemplated deal through emissaries. One of Keene's emissaries offered him an alliance. Keene, he stated, was in a position to secure a writ enjoining the Union Pacific from voting its Southern Pacific stock at the coming annual meeting. Harriman did nothing in the matter.

Then Keene himself managed to meet Harriman. He stated that he, Keene, held a large amount of Southern Pacific; that he would like to join Harriman and buy another large quantity of the shares in the market, or act for Harriman alone. If this buying were done, Keene said, the Union Pacific should take all of the Southern Pacific stock so acquired and issue its own 4 per cent bonds in exchange. He called attention to his skill in conducting large stock market operations, as shown in his manipulation and distribution of U. S. Steel for the Morgan syndicate.

Harriman assured Keene that his turning of the railroad's earnings into improvements, his strengthening and developing of the property, were necessary because of the large bonded indebtedness which would mature within a few years. Keene assured Harriman that he did not want to act in any antagonistic way, and that he would do nothing without giving notice.

The pool acquired a large amount of stock within a comparatively narrow range. It seemed strange to me that so much stock could be bought without advancing the price 15 or 20 points; I concluded that some one with a large block had supplied the pool. The reader may draw his own conclusions from a few additional facts.

Edward Lauterbach was reputed to have informed Harriman that the Keene pool held about 170,000 shares of Southern Pacific, in addition Mr. Keene owned 70,000 shares, and that the latter contemplated legal action which might cause much trouble. He suggested that the pool's holdings could be purchased at $70 per share, and Mr. Keene's at $78. Harriman ignored this suggestion.

Keene and his party now brought suit in the United States Circuit Court at Nashville to enjoin Union Pacific from voting its Southern Pacific shares at the annual meeting to be held at Beechmont, Ky., in April, 1903. Had the writ been granted, Keene and his pool, of course, would have been masters. The case was thrown out, however, on the ground of lack of jurisdiction. The meeting was held; Union Pacific voted its shares and retained control of Southern Pacific.

That is not all, however, of this remarkable piece of Wall Street buccaneering. Harriman had prepared for a possible adverse decision of the Circuit Court by selling to William Rockefeller 300,000 shares of the Union Pacific's holding of Southern Pacific stock. Even if the injunction had been obtained, it would have done the Keene party no good; the shares would have been voted by Harriman's friend, Rockefeller.

I always had the idea that, thus sure of the voting strength of these 300,000 shares, and secure in the control of the market it gave them, the Harriman-Rockefeller party had fed a good deal of stock to the pool when, so eagerly, it was acquiring the shares at high figures.

Upon the court's decision, the wind all escaped from

the Keene balloon, in a market that was curiously devoid of support. I happened to hear of a few things that went on in Keene's office at the time. Undoubtedly he first sold his own stock the moment he found he had lost the suit. He also began to sell out the pool's holdings, now that he had lost his desperate game. He found that other large operators were "helping him along," as is the sardonic phrase: their heavy offerings competed with his. He also learned that certain accounts in T. J. Taylor & Co.'s office were carrying large amounts of Southern Pacific, which he promptly ordered cleaned out.

The market for Southern Pacific continued to break badly. The liquidation of such heavy lines, plus the "helping-along" process, resulted in a smash from the 60s into the 30s. The pool lost $3,000,000. How much was lost in addition by T. J. Taylor & Co., their associates and clients, and by others around the Street and throughout the country who were trading on the long side of Southern Pacific, there is no way of estimating. But while the liquidation was at its height, around the low levels of 39 to 41 some one apparently took on a big line of Southern Pacific. I have always had the idea that much of this was covering of shorts by the insiders, who nailed a profit of from $3,000,000 to $5,000,000 on this operation and that much of the shares which so cannily had been supplied to the pool were now bought back—the Harriman party accumulating large additional lines of Southern Pacific at a price that never has been and probably never will be duplicated.

* * *

The bond business grew dull after the first section of the panic in the spring of 1907, and my mind reverted to the idea of establishing an educational publication in the financial field. Since I myself was so eager to learn all I could about stocks and bonds, investing and trading, I believed there must be thousands of people throughout the country interested in the same subject.

Nothing of the kind existed. There were, of course, a number of daily papers handling financial news; and one weekly. But my idea was of something different. If I could focus the attention of people upon the necessity of understanding the business of trading and investing, I would arouse public interest, building up real circulation, and secure a substantial amount of advertising revenue from brokerage and bond houses.

No one could possibly have been less fitted for the job of editing and publishing a magazine. I knew absolutely nothing about the publishing business. In fact, I didn't realize it was necessary to paste up a dummy before the first copy could be made up and printed.

Nothing in my past experience gave me the impression that I was a writer—even on financial subjects. The business of being a broker has little to do with writing or publishing.

Of how much a magazine of the kind I had in mind would cost me, I had no idea except a vague knowledge of the cost of printing and paper. I had some capital, however, a small office at 43 Exchange Place, and one $10 employee.

My idea was to make it a monthly magazine and sell it for a dollar a year. A friend who knew something about the publishing business suggested that I make it $3 a year, or 25 cents a copy. I took his advice. He showed me how to paste up a dummy.

I started to gather material for "Volume I, No. 1," which was to consist of thirty-odd pages. I soon saw that

I would have to write most of it myself—a large order that. The best thing on hand was the memorandum I had explaining my method in forecasting the turning point of the market in 1904, as shown on another page in this book. Then I had a copy of the *Rules of a Successful Speculator,* written by Dickson G. Watts, successful in cotton. I wrote an article on the finer points of placing orders in stocks; another on the advantage of holding sound investment securities instead of keeping money in the savings banks; I got an article from Hugh McElroy: "Gauging the Cotton Market." I clipped and pasted a few items from other publications, and bought a story on stock trading. Then I was faced with the task of apologizing editorially for the infant thus making its bow. This editorial took up one page.

All business is speculation and speculation is a business, it said. Most men fail in both business and speculation. Ninety-five per cent of those who fail in speculation do so because they are ignorant of the stock market in its very rudiments, and ignorant of its technique. No facilities were available to those who wished to learn the stock market; hence the average man, in most cases, traded without learning how to do it.

The "Editor" believed that by collecting, selecting and boiling down all available data on the subject, and offering this in predigested form, he could increase the public's knowledge of Wall Street. He proposed to measure the value of each article by considering whether it would help put dollars in the pocket of the man who read it. Examples in model trading would be given; the reader's cooperation was requested. The editor invited suggestions that might increase the publication's value to the average trader and investor.

I had to decide on a name for the poor little thing, and I named it—*The Ticker.*

Many an enterprise has started with just an idea and a roll-top desk. Here was another. I have always learned to swim by jumping overboard.

Having got together what you might call the guts of the new magazine, I still had to get it printed. James R. Keene's Graphotype Co., was yet in the non-commercial stage, but he had a development laboratory where the machine was working perfectly, and I knew the manager, Mr. Nicholas. He set up my first number on the Graphotype, and the type was taken to the Berkeley Press in William Street. About a hundred copies were run off, with blank spaces for the advertising.

With some of these copies, I called on firms like Hayden, Stone & Co., Alfred Mestre & Co., Hubbard Bros., Charles Fairchild & Co., Atwood Violett & Co., and sold $300 worth of advertising space before the first number appeared. Violett took a whole page at $50—think of that! The others took a half page at $25. With these six pages of advertising and thirty-odd pages of reading matter, I gave the printer an order for 15,000 copies, which I intended to shower on a thirsty Wall Street public.

Never shall I forget how I thrilled as the big cylinder presses rolled over, turning out the first complete impression. I had a message but didn't know exactly what that message was, nor how it would be received. Not until long afterwards did I realize that my chances for success were about as good as those of one starting from Coney Island to swim to Europe.

When the copies were all run off, my problem was to get them into the hands of people who would read them —and perhaps subscribe. I dug out a list of clients and of people interested in the stock market, also a list of bond, stock and cotton houses, and mailed 10,000 or 12,000 copies. Then I called on Mr. Hart of the American News Co. and showed him *The Ticker* and asked what my chances were to sell it on the newsstands. Mr. Hart told me I had no chance at all.

But among the past clients of Ashwell & Co. was a man named Gregory, who was owner and publisher of *Travel Magazine,* formerly the *Four Track News.* He had bought it from the New York Central Railroad Co., which ran it as a house organ. I went to Gregory.

"Mr. Gregory," I said, "I've started in the publishing business and don't know anything about it. Here's a copy. I've sent out most of my first edition. Please tell me how to get this going on the newsstands."

Gregory was good enough to lend me his circulation man, and with this aid I got up a circular describing the new baby. This was sent out to newsdealers, each copy accompanied by a postal card, addressed to the American News Co., and ordering so many copies of *The Ticker.* Within a few days the American News Co. sent down an order, and then began to send more orders. People, for one thing preferred to buy the magazine at the newsstands; solicited for a three-dollar yearly subscription they looked it over and didn't think it would last a whole year!

* * *

It was in August, 1907, that I began to get material ready for the first *Ticker,* which appeared about on October 1, although I dated it November, so as to get a month's start on the calendar. It was no sooner out than I had to plan, write and prepare the next number. I wrote a story about James R. Keene; another about the results of an office trader's operations; wrote some stuff on trading, and selecting bargains; got some stock market stories; and used, by permission, a chapter from Thomas Gibson's book on Speculation. I started an Inquiry Column, with both questions and answers written by myself. Finally I laid out a double-page spread, offering a fifteen-dollar book, *The Story of Erie,* with each three-dollar subscription to the magazine.

Here was the crowning proof of my ignorance of the publishing game. A fellow had sold me the rights to publish this book, and my double-page spread was so overpowering I thought mobs would fall in line with three-dollar bills. I did get subscriptions, but in offering a fifteen-dollar book for a three dollar subscription I queered myself with the United States Post Office, which now refused me the second-class postal rate. The department's rule was that no premium should have a value of more than half the subscription price. I had made one ten times that half.

For the third number of the magazine, I prevailed upon Edward Wasserman to give me, as a leader, a story on Reading. Then I had big placards printed and hired a man to plaster New York City with them. A rumor got around that this article was the beginning of a new Wasserman bull campaign in Reading, and Reading promptly advanced 15 or 20 points. Eddie Wasserman was so pleased with the results that he offered to buy a half interest in the magazine, but I told him it was not for sale. I knew that he would immediately have elected himself Editor-in-Chief.

It was apparent that I had cut out an awful job for myself if I was going to write most of the magazine; so I went out after contributions—without compensation.

Copyright Brown Brothers

1900. *Edward H. Harriman*

I obtained some good material. Larry Chinn, of Ball & Whicher, Stock Exchange members, wrote me a one-pager. Montgomery Rollins, of Boston, contributed. I wrote several pages on the technique of executing orders and on experiences in arbitraging; I got points on grain trading from E. W. Wagner. Then one day I met Roger W. Babson and he told me that he was writing a book consisting of a series of articles, on his Theory of Financial Statistics. I suggested that he let me run these articles and he consented. I ran the articles through several numbers, and they were used eventually as the basis of Babson's first advertising campaign.

My readers, to my requests for suggestions, were asking for explanations of technical points. I began to write short articles on "The Machinery of Manipulation," "How a Stock is Marked Up." I searched my old data for ideas, and found a number, used them all up, and then had to think up new ones.

These articles seemed to take well, and my readers began to demand a comprehensive article on tape reading; that is, on judging the course of the market by its own action. These requests continued to be so numerous that I saw that many people would subscribe to the magazine if I could promise something along this line. Where to get it was a problem. The only expert I knew in the subject was Mr. Keene and he wouldn't tell what he knew. From observation I knew he got more out of the tape than from anything else, and that the action of the market was life-breath to his trading. Finally I saw that I would have to do the job myself. But I wasn't quite ready to tackle it. Until I was ready, my readers would have to content themselves with short stabs at the subject.

* * *

1908 A BIG BEAR TRAPPED

TRYING TO INFLUENCE THE PRESS—MAKING *The Ticker* TICK

J. BRANDT WALKER was a Western stock market operator of considerable prominence during the bear market of 1907. He was reported to have made a million or two, which was a good deal in those days, and after the operations begun in the West were transferred to Lakewood, he finally came to New York and established quarters uptown.

He saw my magazine and asked me to call. When I arrived he launched into a long discussion on U. S. Steel. He thought the position of the corporation quite weak; he said that the company was unable to continue payment of the preferred dividend. And so on.

"Why," he exclaimed, "do you know that at a recent dinner given to his partners in the steel business, Carnegie said: 'Boys, we are going to be able to buy back our property at ten cents on the dollar! Morgan is going to make a failure of it.' "[1]

"You can see," Walker went on, "why I've good reasons for being very bearish on this stock and why I am heavily short of it. Here is something which I have pre-

[1] In his *Memories of an Active Life,* Charles R. Flint states that when U. S. Steel was selling at about 15, he happened to call upon Carnegie and in the latter's library noted a cartoon burlesquing a painting of Napoleon's retreat from Moscow "in which Morgan and his associates were pictured trudging through the snow—Morgan in the costume of Napoleon surrounded by his generals among whom were Charles M. Schwab and John W. Gates."

pared and which I thought you might like to print in your magazine."

He handed me an article in which what he had told me stood elaborated, backed up by figures, and emphasized till the condition of poor old U. S. Steel seemed hopeless. He then called his secretary and said:

"Put Mr. Wyckoff short of two hundred shares of U. S. Steel at twenty-six," which meant that he was making a trade for me of which I would have the profit, if profit resulted, and of which he would take the loss, if there was a loss.

"Just let me look this over, Mr. Walker," I said, taking the article. I withdrew, read it, and decided I would not print this—much less since my judgment did not agree with it. I would not have *The Ticker* used to further the interests of big traders, no matter which side of the market they were on. Nor, I decided, did I care to be short of U. S. Steel at 26 only a few weeks and a few points away from the low level of the 1907 panic, whether there were any risk in it or not.

So I handed back the article and said: "I'm sorry, Mr. Walker, but I can't print this, and I guess you had better ask your secretary to cancel that short trade in Steel you told him to make for me."

Walker stayed short of Steel, and it was not long before it was reported that the money he had made on the short side was lost. He had not been wise enough to cover while the panic was on; he had overplayed his hand.

* * *

When *The Ticker* was six months old I was still editor, principal contributor, managing editor and make-up man, procurer of articles from others, also advertising solicitor, business manager, and statistician. I got up at seven o'clock; worked at home until two in the afternoon, writing articles and getting material ready for publication; then had lunch and worked at the office until seven. After dinner I resumed work at home until midnight. All articles were written by hand. The chief assistant in the office could plunk a typewriter, but she had enough other work to do. I couldn't write in the office—too many interruptions.

* * *

1909 TAPE READING

PUBLISHING PROBLEMS—TESTING MECHANICAL METHODS—HARRIMAN'S MANIPULATION—STOCK MARKET TECHNIQUE—JUDGING BY THE TAPE—SCALE PLANS—"STUDIES IN TAPE READING"—THE KEY TO SUCCESS

As NUMBER after number of *The Ticker* was prepared, I began to see that I was getting more out of it than anyone else. The articles selected for publication were only a small part of the material examined and considered. Much that was of value, in one way or other, left a residue of new knowledge. Writing articles clarified many things in my mind. Much came out of my head that I did not know was there.

The queries sent in on technical points of investment and speculation were also stimulating. They varied over a wide field, and when my own knowledge did not suffice, I made it my business to ascertain the correct answer before replying.

At that time many thought that the market could be beaten by mechanical methods; that is, by some means other than human judgment. Dow had suggested a few of these. Babson had one or more. All kinds of individuals came forward with ways of beating the stock market; each was certain his method would make a fortune. Few had any money. Always there was some reason why they had not made *their* fortune, even though they possessed the magic key. A few were willing to let me try them out; others were more suspicious, demanded a cash advance of $1,000 to $5,000 before disclosing their secret.

Out of all this welter of plans, a man came along one day with something that looked good. He asked me to test him. He had one of the little pocket manuals containing the past record of the daily high and low prices of many leading active stocks for a long period. I would take the manual and read off the price of Reading or Union Pacific day by day from, say, January 1, 1907. To each high and low price as it came from me, he would quickly say: "Buy" or "Sell short" or "Close out," as if he were watching the tape and giving orders to a broker. And "buy," or "sell out," or "close out" nearly always proved to be what should have been done at the time. I thought at first that there was a trick in it; that he had studied, and remembered, the past movements of these stocks. He always limited his risk to two points, which in markets of that day was the ordinary stop order. He had frequent losses, especially in traders' markets with narrow swings; but when the trend started definitely in one direction and kept going, he kept on the right side and made big profits.

I put him through a lot of tests on various stocks at different periods and concluded that he had something. He then disclosed his method to me and it did seem to be one that would make money. Not long afterward, however, after further study, I decided once for all that methods of this kind, which substitute mechanical plays for judgment, must fail. For the calculations on which they are based omit one fundamental fact, i.e., that the only unchangeable thing about the stock market is its tendency to change. The rigid method sooner or later will break the operator who blindly follows it.

The man in question had no money with which to trade, except in ten share lots; he wanted to find some one who would put up a fair-sized amount of margin and trade in hundred to five hundred share lots. I knew enough about stock market uncertainties to want to do my own trading. Some people tried his method and got good results. Others failed completely, especially after September, 1909, when, owing to the death of E. H. Harriman, the whole character of the market changed.

One might ask: how could this happen? Did one man run the whole market? The answer is that he did not; but Harriman's personality and methods did affect the operations conducted by him and his two chief associates, William Rockefeller and H. H. Rogers, with whom also were allied the National City Bank and Kuhn, Loeb & Co. The manipulation of leading stocks, chiefly of Union Pacific, their market leader, bore the Harriman imprint, was clearly defined, and easy to interpret if one understood manipulation at all. All one had to do was to be able to detect evidence of accumulation when a bullish operation was being prepared. When the stock reached what I called the jumping-off place and was ready for its upward swing, then was the time not only to go with it, but to pyramid.

Harriman's method in such a campaign was first to poke a stock down to as low levels as he thought advisable; then gather in everything he could find within a certain buying zone. There would be drives for the purpose of shaking out weak holders who had placed stops or who could be scared off by signs of weakness. After this, Harriman would keep his stock dead within a range of a few points, for weeks at a time, so that nobody could make any money trading in it and those who held it would be discouraged, throw it out and get into more active issues. In other words, he first shook them out, then he tired them out.

One knowing how to interpret these movements, which were there for everybody to read but were understood by few, would observe that the transactions tapered off to almost nothing just before a real move began. That was because there was no more stock for sale at that level. No use putting it further down now—everybody was shaken out, and a new weakness might bring in fresh and unwelcome buyers. No advantage, either, in putting it up until the last five hundred shares had been gathered in.

Characteristic of a Harriman manipulation it was to see Charlie MacDonald, or some other important Harriman broker, come into the Union Pacific crowd with orders to "put her up." This was readily done under the rules of that period by bidding for round lots of stock such as 10,000 to 25,000 shares without having to accept offers of less. The bid made, he could gather in whatever was offered, then immediately he would bid again, an eighth or quarter higher, for a big lot. Other smaller buyers and shorts were thus forced to raise their bids to the same price, or above; if there was no stock offered he would bid still higher. An atmosphere of urgency filled the crowd; sellers withheld their offerings even though they had orders in hand. This continuous artificial effect of an excess of demand over supply was a vital part of what I designated in my later writings as "the marking-up period."

These manipulative campaigns on the bull side were

Copyright Brown Brothers

1905. *Edward Wasserman*

based on one of Harriman's fundamental marketing principles. Once when asked whether he could unload a line of Southern Pacific at 80, he replied that he did not think so, but that he could put it at 120 and then sell it back to par. The reason for this was that with the stock selling at, say, 70, a ten-point rise would not attract much of a following, while a fifty-point rise would attract an enormous following. Such a broad market would be created that almost any amount of stock could then be sold to people who thought themselves shrewd because at 110 or par the stock looked cheap in comparison with the 120 where it had lately been.

A mechanical method, then, based on the behavior of the market while under domination of the Harriman methods might thus work for a time. It is obvious that after the death of Harriman in 1909 such a method would not operate with the same degree of success. For those who succeeded him to leadership in important stock market operations employed different tactics, lacking his boldness of execution.

My mechanically inclined friend's method took account of the points that I have just mentioned. But he was using tabulated statistics as a substitute for judgment. And, as I afterward learned when I got down to the study of the *action* of the stock market as interpretive of its future course, there is no substitute whatever for human judgment.

Mechanical aids are of benefit simply in this way: No one can remember all the transactions in a given stock over many days, weeks or months. A trader requires records of the stock's previous gyrations. He must know at what points a stock was accumulated and distributed in former campaigns. He must know how the manipulators did the marking up; how they supported it during reactions; how far these reactions were allowed to run, what secondary moves were made. The best way to keep such records is in the form of charts.

The study of mechanical methods submitted to me as editor of *The Ticker* led me deeply into the study of stock market technique and interpretation. (The magazine was then almost wholly devoted to the field of speculation, although it was later developed into more of an investment publication, when the name was changed to the *Magazine of Wall Street.*)

I saw more and more that the action of stocks reflected the plans and purposes of those who dominated them. I began to see possibilities of judging from the very tape what these master minds were doing. My editorial work was proving a most valuable means of self-education. In gathering material that would benefit my readers, I was actively searching out the stuff that would aid me personally. While my subscribers were given the best of what I collected, there was much in material discarded which helped to build up what I might call a code of enlightened procedure for use in this greatest of all the world's games.

I had a friend who had been a member of the Exchange and who was well up on the technique of the market from the standpoint of the floor trader. We often discussed the difference between reading the tape simply to follow price changes (as most clients did) and reading the tape in order to judge the probable action of stocks in the immediate future.

Starting from the simple ground that the logical action of a stock was to decline when offerings exceeded the number of shares bid for, and to advance when the amount bid for was greater than the amount offered, we agreed that the quantity or volume of stock changing hands in each succeeding transaction was of great importance. Anyone who undertook to read the minds of the momentary buyers and sellers was able to measure, to a certain degree, their eagerness or anxiety to buy or sell. Also to measure the force of the buying power or selling power as shown by the number of shares. And to judge of the purpose behind the action—whether it was to buy without advancing the price, or to force the price up, or to mark it down, or to discourage buying or selling by others, as the case might be.

Each transaction carried with it certain evidence, although it was not always possible to interpret that evidence. All stocks no matter by whom they were owned, bought or sold, looked alike on the tape. But the purposes behind this buying and this selling were different and these might be fairly clear to those who understood stock market psychology.

Each transaction, although recorded only once, represented a meeting of minds; those of a buyer and a seller. This meeting of minds took place at a certain post on the floor of the Stock Exchange, even though the buyer might be in the far West and the seller in Europe.

Not all transactions were significant, but the interpreter must detect those which were. He must see that some indicated a purpose. Some one or some group was carrying, or attempting to carry, something through. He must take advantage of that.

Having had years of actual trading experience, my friend described the trained tape reader as one clever, alert, and not only quick to act, but able to reverse his position at a moment's notice—turn a complete somersault if required. Such a trader might be long of a stock one moment, then neutral, then short. Often he would be out of the market for hours or days, watching every possible turn, detecting what appeared to be opportunities, only to see them fade out, but taking instant advantage of real ones when they did come along.

This ideal tape operator should have no hopes or fears. He must play the game without a sign of nerves or mental strain; look upon profits or losses with equal equanimity. He must develop the kind of intuition that becomes a sixth sense in trading.

Such an operator, we agreed, was generally evolved from a series of failures over many months or years; his education could be completed only through a long series of transactions, spread over long periods, which would perfect his operating personality into one that could play the game cold. He must have persistence to carry him through adverse times without discouragement, until his expertness and self-confidence match that of the surgeon who performs many operations, losing some patients but never losing his nerve. Such a man, with such a character and with that experience, should be a success at reading the tape.

* * *

Many mechanical plans and "systems" were submitted to me. Sometimes I would work till three o'clock in the morning examining and testing them.

One, widely discussed at the time, was known as the Dow scale plan. This recommended buying a stock on its investment value, when, in the judgment of the investor, it became cheap, and buying additional amounts every 5 or 10 points down in case of a severe decline.

Copyright Brown Brothers

1907. *James R. Keene at the Races*

This plan looked sound on paper, but I have seen many a man go broke playing it.

For instance, when Union Pacific was put on a 10 per cent basis in 1906, the stock rose to 195⅜. On the subsequent decline, it looked cheap at 185 to a friend of mine with an eye on the dividend. He began buying at about that level, then at 160. It kept declining and he bought more at 135, thinking he was getting a great bargain, for the cost of his stock now averaged 160, and the investment netted about 6 1/3 per cent. But in the panic of 1907, this stock suffered a further slump. After putting up all his money, my friend saw his account sold out by his broker, with Union Pacific at 116. Finally, when the stock touched the low point of par, he had no money with which to buy it back.

Such a weakness appeared somewhere or other in about every plan which substituted a mechanical operation for the use of judgment. I examined hundreds in the first few years of the *Ticker*. They would all make money while the market was suited to their operations; then the time would come when the capital they employed would be slowly sapped, or suddenly annihilated.

More and more I became impressed with the possibilities of making money through study of the action of the market itself rather than the study of statistics. I wanted more knowledge on the subject; my subscribers continued to request more light. In many offices, active traders, more or less expert, scanned every transaction that appeared on the tape, evidently trying to scent out coming moves. They ignored statistics or earnings or such information, but they had great respect for previous swings, high and low prices, and other technical indications.

Many of these traders sitting on high stools by the tickers had no other vocation; they devoted their entire time to this business of trading in stocks. As they became more expert, they seemed to operate a good deal on intuition. They were especially quick to detect the starting point of new moves, up or down, in stocks which had previously been inactive.

I had customers of this kind in the brokerage business. They were among the best of my clients because they were always trading. They made far more money out of the market than the average customer; they were never found long of a lot of stocks with the market going badly against them, for they worked in harmony with its trend, trading on either the long or the short side as the situation demanded, and using stop orders one or two points away—never more than two.

Reasoning the problem out and analyzing the difficulties as I went along, I succeeded in writing much that was of great value to myself as well as to others. Along with the writing, I was continually experimenting in order to put my ideas to a practical test; but although I was losing money on the *Ticker* and might have been justified in taking larger chances in the stock market, I bided my time, knowing that I would have less difficulty once I developed the right method.

So while I worked away, and gave [1] the benefit of my discoveries to my readers, along with articles from the most intelligent people I could induce to write, my ambition to solve the problem grew with the number of copies that were being run off the press. The more I worked and

[1] Helpful material of this kind, obtainable nowhere else, was practically a gift at $3 a year—twelve issues—on which I was losing money.

studied, the more I pitied the fellows who were sloshing around the stock market without any real idea of what governed the machinery. And the more I progressed the more possible it seemed to me to help, educate and actually make money for the people who were buying my magazine, in their speculations and their investments.

* * *

I now began a series of articles entitled—since I was still but a student of the subject—*Studies in Tape Reading.*

The unexpected part of this business was that I soon found that I had already learned more of this question of playing the market by the tape than I possibly could put into print. I had, for instance, greatly developed my intuition, the immediate perception of a situation without conscious reasoning.

I was developing for my own benefit and that of many thousands of people the basic principles of success in the stock market. This was to be proved during the twenty years between the writing of the *Studies in Tape Reading* and the writing of this present book.

The articles attracted wide attention as the first of the kind ever published.

The law of supply and demand controls the movements of both the market as a whole and of individual stocks, they said. The solution of the stock market problem lay, therefore, in an understanding of this principle and in the ability to interpret supply and demand correctly.

Studies in Tape Reading [2] ran through the numbers of

[2] The articles were later published in book form under the title of *Studies in Tape Reading.* This book had a steady sale for eighteen years, and was our best seller much of that time. The method set forth in it was used by me later in forecasting the course of the stock market both in the *Magazine of Wall Street* and in most of the

The Ticker from November, 1908, to October, 1909. The letters I received seemed to show that I was giving the public something it wanted. I seemed to be on the right track in presenting a practical method for operating in the stock market. The series dealt with methods of determining the trend; playing panics; trading for small and long swings; mechanical trading; arbitraging; dealing in puts and calls, etc.

My basic proposition was that the stock market, by its own action, continually indicates the probable direction of the immediate trend, and that anyone able to interpret this action with fair accuracy should attain success in his trading.

I demonstrated the fact that the law of supply and demand controls the prices of stocks just as it does the prices of wheat, corn, labor and materials of all kinds.

Up to that time practically everyone, except the traders on the floor of the Stock Exchange and a few large operators, worked on fundamentals; that is, they studied the condition of the money market, of the crops, of business, and so on. They ignored manipulation, which is the cause of a large proportion of the moves in the leading speculative stocks.

The technique which I had begun to work out and explain in this series was unknown to the speculative public; when I began to publish articles showing how the

---

advisory services I have conducted. And the principles stated in it have operated in every kind of market since that time—bull and bear markets, booms and panics; through changing leadership, increasing breadth of the market and growing volume of trading. The original volume was written by me under the name of Rollo Tape. This *nom de plume* was chosen because the roll o' tape is the nearest thing to the ticker. *Studies in Tape Reading* has been out of print for some time and the publishers have announced that they do not intend to republish it.

market's immediate trend might be ascertained and the course of the market forecasted, and how trading could be done with this technical knowledge as a basis, there was a howl from the fundamentalists who published and reiterated the fact that I didn't know what I was writing about; that fundamentals offered the sole road to the golden gate of success.

I let them howl, and went on proving that the real solution of the stock market problem, for office traders at least, lay in a study of the forces behind the market and their power to lift or depress the prices of stock. These forces might be natural or artificial; that is, they might result from buying or selling by the public, or they might consist largely of manipulative operations which were purely artificial. These were planned and executed for the purpose of inducing the public to do the opposite of what the manipulators wished to do: when the latter desired to accumulate, they would mark down the price of a stock, spread bear rumors, and try to shake out or tire the outsiders until they sold. When they wished to distribute, prices would be artificially stimulated, glowing reports spread broadcast and the public induced to buy on the bulges.

Coming events were foreshadowed on the tape because insiders expressed their anticipation of an advance or decline by purchasing or selling. By the time the public became aware of what was happening, prices were already away up or down from the levels at which the insiders had begun operations. If one were to become sufficiently expert to judge by the action of stocks what was in the mind of the insider or manipulator, one could scent the moves, go with them, and benefit by having these big operators working for one.

I make no claim of having discovered a new principle: this is as old as Adam. But I do claim that no one had reasoned it out and put it into print as a method of operating in the stock market.

I was trying to show how a trader in a brokerage office could operate on this law of supply and demand, just as traders on the floor of the Stock Exchange were doing. The floor trader had a great advantage in not having to pay commissions; nothing could overcome this handicap. And at the time we were not having any such wide swings in the market as prevailed years later. The average daily fluctuations in the leading active stocks were from one to two and a half points and only the leaders could be traded in profitably by people who were getting in and out and closing their trades daily.

The purpose of the self-training and the continued application of the methods suggested in *Studies in Tape Reading* was to develop an intuitive judgment, which would be the natural outcome of spending twenty-seven hours a week at the ticker over many months and years. Every dealer in any fluctuating commodity such as wheat, corn, cotton, rubber, etc., learns in time to sense the trend of the market and after years of practice develops this sort of judgment in his own field.

The *Studies* represented a person studying the tape under the suggested plan as one looking upon a large room where a social gathering is being held. At first glance one would merely be seeing a lot of people; closer observation would disclose some individual traits. But by going in and mingling with them, the student would be able to detect many of their personal qualities—their hopes, wishes, desires; their habits, their weak and

Photo H. N. Tiemann Company

1909. *View of Wall Street*

strong points; their probable actions under certain conditions.

Another way was to look at the market as if all of the transactions were made by one person. I called this person the *composite operator.* The successful trader must endeavor to ascertain what is in the back of the head of that fellow and to anticipate his moves; for he is constantly expressing his intentions by what he does and the way he does it; by the urgent or leisurely character of his buying or selling; by the volume of the stocks he deals in, the width of their swings, especially in the leaders.

Remembering this, one would see, on the tape, a number of transactions in various stocks; one would see the volume of the trading, the prices at which the trades were made. Closer study would reveal individual peculiarities. Some stocks would be dealt in more actively than others; fluctuate over a wider range, daily, weekly and monthly; appear subject to little or much manipulation. Others might seem entirely neglected for days at a time, offering no trading opportunities. Some would afford sudden and highly attractive openings for profitable trading. Determination to reach clear understanding of all this, continuous self-training, persistent experimenting, were indispensable.

The trend was along the line of least resistance; stocks flow like water. Manipulators, while accumulating and distributing a certain stock, held it within a certain range; when the stock broke out of the range, this meant that it was on its way to the level, higher or lower, where the operator wished it to be. Of course, the operator might make false moves.

Bringing down these general observations to the individual attempting to derive a profit from the fluctuations in the stock market, I went into much detail. The necessity of limiting the risk in every transaction was emphasized; no one could expect to be right in every case; Mr. Keene himself had said that success meant that three out of five of his trades were profitable. Stop orders should be placed at the time the trades were made; they should be moved from time to time in such a way as to reduce the risk; and eventually be placed, if possible, where a profit was certain even if the stop were caught.

I found myself obliged to invent terms that more clearly described the various phases. One of these was "point of resistance"—a term which has since been widely used as indicating the level where, at the end of a decline, the buying power at length begins to overcome the selling, or the level where, after a rise, the selling begins to balance the buying.

Studies in Tape Reading was originally written to demonstrate a method of continuous trading from a broker's office. The changing character of the stock market over a number of years, however, brought a new and better application for this method: I was to use it later in forecasting the important swings of the stock market and as the basis for the predictions published in my magazine and in my "Trend Letter," publications which had a most successful career for many years.

The book contains what is still a highly practical way of judging the future of the market and of different stocks. It fits the requirements of those who wish to trade not too often but successfully. The trader today, who waits for swings of 5, 10 or 20 points to develop, as they do more often than ever before in Wall Street history, has a better chance than ever. In contradiction of those who believe that tape reading is an obsolete practice, I affirm that a knowledge of it is the most valuable equipment a Wall Street trader can possess.

If I were beginning my Wall Street career now, and knew what forty years of it have taught me, I should apply myself first of all to this business of judging and forecasting the stock market by its own action. It is something that requires long study and continuous practice. Practice in actual trading; paper trading lacks the element of risk. The feeling of uncertainty and of danger, the hope of profit, as well as the fear of loss—these are all obstacles to be overcome by anyone who desires to master the subject. In doing this he must risk his money; he must subject himself to all the emotions that accompany regular trades. After he has made hundreds of trades he may find that he is one who can work without hope or fear. He will gather experience from long series of transactions, each requiring a summarizing of the factors upon which decisions are based; each demanding that he "follow through" the trade until he decides upon the closing of it after due deliberation. Thus he will gradually evolve a trading character or personality. He will be able to decide whether he is adapted to the job. Comparatively few are. Something in the very nature of most men seems to work against them.

The greatest danger lies in overtrading. I am convinced that most people fail because they take on amounts of stock out of proportion with their capital and their experience. That is why learning should be done by trading in small lots while preserving a margin enabling one to sustain a series of losses, for losses there will be during that period of education.

No one, from what I have written, should derive the idea that the stock market is an easy nut to crack. That is the public's fallacy, especially in bull markets. It should be remembered that many of the biggest, most active and wealthy traders did not begin with large capital, but by trading in small lots in the bucket shops, where their margin in those days was only two points, or $20. This is true of such important traders as Field, Manning and Livermore. They might have been failures if they had begun with capitals of $25,000 to $50,000.

One should remember that the stock market is the world's greatest game; that it is played by the wealthiest, most influential and most powerful individuals, bankers, pools, cliques and organizations. Some of these are able to influence not only the stock market, but, most of the time, the money market. Some are in position to influence business conditions to a certain extent and public sentiment to a large degree.

* * *

1910 PREPARING TO SHOOT

THE HOCKING COAL & IRON POOL— KEENE GETS AWAY—A JOB TO TIDE OVER —DETECTING ACCUMULATION— W. B. THOMPSON'S NIPISSING DEAL

AMONG my personal clients when I was in partnership with Harrison was William H. Ziegler, one of the wealthiest men in Brooklyn and interested in the Columbus and Hocking Coal and Iron Co., a non-dividend payer selling on the New York Stock Exchange at 15 to 20.

In preparation for a new issue of stock, the finance committee of that company organized a junketing party of prominent brokerage and newspaper men. We left New York in a private car and inspected the company's properties in the Hocking district of Ohio. The company appeared to me rather a one-horse affair.

Ziegler and his friends now began to work the stock upward to 25, and around the high point I was given orders to sell a considerable number of shares, the proceeds of which went into the company's treasury. During the next year or two the stock declined to around 8, and then along in 1909, without any apparent improvement in the company's affairs, it began to work upward into the 40s. There were only 70,000 shares of it, making it an easy stock to manipulate. At 45 the stock was selling away above its value. The company succeeded in paying dividends for only one or two years in the twenty-five of its existence. It was being choked off by the railroad-owned coal properties surrounding it, and my observations while on the inspecting trip had convinced me that the proposition was unlikely ever to amount to much.

The stock was being manipulated by James R. Keene, as manager of a pool in which several Stock Exchange houses were interested. When the stock got up into the 60s Keene had advised the pool to liquidate, because even at that time the stock was selling away above its value. Certain members of the pool did not want to quit, and Keene continued the deal against his judgment. Many people had then sold the stock short. With the stock more or less cornered Keene then worked it upwards and forced these shorts to buy at the higher levels. Finally the stock rose to around 90.

From 88½ on January 19, 1910, the stock broke, with hardly a rally, to 25. The effect upon the stock market in general can be imagined, and on the firms involved, and on the unfortunate broker who had the order to buy 500 shares every quarter point down until he had taken 20,000 or 25,000 shares with no place to put them.

I always had my suspicions as to who really got the money out of the pool. Certainly not the firms which failed, the combined liabilities of two of them amounting to over $8,000,000. Certainly not those individuals who subscribed to the pool. Perhaps it was the shrewd old gentleman who was such an adept at such operations, for, before the smoke had cleared away, he was on his way to Europe, beyond the reach of process servers and investigating committees.

* * *

During the fall of this year *The Ticker,* then three years old, was meeting the approval of its readers, but these were not numerous enough to produce much money at $3 per annum. Advertising was scarce; the periodical's limited circulation did not greatly attract those who were endeavoring to secure margin accounts and investment business from the public. As I had no advertising solicitor and little time to get around, the advertising columns developed but slowly.

My appeal at that time was to students of the stock market rather than to people seeking investment. My great interest lay in stock trading, and the *Magazine* was an expression of this interest. Its purpose was to teach its readers how to trade and invest successfully. It showed them how to make money. But meanwhile I was losing money. I was not getting even a living out of the enterprise. I now looked around for a concern with whom I might get a job to tide me over to the time when *The Ticker* would become a money-maker.

The firm of Thompson, Towle & Co., recently organized, was one of the most enterprising in Wall Street. Colonel William B. Thompson, who had gained considerable prominence through his deal in Nipissing in 1906, and who now was promoting Inspiration Copper, was at the head of it; associated with him were his brother, J. E. Thompson, and Messrs. Towle, Bartholomew and Lovett of Boston. The firm was spending $50,000 a year in advertising and publicity; the office took up the entire fifteenth floor in 25 Broad Street.

Here was a chance to apply the mail-order method, which had cost me much time and money; I could be of value to such a concern. I called, said I did not have, and did not wish to have, any personal clients, that no job as a customers' man would interest me, but that I could show them how to add to their own clientele economically and profitably.

I got the job. There was a living in it for me. I worked there from nine to five; then went to my magazine office until about seven. Working at home a few nights a week, besides, I was able to keep it going.

All the while I was studying the stock market in two ways: First, by means of "Studies in Stock Speculation," another series of articles which I was pondering and writing; second, by watching the market analytically during the day and making experimental odd-lot transactions now and then.

Confidence in my ability to judge the market was growing. I began sending opinions over the private wires to Boston and working up a reputation for accurate foresight. Mr. Bartholomew, widely known in Boston and New York as "Bart," took an especial interest in my advisory work and often would test me thus:

Bart: What do you think of Steel common now, Wycky?

Wycky: It looks like big accumulation to me.

Bart: You're right; we are doing the accumulating; our order is to buy fifty thousand shares.

I worked up a lot of special features for Thompson, Towle & Co. For instance, we had some inquiries on Standard Oil of New Jersey. This was before the United States Supreme Court decision, which dissolved the trust, and the stock was selling in the 500s. I obtained information from a Standard Oil man that the company had oil above ground not shown in its balance sheets, and that this oil was worth $300 per share. I relayed this information to important clients but, strange to say, with no result. Nobody would buy gold dollars at 20 cents.

However, my principal work was the organization of a department that got business by advertising and by follow-up methods. This began to bring in customers within a few weeks after I was engaged; soon they were coming in one a day, then two or three a day.

The firm's clientele, though fairly large, had been scarcely enough to support several partners, big offices and heavy publicity expense. It had not been growing as it should have. Customers' men were employed, and the time-worn practice of nine brokerage houses out of ten was followed. I built a piece of business-getting machinery, in which most of the work was done by girls paid from $12 to $25 a week, and began to increase the clientele in a way that surprised and pleased the partners.

This was my first contact with Colonel Thompson. He was now a growing factor in Wall Street's machinery. The millions he had taken out of his Nipissing promotion had been kept active in deals like the Cumberland-Ely mining stock operations, in which he never got the worst of it. Well as he understood the mining business—and he had capable engineers—he understood the mining *stock* business even better.

In addition to his controlling holdings of Inspiration Copper, he had 50,000 shares of Utah Copper, then selling in the 50s, to say nothing of other securities, and quantities of stock in other mines.

In his Nipissing transaction, he and his associates acquired control of the property at cents per share. In 1906, a friend of mine had called my attention to this mine, and I had made some money out of it.

It was in that same year the big move in Nipissing

took place. Thompson had given the Guggenheims an option on a raft of the stock at $25 per share. The price began to go up and up because people were beginning to realize that here was a valuable mining property and because the insiders were not bashful in announcing the fact.

By the time Nipissing got up into the high 20s and low 30s, the public was buying its head off, and there was a tremendous market for the stock on the Curb. Rumor said the Guggenheims were, of course, going to exercise their option. They called the Colonel over to talk about it. But curiously enough, they kept him waiting in the anteroom for nearly an hour. He became suspicious, grabbed a telephone and asked about the price of Nipissing. Heavy liquidation had set in; the stock was very weak; some one was unloading. He suspected that while he sat there in the anteroom those who were in the inside office, keeping him waiting, were selling out at above 30 the stock which presently, exercising their option, they would buy from him at 25.

Well, the Colonel beat them to it. He bolted around to his office, and began to sell Nipissing so fast that it was soon down below the 25 price at which the other fellows could sell only at a loss. Then he poured out all the rest of the stock that he owned, which as I have said cost him cents per share. When the smoke cleared away he was $12,000,000 to the good.

At the time described, that is, when I first became associated with Thompson's firm, these millions had grown out of all proportion to what their number would have been in ordinary hands. I hate to think what some people would have done with so much money acquired so quickly and in a single deal. Thompson's practice was to take a few hundred thousand and build that into more millions. While I did not keep his books, there was reason to suspect that in the five or six years following the Nipissing maneuver, he had doubled his original roll a few times.

Well, I had a profitable experience with that firm. I did not make any money out of the market there, however. I had no working capital; the magazine absorbed everything I had. Also, I was skeptical about inside information. It was my belief that insiders were often the worst judges of their own properties; also that the insider who gave you a piece of advice had an ax to grind. When Colonel Thompson would drop into my little private office in the very corner of the building at Broad and Exchange Place, where I had a ticker and a telephone, and was then studying the market closely and in solitude, and when he would say: "Wyckoff, tell your people to buy Inspiration," I would take the receiver off the hook and say: "Quote Inspiration." Before the quotation came back he would be out of the office, and I would have placed no order to buy Inspiration, nor advised anyone to buy it. I do not think this laid me open to the charge of disloyalty, although there was an unwritten law in the office that whatever W. B. said "went," and the folks were all expected to bull things he wanted bulled. But I could get far better results in doping out the probable action of Steel and Union Pacific and Reading, than in buying Inspiration, which did not respond until later to the Colonel's bull tips.

* * *

1911 THE NEW TREND

GETTING A REPUTATION—FORECASTING THE MARKET—STARTING THE TREND LETTER—ON MY FEET AGAIN

BY THE summer of 1911, I had begun to acquire a little prestige in forecasting. I was interpreting the action of the stock market, both for the clients of Thompson, Towle & Co. and for the readers of *The Ticker.* For some time I had been printing in the front of each issue a "Market Outlook." This examined the principal factors used by the ordinary market student and analyst; viz., money, earnings, crops, business, etc. While my discussions were upon these so-called fundamental factors, only my closest associates knew that my conclusions were not based on them, but upon the action of the market. The average man—trader, investor or stock broker—could not at that time have understood any other kind of language. To write a market outlook based on the action of the market alone would have been far over their heads. This is not stated egotistically but because I knew from personal contact with thousands of clients and hundreds of brokers that they did not study the stock market as I had done and was doing. They read news slips, news tickers and dope sheets put out by tipsters; they followed bank statements, reports, earnings, other statistics. For me to state in print that, owing to certain technical considerations (the tools with which I worked), I believed prices were about to advance would have gained neither their attention nor their respect. I clothed my own thoughts in their language, and by means of a long series of accurate predictions gained a substantial following.

My readers were asking if some way could not be found to bring my forecasts to them more frequently. I decided on a weekly service, and about October, 1911, announced *The Trend Letter.*

The response of my readers was almost instantaneous. Within a week or two the subscriptions to the new *Letter* had assured the solution of all my financial and publishing problems.

I knew already what the new subscribers wanted. They were not so much interested in general methods by which money-making ability in the stock market could be acquired; more specifically, *they wanted to be told what to buy or sell and when to do it.* They were willing to pay me more money in a month for this than they had been paying me in a year for the other. The price of the *Trend Letter* was $5 a month, or $50 a year.

I had, for the first time in my life, run into debt, in attempting to put over a publication which taught the public how to play the market. I had succeeded in training myself—and in finding out that the public did not want to be trained, but wanted me to do the "doping out" for them. I knew I could do that better than the average man. I had only to keep on doing it better and better to gain an increased following and a larger income.

Within a few months this income had risen to $60,000 a year.

The *Trend Letter* was a one-page multigraphed sheet. But it might have been done with pen and ink on wrapping paper; what got the money were my forecasts of the market, correct *most* of the time.

I had put myself on my financial feet once more; I could now develop my magazine. With my assistant editor, George C. Selden, I had been writing a good part of the contents. I now augmented my staff so that I could study the market from 10:00 to 3:00 every day, and do my share of the writing after the close.

Resigning from Thompson, Towle & Co., I left them a business-getting plant, completely equipped. I continued to make my headquarters there. They supplied me with a good private office. I gave them business more than enough to compensate for the office, equipment and facilities.

* * *

1912 REFUSING A GOOD BID

HAYDEN, STONE & CO.'S OFFER—A BIG TRADING CLIENT—TURNING DOWN A GOOD PROPOSITION

ONE day N. Bruce MacKelvie, managing partner of Hayden, Stone & Co.'s New York office, asked me what I was doing. "I hear you have resigned from Thompson's," he said.

I replied that I had. That I was publishing *The Ticker,* writing the *Trend Letter* and doing well with it.

"What will you take to come in here with us?" he asked. "And develop this business just as you did Thompson's—as if it were your own?"

"I'll take a partnership."

"That's all right as far as I'm concerned," said MacKelvie, "but neither Mr. Hayden nor Mr. Stone knows you as well as I do. I'd like them to get acquainted with you. Suppose you come in here on a salary until they have a chance to do this."

"No," I said. "I have decided never to build up any other fellow's brokerage business again unless I have an interest in the firm."

A date was set at which I would see the other two partners, and meanwhile something occurred which put me in a position to give them a little demonstration in business-getting. A certain large trader, whose dealings ran into big totals and who had been interested in my methods of forecasting, now came to me.

"If you will get a headquarters in some good brokerage house," he said, "I will give you some business."

I told MacKelvie this, and asked him to postpone that interview with his partners. He arranged for me to occupy one of the firm's private offices, and I moved in with my trader. Other personal clients followed me, and for some months there came out of that private office a daily commission business of from 1 to 2 per cent of the total number of shares dealt in on the New York Stock Exchange.

At the end of that time I had another talk with MacKelvie and asked him how he and his partners liked my demonstration. They liked it very well, he said, but they would like to have me for another year on a salary. How much did I want? "Twenty-five thousand dollars for the year," I replied. He offered me twelve thousand dollars.

"You'd better think it over carefully," he suggested. "It wasn't many years ago that I was posting quotations on Hayden, Stone & Co.'s board in the Boston customers' room. My interest in the firm thus far has made me away over a million dollars."

I said: "If I undertook to build you, in one year, a business-getting plant on a twelve thousand dollar salary, it is true that I would have the twelve thousand. But you would have the machinery, the ideas, the system. I would have twelve thousand and you would have something worth hundreds of thousands of dollars. And if then, at the end of the year, we should fail to come to terms, I would be just where I am now. I guess we don't get together."

I then began to consider going into the brokerage business as a partner in another firm. Many clients were coming my way; I might as well have a place for them.

1910. *J. P. Morgan, His Son, and His Daughter, Mrs. Satterlee*

They were a by-product of the *Trend Letter;* not a few insisted upon establishing more personal relations. But I did not care for this, and kept myself in seclusion most of the time. The more time and thought I put into a close study of the market, the better my judgment.

* * *

My magazine was now less speculative; an increasing number of its pages were devoted to articles on investment and finance.

I, therefore, decided to change its name to *The Magazine of Wall Street.*

* * *

1913 PICKING A REAL ONE

A BROKER AGAIN—SELECTING THE BEST STOCK—FORECASTING EARNINGS—AN OPTION ON GENERAL MOTORS—BUYING IT AROUND THE LOW

THIS year I joined the Stock Exchange house of Alfred Mestre & Co. as a special partner, putting some capital into the firm.

I continued to develop the *Magazine,* to write the *Trend Letter,* studying the market the while, doing some trading, and mentally investigating the possibilities of broadening the firm's business. But the firm was not equipped for what I had in mind. Mr. Mestre, a member of the Governing Committee of the New York Stock Exchange, was once a partner of Mr. Noble (President of the Exchange in 1913), on the same floor as were Hazard & Parker's offices twenty-six years before, when I was office boy. He was of the old line of brokers and could not be induced to see the business and its possibilities in a big way.

A certain amount of new business was coming in without my going after it. I continued to write articles for the *Magazine*—some analyzing the action of the market and defining its position and prospects, others upon special subjects. I wrote a series on "Buying stocks for future income." [1] These articles dealt with the selection

[1] This title suggested the department "Building Your Future Income," which has been a feature in the *Magazine of Wall Street* for many years.

of stocks in companies with clearly defined futures, not so much for what they then paid as in view of a probable larger return indicated by available data.

Another series, "Which kind of a stock is best?" answered this question. Preparing these, I grouped all the stocks listed on the Stock Exchange according to the industries they represented. Even at that time there were several hundred stocks, but there were only a few scores of industries. My analysis showed definitely that the greatest prospects at that time were in the chain store and mail order companies. The chain stores I designated the "guinea pigs of finance" because these chains of stores begat other little stores out of their earnings, and did it rapidly. Other industries might issue bonds and preferred stocks to finance their extensions, but these outfits rarely asked for a dollar of new capital. S. S. Kresge, for example, told me he started with less than $5,000.

I wanted to find for my subscribers the particular industries in which their money would grow the fastest. The development of chain stores during the following fifteen years was to verify the indications available at the time I made my study.

The mail order houses also—taking Sears Roebuck & Co. as an example—forecasted their own possibilities. Their statements over several years showed that their gross earnings had increased at the rate of about 10 per cent per annum, and that their net profits were about 9 or 10 cents on the dollar of business done. Hence, it was easy to forecast the future and to anticipate increased cash dividends and melon cuttings.

* * *

In this year, 1913, General Motors was selling on the New York Stock Exchange around $30 a share. There were only 164,000 shares of common stock outstanding on which no dividends were being paid. The company had found itself in financial difficulties a few years before, had been forced to borrow $15,000,000 on pawnbrokers' terms, and the bankers lending the money had secured control by means of a voting trust.

Obtaining now some inside information as to what the company was doing, and believing that it had a great future, I visited these bankers, one after the other, in an endeavor to get an option on 10,000 shares of the stock at $30 a share. This would have represented about one-sixteenth of the outstanding stock. I intended to take part of this myself and to place the rest where it would not come back on the market for a long time. I reminded these bankers of what they already knew: the stock was dragging along, very little was being traded in. If they would give me the option, I said, I had ways and means of stirring up a market in the stock and of greatly increasing public interest.

Some of the bankers seemed interested but the final decision rested with one of the Seligmans. "I admit that there isn't much doing in the stock at present," he said, "but it is being gradually absorbed by investors, and in the course of time we hope to see a better market for it. I am afraid we can't let you have the option."

I asked if a higher price than $30 would interest him.

"No," he answered, "I think we will stand pat."

Thirty dollars a share made the entire outstanding stock worth about $5,000,000. Fifteen years later it had a $4,000,000,000 valuation. The low point for General Motors in the year of my negotiation was 25. Within three years that same stock sold at 850.

* * *

1914 THE PRE-WAR MARKET

MYSTERIOUS SELLING—THE CRASH—STOCK EXCHANGE CLOSED—CUTTING EXPENSES—THE WAR BRIDES BOIL

THE first half of this year was marked by a dull, dragging, slowly declining market. There was little buying power, but a steady and persistent liquidation that appeared to have a mysterious source. Stocks were not hurriedly sold; just enough was laid gently onto the buyers, in such a way as not to discourage them; if a thousand shares were wanted, not more than five hundred would be supplied at the price. A lot of somebodys were getting out—slowly, patiently, steadily. The volume was small and tended to shrink. Fluctuations were narrow. There was little opportunity to make money. It was just as if some one were trying to kill off speculation.

When the first definite probabilities of war appeared, the source of all the wise selling became apparent. Large interests abroad and here, including bankers, diplomats and their close friends, had been turning everything into cash in preparation for the catastrophe. Governments were buying all the grain they could get hold of. The action of wheat and other commodities on the Chicago Board of Trade indicated, to anyone familiar with such signs, that a volcano was about to erupt; yet most people doubted what was forecasted. Few would believe that in these so-called civilized times any great country could go to war.

When the European armies finally were mobilized and panic broke out on the New York Stock Exchange, the decline was so swift in the brief sessions remaining before the Stock Exchange closed that most traders were mentally paralyzed; they seemed to hope that at the last moment the cataclysm would be averted. Those interested in the stock market who have never been through a panic cannot imagine what it means to the ordinary man who is long of stock to see his fortune being wiped out and the ground cut from under his feet by the closing of the Stock Exchange.

Having been through several panics, I knew how to take care of myself. The first thing I did was to reduce the expenses of the publishing business so that I could carry through with the minimum of loss. There being no stock market except the illegitimate trading that was done in what was called the "gutter market," the *Trend Letter* was of no value to its subscribers. I continued to issue it, but made no charge for the period when the Stock Exchange was closed. With Mr. Selden I wrote nearly the whole *Magazine,* the earning power of which was represented by a minus sign.

The Stock Exchange resumed operations in December, and at the low levels represented by the initial quotations there was a great increase in public interest. Bargain-hunters' money came out of the banks and poured into stocks and bonds. Demand for the *Magazine of Wall Street* and the *Trend Letter* increased heavily. Stocks of war-bride companies boiled. Barrels of money were made by those who got into the right ones. The market became broader than at any time during the past two or three years.

* * *

1915 FINANCING AN ENTERPRISE

PHONOGRAPHS—BUCKING THE COMBINATION—A SPONTANEOUS MARKET—INVENTION OF A NEW RECORD

FROM the time the *Magazine* first appeared people began to come to me now and then with inventions or enterprises that required financing. It seemed to them that the publisher of a financial magazine must be in touch with everybody in the Street who had money and who would be willing to chance that money. Mostly I gave no heed to such overtures; now and then I gave the caller a letter of introduction to some one who might be of assistance.

Most men make money in their own line of business and lose it in the other fellow's. Nevertheless, we gain in such losses what is often more valuable than money. While undoubtedly I would have been better off in the long run if I had never touched any of these propositions that came to me, my participation in some—regrettable as it proved sometimes—gave me an insight into many corporation affairs related to the stock market which I would not have got otherwise.

For some years I had known Victor H. Emerson, head of the recording department of the Columbia Graphophone Co. He had had long experience and was an inventor in the record-making field, having been the one who originated the idea of putting music on a phonograph record. It was he who first used Edison's invention for entertainment and amusement. He had made the first musical records from a German band which happened to be playing in the street below his window. He recorded their music upon some of the little cylinders (then used for dictating letters) and charged 25 cents to those who wished to "hear music come out of a phonograph" through the old-style ear tubes.

After the war broke out Emerson told me of his plan for producing a 10-cent phonograph record, and it was not long before these "Little Wonders" were sold by the millions in the Woolworth stores.

One night he asked me to come around to his house to see something new. He had developed a small phonograph which he believed could be made to sell at $3 retail. Fifteen dollars was then the lowest price for a phonograph. His idea was that large quantities of this new machine could be sold, at its low price, to people who would then buy a still greater quantity of "Little Wonder" records, made by the Columbia Graphophone Co., or others which he proposed to manufacture.

At that time the Pathé Frères were making a record in France which had a large sale in this country through a subsidiary in New York. Emerson had secured from Pathé the right to transfer these selections to 6-inch disks which could be sold at retail for 10 cents. The Pathé repertoire included selections by Enrico Caruso, John McCormack and other leading operatic stars who were feature artists of the Victor Talking Machine Co.

Emerson explained that his real purpose was to create a tremendous market for small records. His 3-dollar phonograph, once on the market, would stimulate the production of cheap machines by other manufacturers; people who bought these would buy many, many records. He saw a great opportunity, not only for the 10-cent disks, but for another of a little larger size which he could retail at 25 cents—the first of its size in this field.

He asked me if I could raise $200,000 as working capital for this new enterprise. I expressed confidence in my ability to raise this money and, after the papers were signed and the Emerson Phonograph Co. was incorporated, set off about it.

I wrote some friends that this stock was going to be dealt in on the Curb at from $5 to $7.50 per share, that the market would open for it within a week or so and told them that it would be a good speculative purchase. Soon afterward my broker called me up one day to say there were bids on the Curb at $7 a share for Emerson Phonograph Co. stock. A little later he called back again and said $8, $9 and $10 was bid for Emerson. I hadn't done a thing about the market. It had opened itself. Within a couple of days there were big transactions at from $11 to $12 a share, and within a few weeks, by selling treasury stock, I had the $200,000 necessary to start the company in business.

Emerson Phonograph Co. stock continued to be dealt in heavily on the Curb and within the first few months of its existence sold as high as $16 per share. A contract for the manufacture of 200,000 3-dollar phonographs was signed with a concern in Brooklyn, and it began turning them out rapidly within the next few months.

Meanwhile the Pathé Co. in Paris was making the dies for the small records and as soon as these arrived in New York we started to manufacture them. The first were of selections by Caruso and McCormack. While the Victor Co. sold its records up in the dollars, we advertised ours for 10 cents in the Woolworth stores! The Victor Co. got out bulletins and placards claiming that they had the exclusive right to make and sell records by these artists in the United States. But they could not interfere with our sales, for these artists had sung for the Pathé Co. in Paris before they signed with the Victor, and we had acquired the rights from Pathé.

My part in the enterprise was supposed to be only the raising of the working capital; but I had not gone far before I saw that many people had invested on the strength of my being identified with the company, and were depending upon me more than upon Emerson. It also became apparent that I would have to stay on the job to keep the company's capital from being ventured in the development of new inventions and in new and inadvisable deals.

During the first year of the war most of the material for the *Magazine,* which had not yet made a dollar of profit, was being written or prepared by George C. Selden, my Associate Editor, and Frederick Lownhoupt who was assisting him. I divided my time between the *Magazine,* the *Trend Letter,* and the Emerson Phonograph Co. The work I had to do for the latter I detested. But I was caught. I now felt that if the company went wrong this might reflect upon me.

The sale of the Pathé style of records was under a handicap at the start, because anyone playing them on a Victor or Columbia phonograph was obliged to use an attachment, the records being made by a process similar to Edison's, and differing from that used by Victor and Columbia. One day while at Emerson's house, playing a Pathé record on one of our small machines, I chanced to put the sound-box in an oblique position and a little sideways. Somehow it played the record to a fairly audible degree without the use of an attachment. Emerson, sitting across the room, gave me a quick, inquisitive look and said:

"How did you make it play? Let me see what you did to it."

I showed him how I had placed the sound-box and he became thoughtful. Within a few weeks, as a result of that accidental occurrence, he had invented a new record that would play on the Edison or Pathé, as well as on the Victor and Columbia phonographs. This invention again greatly widened our field. We began to count on a rapid expansion of the company's business.

* * *

1916 WAR BRIDES

A REAL MARKET—WIDE SWINGS—RUNNING CAMPAIGNS—LANDING PROFITS—TEN MILLION RECORDS

THE stock market was responding almost entirely to conditions growing out of the war. The panicky liquidation which had occurred upon the outbreak of hostilities and the extreme low prices made in the "gutter market" of that summer and fall had been followed by a slow and feverish recovery. In 1915 we had begun to get a real market in which money could be made because there were activity and wide swings. Baldwin rose from 27 to 154 in 1915 and the following year fluctuated between 52 and 118½. Bethlehem Steel, which was below 50 at one time in 1915, rose to 600 that year and to 700 in 1916. General Motors went to 850. U. S. Steel, which had sold at 38 in 1915, rose nearly to 130 in 1916.

The *Trend Letter* was run in weekly editions with supplementary letters whenever especially important changes occurred between the regular dates of issue. While leading market influences were briefly touched upon, my main discussion related to the technical position of the market and the definition of its trend. Advices were in the form of campaigns. Most of the leading speculative stocks were swinging up or down, more or less as a unit. My task was to ascertain whether accumulation, distribution, marking up or marking down was in progress, and to advise my subscribers to take a position either on the long or the short side of the market as near to the turning points as these could be ascertained.

The market was being handled in an expert manner. Leading bankers were in the saddle and with a few exceptions prices were more or less controlled. At times the public would break loose, and take the market out of the bankers' hands. There would be intervals, of course, when the trend was indistinguishable, at least to me, and at these periods I would take a neutral position; but when preparation for an important advance or decline showed itself in the transactions, the purchase or sale of a line of stocks would be advised. Preferably these were of important leaders which had wide swings—especially those which indicated, by their action, the volume of their transactions, etc., that they would be the ones most likely to be manipulated upward or downward to the greatest extent in the shortest length of time. I aimed to have my followers on the fastest horses. As soon as I discovered an opportunity I told them to hop on its back, letting the manipulators drive it, and thus to enjoy the pleasure of having the big fellows work for their benefit.

Of course, there was a risk in this business. Subscribers were clearly told that they must expect occasional losses. But as the risk on practically every trade was limited to three points, my problem was to see that profits exceeded losses, commissions and the cost of the service, which by 1916 had been increased to $90 a year.

As a result of a series of successful campaigns, profits for the subscribers were rolling up. On September 8, 1916, we took the following points profit on stocks, bought one month previous to that date: Steel, 17⅞; Baldwin, 12½; Smelters, 9⅞; Union Pacific, 7⅛; Pressed Car, 6⅝—a total of 54 points on 5 stocks. (A point, as everyone knows, means a dollar per share.) Then we stayed out of the market until October 5 and took the short side. Within a few days, profits of from 4 to 8 points appeared and we moved the stops down so that 3-point profits were assured. These stops were caught on a rally, with smaller profits than in the previous campaign, and then on a further rally we took the short side again and had some losses. Next we put everybody into Magma Copper at 30 and saw it above 60 in a month; otherwise kept a neutral position until November 27; then went short again until December 14, when the following profits appeared: Steel, 13; Smelters, 12¼; Central Leather, 16⅛; Baldwin, 14; Pressed Car, 7.

* * *

The first year of the Emerson Phonograph Co. had been one of preparation. Enemies had criticized and called the company more or less of a fake. I went right ahead devoting more of my time to the phonograph business, digging in harder than ever, in order to justify confidence in the company's future and to make good on the moral obligations I had assumed.

War conditions prevailed. Materials were high and deliveries difficult. The company had not yet established its credit but it was doing sufficient business to yield encouragement. Then, after the new style of record was ready for production, I signed a contract with a concern in Pennsylvania for 10,000,000 records to retail at 25 cents, and told them I was going to give them so many orders they would have to build a new factory. We began to do an increasing business; but the factories couldn't supply us fast enough, so that our growth was comparatively slow. We were selling two or three records on orders for every one we could deliver.

The company's business was growing so fast that we needed more capital. I couldn't get it because of the way certain insiders were mussing up the market for the stock and limiting the company's credit with the banks. During the second or third year of the company's career I loaned it over $100,000 on promissory notes. Not only my reputation, but my time, money and, as it eventually proved, my health were at stake.

* * *

1917 A BEAR RAID

SO MANY PROFITS BRING TOO MUCH FOLLOWING—PARASITES—SMASHING STEEL COMMON—TEN YEARS OF PUBLISHING

In 1917 the *Trend Letter* was successful in profits secured for clients. On May 14 we took the long side of a number of leading active stocks with 3-point stops. On May 31 we closed these out. Profits: Steel, 14⅛; Bethlehem, 12; Crucible, 11¼; Lackawanna Steel, 10; others, from 8⅜ to 6¾ points. We had one loss, 3¼ in Studebaker. We had averaged over 8 points profit on the 10 stocks.

After remaining neutral for a week, we took the short side, got a good break, took profits the next month. Then, July 27, we went long of 10 active stocks and got out with a fractional average loss. August 15 we were on the short side again. By the twenty-third the 10 stocks showed 66 points profit. This was considerably increased by the end of the month and on September 4 we advised all subscribers to take profits, which were as follows:

Stocks Sold Short	*Selling Price*	*Price Sept. 4*	*Profits*
U. S. Steel	124⅛	104¾*	15⅛
Crucible	81¼	66¼	15
Baldwin	70¼	56	14¼
Republic Steel	89½	77⅞	11⅝
Bethlehem B	115	104	11

1910. *The Curb Market before It Went under Cover*

Lackawanna Steel	90¾	77½	13¼
Am. Locomotive	69¾	57½	12¼
Beet Sugar	94¼	81	13¼
Central Leather	92⅛	79	13⅛
Pittsburgh Coal	54¼	46⅜	7⅞

* X Div. 4¼

That campaign was one of a long series in which we had some losses but a whole lot of liberal profits which far exceeded all losses, commissions, etc. Subscribers now had such fat equities in their brokerage accounts that the *Trend Letter* was the object of admiration in the brokerage offices throughout the country. Business began piling in so fast that I saw we were likely to secure too large and unwieldy a following. I raised the subscription price from $90 to $150 a year. Subscribers responded by mailing in their checks to the amount of $60,000 within the next six weeks.

Instead of reducing the number of subscribers, the new subscription price seemed only to increase it. People subscribed whose names we did not have and who said they had heard about our successful advices. Brokers around the country began to subscribe, and send our letter's advices over their wires word for word, as if these represented their own opinions. When we issued advices to buy, the stocks selected opened from 1 to 3 points above their previous day's close, and when we advised taking profits or selling short, our stocks opened down from 1 to 3 points the following morning.

This was a serious handicap; it came because our subscribers placed their orders "at the market price," and because to these were added the orders poured into brokerage houses that passed along the gist of the *Trend Letter's* information. Houses in Buffalo, Chicago, Kansas City and elsewhere, to say nothing of the local brokerage offices, continued to shoot our stuff over their wires. When their customers' men, and those of their branches, and those of their correspondents, slid these on to clients by phone, wire and mail, there was a rush to buy or sell, as the case might be, all concentrated in the very stocks we had selected.

Subscribers who were paying money for my advice were thus crowded out of their rightful purchasing prices by hundreds of other buyers who didn't pay us a cent, and whose brokers were simply parasites feeding on our service. If we advised the purchase of Steel at 120 with a 3-point stop, it would open perhaps at 123 and the stop order would then have to be placed at 120, which was the previous night's close. This made an artificial jump of three points, which would undoubtedly not have occurred had it been possible to keep the advices confined to the subscribers. Certain houses boasted that they were able to secure the meat of the *Trend Letter* a short time after it was dictated. This meant that they began sending out their advices on the very afternoon that ours were transmitted to subscribers, and resulted in an amount of competition for the next morning's opening that was out of all proportion to the number of shares our people would have dealt in.

Repeated warnings were issued in the *Trend Letter* against placing buying or selling orders at the opening; for brokers having such orders on the floor of the Exchange all endeavored to execute them at the same moment. We stated that much more satisfactory results would be obtained by holding orders until after the opening and by avoiding the purchase or sale of any large lots all at once. We also warned against letting brokers know what the orders were until they were given to them to execute at the market price. Even though a brokerage house should have no advance information on the *Trend Letter's* advice, our subscribers were known; when their orders came in, the customers' men and order clerks knew: "Wyckoff was buying stocks." This would develop a further following which trailed in from a few minutes to a few hours after we had taken our position.

This became a serious matter. Continued success in judging the market would automatically develop into failure. The parasites were killing the game. While I did not want to see many losses occur, I began to wish at times for a fair amount of them; they might shake off some of this unwelcome following.

I had been issuing these advices for six years, trying my utmost to make them profitable to subscribers, working my head off on the Emerson promotion which I should never have gone into, and in the one hour a day that I could devote to the stock market, turning out opinions and advices that exceeded, in accuracy and in profits to subscribers, anything that had ever been issued or published in Wall Street. The net result left me in the position of a farmer who, having worn out his knees praying for rain, was now presented with a deluge that threatened to wash out all his crops.

* * *

It was not until some time afterward that I realized that being limited to one hour in the middle of each day was an advantage in my concentrated study of the position of the market and its action. Had I been an active trader, this would not have been true, but in defining the trend of the market, anticipating the important turning points, and selecting the best stocks for making the most profits in the shortest time, the hour-a-day method was ideal. Each hourly section was compared with those of the preceding days. The comparative strength or weakness, the response of the market to bullish or bearish influences, the nature of the manipulation, and the evident purposes of the manipulators became more clear thus in comparisons of hours side by side.

* * *

An interesting episode at the end of October further emphasized the disadvantages of "hangers-on." The average price of 50 stocks had been working around the 70 level with continuous liquidation in many of the high-grade rails. The market was within a couple of months of the extreme low point of the rails which occurred when the government took over control of all the railroads.

On October 29, the tape told me that the market was on the verge of a further important decline. I put my people short of U. S. Steel, Bethlehem, Baldwin and 7 other stocks. Next day there was a big market, especially in U. S. Steel, and on the thirty-first 352,000 shares of Steel were dealt in, out of a total of 1,127,000 shares of all stocks for the day. Fully satisfied that some big people were either unloading a big line of Steel, or going short of it, or doing both, I figured the market to be in a most critical position. These big bankers and operators would not be selling heavy quantities unless they anticipated a considerable break. As it was always my purpose to endeavor to detect what the largest operators were doing and to go along with them, I waited until the following morning for further confirmation of this coming weakness in Steel, and, seeing the downward tendency more marked than ever, issued the following telegraphic advice to my subscribers:

"*Steel common should decline to* 85.

"*Sell it short at the market and sell an equal amount every one point down, with a* 3-*point stop on every individual lot. Do not fail to use these stops. The trend is strongly downward.*"

The market that day was weak on false rumors that the Governing Committee intended to set minimum prices at which stocks could be sold. Most of the leading active issues were down 1 or 2 points for the day, and some as much as 7 points. Steel fluctuated between 102 and 99 and closed at 100¾. What followed the next morning is best described by referring to the newspapers of that day: The New York *Herald* said: "U. S. Steel was the center of attack—for that there was a concerted attack is without question. The 'premier industrial' opened off 1¾ at 99, was 98 in a minute, sold at 96 before midday and in the afternoon touched 93¼, a net fall of 7½ for that day and with only a fractional recovery at the close."

The New York *World* referred to the fact that a certain agency had "sent broadcast a telegram urging the west to go short of Steel at every point down from 95 and not to cover until the stock had touched 85. This advice was largely responsible for enormous selling in the last hour when U. S. Steel broke to 93¼ with total sales of the stock over 500,000 shares, the largest volume since the panic that followed the Lusitania disaster."

Judging from what friends of mine (members who were on the floor of the Stock Exchange that day) described to me, half the brokers on the floor were around the Steel post selling the stock steadily all day. Buyers were simply swamped. Naturally, the price of the stock melted away.

The decline of several points in U. S. Steel, the undisputed market leader, combined with such a tremendous volume of trading, produced a sensation. There had been rumors of organized raids against the market by bear operators and no doubt some big campaigns of this kind were under way. Undoubtedly those high in the confidence of the administration knew that the disastrous condition of the country's railroads—its transportation plant—would result in a crisis of some sort. The weakness in the leading railway shares was proof that enough wise people knew what was going to make an impression on the market. But this sudden weakness in Steel produced such a loss of confidence on the part of investors and such a panicky feeling in the financial district that something drastic had to be done.

After the close of the market, the Governing Committee of the Stock Exchange held a special meeting requiring all members to furnish, daily, a list of all stocks which were borrowed, giving the names of the customers for whose accounts such stocks were borrowed.

It was perfectly obvious that in sending these special advices to my clients I had unintentionally turned loose the lightning; not because my comparatively limited number of subscribers were powerful enough to force the market down to that extent, but because the advice was so unusual and sensational that it was passed along by telephone and telegraph until the whole country had it and everybody was plunging on the short side of Steel, selling more and more as the price declined. Probably for every 100 shares my subscribers sold, other people sold 500 or 1,000 shares. At the rate Steel was declining, it easily would have reached 85 the next day, but my objection to this sudden consummation of the predictions expressed in the *Trend Letter* was this: All these enthusiastic sellers, made up of my following, plus many others, would endeavor to cover their shorts around 85 and produce a stampede on the upside, similar to, or perhaps worse than, the one which had occurred on the way down.

If the advice had been acted upon by my people alone, Steel might have taken a week or ten days to reach 85 and their shorts could then have been covered without disturbing the market. But with this mob hanging to our heels there was no telling what the consequence would be, either to the subscribers or to the mob. The former were short of Steel at 102⅞, sold in a separate campaign, along with the other 9 stocks, on October 29.

Only one course was left to me: I was compelled to get rid of this outside following, and therefore issued in my regular *Letter* of November 1 the following advice:

"The Steel sold on our Special Letter of October 31st should be covered at the opening tomorrow because today's extreme weakness might lead to a sharp rally of three or four points."

This, of course, was not a good reason for covering, but it was enough to scare off the parasites. Most of my people were not likely to change their position on such a slender excuse. At any rate they would stay short of the other lot of Steel sold higher up.

Next morning there was one grand scramble to cover Steel, which had closed the night before at 93⅞. When the market opened Steel sold at 98½ on one side of the crowd and 97 on the other, and then dipped to 95⅛.

The New York *World* said: "A copy of the much-talked-of bear letter on Steel sent out on Wednesday was obtained yesterday by the Governors of the Stock Exchange. As it turned out, the Letter did not make the specific statement that Steel would go to 85 within a specified time. It was sent out by the *Magazine of Wall Street* of No. 42 Broadway, a financial publication which contains a market information bureau in connection with its publication business."

The *World* then repeated the advice which was contained in the *Letter* and continued: "A representative of the *Magazine of Wall Street* said there was nothing at all mysterious about the communication and that it went out in the usual course of the concern's stock market service. He also pointed out that the letters to subscribers are confidential and subscribers are warned against showing them to persons who are not subscribers. He said they do not pretend to have any inside information as to the trend of the market."

That was true. The tape told me that other big people were selling heavily and the tape is better than any inside information if one knows how to interpret it.

Proof that the advice was correct was found in the subsequent action of Steel. After the rally to 98, caused by the covering, the stock slipped on down again.

We stayed short of our original commitments in Steel and 9 other stocks and had the satisfaction of seeing, in the next two weeks, the average price of 50 stocks decline to levels equal to those of December, 1914 (when the Stock Exchange reopened after its long adjournment following the outbreak of the war).

Steel went to 90. After this and other stocks were covered at a profit, we again sold short and in three weeks U. S. Steel was down a dozen points, to below 80.

* * *

I had often been told that I had a personal following larger than that of any individual in Wall Street since the days of Governor Flower in the 'nineties. But I was not proud or boastful of this. I was more cautious in every move, more concerned as to the final result. I did not seek or desire such a following; I dreaded it. No one knew better than I that this same public which was now reveling in profits through me would slander me whenever my judgment deteriorated.

At times, knowing that their throats were bared to the knife, I could have created situations that would have profited me enormously. But I had no desire to make money by betraying these followers, even though most of them were strangers to me and were actually stealing my goods.

The U. S. Steel campaign had fully demonstrated that correctly-timed advice in a stock that was in a strong or weak technical position and ready to move up or down could be *forced* in the desired direction by the weight of our buying or selling. There were ways in which the number of people thus acting simultaneously could have been multiplied.

But instead of more dynamite in my hands, I wanted less. Rather than have my name on everyone's lips, I preferred not to be recognized. It better suited my plans to restrict those who acted on my advice to subscribers only, and not too many of these. I wished my advisory business to proceed in a sane, orderly and healthy manner, with no excitement and no effect on the stock market. I wished to judge the market with an unbiased mind, and to do this I must not be responsible for any of its moves.

* * *

The *Magazine* was now ten years old, an encouraging fact, considering the predictions of croakers who said, when it started, that it wouldn't last a year. Numerous testimonials from men prominent in the financial field helped to celebrate this occasion, among them being those of Charles Hayden, of Hayden, Stone & Co., S. R. Guggenheim, of American Smelting & Refining Co., Ivy L. Lee, of John D. Rockefeller's advisory staff, and those of a number of other banking, industrial and corporation leaders. Jacob H. Schiff, of Kuhn, Loeb & Co., wrote: "May I attest to the substantial value of the *Magazine of Wall Street?* I have frequently found in the *Magazine* information and views by which I have profited. I wish the *Magazine* a continued successful career."

Mr. Bernheimer, president of the Columbia Bank, had told me that he frequently accompanied Mr. Schiff to Seabright on the Sandy Hook boat. He often saw Mr. Schiff reading the *Magazine of Wall Street,* and Mr. Schiff had once said: "Yes, I like this magazine. I always read it through."

The first ten years had proved the soundness of the idea given to me by that old Yankee merchant in a small Connecticut town: "Young man, if you want people to do business with you, make it to *their* advantage." Therefore, I determined that the next ten years must witness a more complete development of the publication and that a magazine must be produced that would far outstrip the one which had gone before.

Contact with readers had given a clear understanding

of their needs. At the beginning the majority of them seemed to have the impression that Wall Street was a get-rich-quick gambling place. The *Magazine* had endeavored to show that trading and investing are highly specialized businesses, as intricate perhaps as the professions of law or medicine.

In its progress toward helping to create "A Nation of Intelligent Investors" (one of our slogans), the *Magazine* had benefited by much cooperation of its readers. They told us of their desires, of their difficulties, aims, hopes and ambitions. We frequently sent them forms in which they indicated the features they preferred and those which they would like to see also included.

George C. Selden was my Associate Editor; Barnard Powers was Managing Editor, and Robert L. Smitley, the Business Manager. Planning a bigger and broader *Magazine,* we began to enlist the further cooperation of prominent financiers and brokers of the time, some of our contributors being Hon. Theodore E. Burton, Frank A. Vanderlip, and J. W. Harriman. We were greatly to augment the contents and improve the character of the publication.

* * *

1918 MAKING RECORDS

WE BEAT THE VICTOR—A DEAL IN SOUTHERN PACIFIC—A WILD OPENING—TAKING MONEY OUT OF WALL STREET

FAST as the Emerson Co. manufacturing facilities were expanded, they failed to meet the demand for records. During the war everybody wanted all the music they could get. We began to make a 10-inch record to retail at 50 cents in competition with the 65-cent and 75-cent records of the same size made by the Victor and Columbia companies. And we had not been in this field long before the business developed to a point where we were shipping $500,000 worth of records per month and could have shipped from $1,000,000 to $1,500,000 worth per month had we had them.

The DuPonts meanwhile had secured control of the Columbia Graphophone Co. and discussions were being held as to the possibility of consolidating the Columbia, Victor and Emerson companies. Mr. Whitten, president of the Columbia Co., visited our plant. Our product was hurting the market of the two big companies; the Victor people admitted to one of our officers that the Emerson sales organization was the only one among their competitors which had ever given them any concern.

Of course these others, too, were doing a land office business in records and machines, but we were underselling them and our lower-priced record was gradually absorbing a larger and larger percentage of their combined market.

The Victor Co. started suit against us, alleging infringement of their patents. The case was decided in our favor in the United States District Court in New York City on December 9, 1918, by Judge Julius M. Mayer. We not only defeated the Victor Co., but, unfortunately for us, for them, and for Columbia, the evidence in the case threw grave doubt on the validity of the original Victor patents, under which Columbia was also manufacturing, and this opened the field to a number of new competitors who began to make records identical with Victor and Columbia.

The Emerson Co.'s business was going along nicely and showing a substantial net surplus. I had labored unceasingly to put this company on its feet. My editorial work on the *Magazine* had been turned over more and more to Mr. Selden and his assistants. For three years I had been working from nine to six every day, including all Saturdays and many Sundays, also two or three evenings a week, mostly for the Emerson Co. This ceaseless labor, without proper rest and relaxation, was telling on my health so that I was near nervous exhaustion, with scarcely strength enough to lift my hand. It was then a question of going on and killing myself, or getting some one else to run the company, for by that time I had less confidence than ever in the ability of my principal associates as executives. Emerson was an inventor, with all the characteristics of the creative mind; the company needed a set of business brains.

Upon finding the man who appeared qualified, I resigned my executive position. I continued, with Emerson, to control the majority of the capital stock which had been placed in a voting trust when the company was organized.

* * *

Trend Letter campaigns averaged about one a month. Some showed small losses; they could not be large because all ventures were now protected by 3-point stops. Our profits were substantial and for any subscriber the result of a year's trading was a big net profit.

We took the long and the short side with equal facility, and were out of the market for days or weeks at a time when it appeared to be in a trading position, offering no good opportunities.

Often we would pyramid. For example, August 26, 1918, we bought Steel at 107 and advised the purchase of additional lots, every two points up, to the extent of one-quarter of the original lot; if a trader bought 400 shares at 107, he would buy 100 shares more at 109, 111, 113, etc. Two weeks later Steel touched 114½ ex 4¼ points dividend, equal to 118¾, so that by closing out at that price, subscribers realized over 18 points on their original plus pryamided purchases.

Frequently campaigns would be conducted in only one stock. This was true of Southern Pacific in October, Mexican Petroleum, U. S. Steel and others.

* * *

The following campaign is described to show what real inside information is. Also to show that others than those in the management of corporations may sometimes obtain advance knowledge of coming events. Lastly, it proves that the most promising of situations may be spoiled by unexpected developments.

The avenues through which this information was secured were open to everyone. There were no indications of any pool activities. To all appearances the stock in which this campaign was to be conducted was lying dead and appeared to offer no greater possibilities than any railroad stock paying a similar dividend. This stock was Southern Pacific.

For some years I had been keeping an eye on the government's suits against the Southern Pacific for the recovery of certain oil lands of enormous value in California. These were lying undeveloped meanwhile. One case was known as Civil Case 46, which was then pending in the United States District Court at Los Angeles, and the other was the Elk Hills Case, before the United States Supreme Court at Washington.

In 1917 the Government Commission appointed for the purpose appraised the minimum value of these lands at $439,000,000.

Every so often I would get in touch with the Department of Justice in Washington with the query: When will these cases come up? Early in 1918 there were preliminary signs of activity and late in the summer I decided it was time to get busy. I sent an investigator to Washington, told him to make a thorough examination of the history of the land grants in litigation. This was to include study of the United States Land Office records, of the Geographical Survey, of California State geological records, and whatever else he might find in the Congressional Library. He was directed to inspect bills of complaint and the answers; the briefs on both sides from the very beginning of these cases; the testimony of witnesses; official maps and all documents bearing on the case. He was told to stay until he got the answer, which must be one of three: (1) The government will win. (2) It will not win. (3) The outcome is uncertain.

He went to Washington and I did not hear from him for three weeks. Then he called me on the telephone, and gave as the result of his investigation: "The Southern Pacific is bound to win," he said. "The government hasn't a leg to stand on."

Of course, there was no guarantee that the court's decision would verify this prognostic. But then, there are few sure things in Wall Street.

When my man returned from Washington I went over and digested all his facts and figures, putting them in the form of condensed memoranda with the necessary exhibits, and submitted these to a firm of eminent corporation attorneys. They decided that my findings justified publication of them. Then came the question of releasing the information in the way that would be of the most benefit to my subscribers. It is one thing to call attention to a number of stocks of merit and another to point out an outstanding opportunity. If this be done by one who has a large following, much responsibility lies on him for what ensues.

Southern Pacific was a big issue. There were over 2,700,000 shares outstanding and its market movements were usually more or less sedate. The stock was widely held both in this country and abroad, and, like many other first-class rails, much was carried on margin and with the certificates standing in brokers' names.

The data I had shown my lawyers leaked to the head of a certain large trust company. This man evidently decided that the Southern Pacific had an overwhelming chance to win the oil lands suits, and it was not long before the stock began to creep up. The action was so distinct from

1920's. *New York Stock Exchange and Entrance to J. P. Morgan & Company's Building*

that which had prevailed before anyone knew what I had up my sleeve that I became convinced that this banker was starting a Southern Pacific campaign of his own. His publicity mill began to grind out bullish talk, an indication that he had already acquired his line. The stock continued to show strength, activity and large volume. Up to 93 this buying appeared to be careful but persistent.

Meanwhile I was preparing a series of articles for the *Magazine of Wall Street,* and planned to release advices to *Trend Letter* subscribers at about the same time as I printed the vital points in the *Magazine.*

Southern Pacific worked up another couple of points to 95. The buying campaign of the banker who had got hold of my data was freely discussed in brokerage circles where he was known. His operations, and the buying of his associates in the insurance field, were prominently mentioned in financial columns.

A magazine is not like a newspaper. It takes some days to get it out. While I was thus handicapped, the effect of the banker's buying had resulted in an advance of Southern Pacific to 98. This would make my people pay a higher price, but also it lessened the danger of an explosive opening. With Southern Pacific lying quiet in the low 90s, the sudden infusion of my information into the minds of my 200,000 followers would have caused such competitive buying that the price would have opened away up and hopped from, say, 92 to par without profiting anybody very much. Whereas the heavy purchases between 91 and 98 had not only broadened the market but had put the banker in possession of a quantity of stock which he would probably sell on a further bulge. The market would thus be kept fairly within bounds.

On October 18 the stock rose to 99¾. Next day the low was 98½ and the high 100⅜. I decided that I could wait no longer; they would have the stock up to 110 without my following getting a share. On Saturday, October 19, I issued a Special *Trend Letter* advising subscribers to buy Southern Pacific at the market price *after* the opening on Monday, and warned them against letting their brokers know they intended to buy, until they gave their orders.

My reason for telling them to wait until after the opening was this: If their orders were all placed at the market before the opening, the specialists and traders, seeing so many brokers flock into the Southern Pacific crowd on the floor, would be sure to make the stock open very high—how high no one could tell. If every one of my subscribers refrained from placing his order until after the stock had had a natural opening (which would probably be around the 98½ price at which it had closed in the previous session) their orders could come in, say, a minute or more afterward, or later, and their buying could start at a little above that figure.

But I had no control over my subscribers' actions. Two things were working against me. One was the tendency on the part of some smart alecks to say: "I'll let the other fellows wait until after the opening but I'll get mine first crack out of the box." The other was the existence of hangers-on among brokers and customers' men who obtained my advice through underground channels within a few minutes after it was issued.

The *Trend Letter* was not dictated until after the close of the market, and not even my employees knew until then what it was going to contain. Those subscribers too far away to be served by mail were always advised to have the information telegraphed to them, so that it be available before the next day's opening. Whatever poached advices got onto brokers' private wires could not be used until the next morning's opening, but it did become effective in the market at the very moment when my subscribers were having their orders executed.

Whenever an especially favorable opportunity appeared, I would advise my subscribers to pyramid. In this Special Letter I advised the purchase of additional lots every 2 points up to the extent of one-quarter of their first purchases. That is, for every 100 shares they bought in their initial transaction, they were to buy 25 shares more at each 2 points advance.

Monday morning's opening was pandemonium in the Southern Pacific crowd. There was a spread opening from 101 to 104, and immediately 105 was bid. This proved not only that many subscribers had entered their orders to buy at the market, but that contrary to instructions they had placed these with their brokers before the opening. Also that most of the deadheads in the brokerage offices throughout the country had filed their orders in the same fashion. The whole situation was further aggravated by a great accumulation of odd lot orders which the dealers filled at the highest prices.

Upon witnessing this extraordinary situation, this wild scramble for the stock, as though buyers feared there would be none for sale if they waited five minutes, I finally decided that I would have to find some other way of handling this enormous following, either by raising the subscription price of the *Trend Letter* to an almost prohibitive figure, or by so altering the method of issuing advices that the market effect would not be to the subscribers' disadvantage, if they disobeyed instructions. It is one thing to drill a regiment of soldiers who are disciplined and another to try to control a group of people within a sort of loose enclosure, with a howling mob outside, peeking through holes in the fence and throwing rocks at inopportune moments.

Southern Pacific went on up to 110 in a broad market. Then the Pennsylvania Railroad Company, which held some 380,000 shares of Southern Pacific, decided that this big market afforded a good opportunity to unload. (The rumor got around the Street that I had been hired to create this big market in Southern Pacific for Pennsylvania; the truth was that I had originated the campaign and that Pennsylvania had queered it.)

Had it not been for the Pennsylvania sales, I believe my people would have seen their stock at 125 in short order. As it was they got out with a substantial profit.

There were indications that most of the Pennsylvania shares were purchased by certain leading Standard Oil interests who scented a killing just ahead. Further accumulation of Southern Pacific was apparent on all declines. It was obvious to me that, sooner or later, those Southern Pacific oil lands, which Mr. Doheny had stated were of "incalculable value," were all going into the basket held by the big boys at 26 Broadway, and at figures ridiculously cheap.

Fourteen months afterward, the United States Attorney General announced that the government would discontinue the Southern Pacific Oil Land suits; there was no possibility of winning them.

A year after—two years after our series of articles—the Southern Pacific segregated its oil lands through the formation of the Pacific Oil Company. That corporation took over all of the oil properties which had been in-

One of the Trading-posts on the Floor of the New York Stock Exchange

volved in litigation; also control of the Associated Oil Company, Southern Pacific's producing subsidiary. Stockholders of Southern Pacific were given a right to purchase one share of Pacific Oil at $15 per share for each share of Southern Pacific held.

After trading in these rights began, a raid pushed them to around $20. With $15 paid in, the Pacific Oil stock cost buyers about $35.

At this time—in 1920—I advised subscribers to sell their Southern Pacific and buy, with the proceeds, three times as many shares of Pacific Oil; it was clear the big move was to be in that stock. Pacific Oil rose into the 50s and 60s and ultimately exchanged share for share of Standard Oil of California.

* * *

Some of my readers will now bring forward the inevitable question put to every man who undertakes to advise others in the stock market, whether he be a broker, customers' man or expert: If you could make all these millions for other people, why didn't you make many millions for yourself and why did you want to bother with publishing a magazine and selling advice? This is a fair question. Here is the answer:

Those seven and a half years yielded all the money I needed to make me financially independent. Between the *Trend Letter* income, the profits from stock market operations, and other enterprises, I was getting ahead fast enough. I had no desire to be known as a big plunger and never staked everything on a single campaign as most of such men do. Nor did I wish to pile up a lot of millions. This was not necessary as a provision for my future, and I had no desire thus to maximize my ego.

When a subscription to the *Trend Letter* was accepted, it was not considered an asset but a liability. It was carried as such on the books. In accepting a man's subscription I bound myself to give him the Service. No matter how small or large a trader he was, I did my utmost to make him a big profit. His interest and not mine had first consideration. If I found that my personal commitments in the market were influencing my judgment, I closed them out whether there was a profit or a loss and awaited a time when my trading could be done without bias. For this reason there were often times in the market when I did not have a share of stock on either side. When I did have commitments, I gave them less attention than they should have had. Often, believe it or not, I completely forgot and had to be reminded of them. At other times I traded in fairly large lots so that my business amounted to 8,000 or 10,000 shares a day; that was when I made the most money. Often it was the comparatively small commitments which bothered me the most in judging and forecasting the market.

There is something else which seldom occurs to those who are looking at the business from the outside: A man may be an excellent judge of the stock market without possessing the qualifications of a Jim Keene or a Jesse Livermore. His judgment for others may be better than that which he applies to his own ventures. This was true of me at times; other periods would find me using better judgment for myself than for others. But all through the years of writing the *Trend Letter* the average quality of the judgment I sold was better than that of the judgment I used for myself.

The public impression that a man who understands the stock market can make millions of dollars overnight is entirely unfounded. Big operators do make large and quick profits sometimes; but they do not make a million this year, three million the next, five million the next and so on. Their opportunities, the character of the market, and their judgment all vary, so that they will be successful at one moment, and then, at another, will lose money heavily—perhaps all they have and more. Such is the character of their calling. There is nothing in the world more uncertain than the future course of the stock market. Forecasting it is a good deal like attempting to predict the temperature in New York City at noon on a certain day three weeks from now. No one knows what influences will rule at any moment. The largest interests who are working in the market, and more or less dominating it, do not know what obstacles they will encounter nor how frequently and radically they will be obliged to change their plans.

Only a novice can think that making money in the stock market, year in and year out, by means of more or less continuous trading, is an easy proposition. There are times when it is easy. But let the novice keep at it for two or three years. He will change his opinion.

My experience proved to me that a man can do only one thing at a time if he does it well. I paid a heavy penalty, in the long run, for my departures from my own business, even though some of these proved highly profitable. Mine was the business of furnishing money-making advice to subscribers. Whatever was done outside of this field—whether it involved trading for myself, the promoting of companies, or helping other people in their promotion operations—took just time, attention and energy from that business. And though I made money in other fields while making money in the market for my subscribers, if I were to begin again I would do only one thing at one time. This is not an apology; it is merely a statement of something learned through experience. I have seen this illustrated thousands of times by people who believed that because they were successful manufacturers, business men, or specialists in certain lines, they could, with little or no experience, master the stock market. A man, because he can make money in one specialty is not, therefore, qualified to make money in another without the long course of study which will equip him for it.

Going back to the *Trend Letter,* let me state that this business of advising other people in the stock market is one of the most nerve-racking occupations anyone can undertake. I did not deliberately choose it and cannot consistently advise others to do so. What is more, the field is becoming overcrowded.

Arthur Brisbane has said in an editorial:

"When advice is good, its origin is forgotten and the buyer rejoices in his own intelligence. If bad, the giver of the advice is hated."

We made $40,000 profit for a man one year; we made only $15,000 for him the next and he canceled his subscription because his profits were not what they used to be. He probably would have lost $20,000 a year if he had acted on his own judgment.

At times when results over a long period were profitable to those who followed our advices, our correspondence would be reduced to practically nothing, but when a losing campaign came along, we would be greeted with sarcasm, complaints, anonymous letters, howls of derision, and accusations.

As in any other business, there were bad spells as well

as good ones. The market was easy to read at times and difficult at others. A series of successful months might be followed by adverse ones. Then people canceled subscriptions and went around to their friends and damned us.

It is the same with brokers. They and their customers men are constantly called upon to give advice. They are expected to know more about the market and about stocks than their clients, and for the most part they do. But they are cursed when they are wrong. And when they are right, it is the client who sticks out his chest, and puffs his cigar, and gloats, and boasts of his own shrewdness.

* * *

1919 MISSING A COUPLE OF MILLIONS

REFUSING TO SELL—STOCK EXCHANGE FAILURES—SUGGESTIONS FOR AVOIDING THESE—PRESSURE BY THE PUBLIC—A MILLION IN SIXTY DAYS—SHOT AT BY GIANTS—STOPPING THE TREND LETTER—TRIP TO ALASKA

THE proposed consolidation of the Victor, Columbia, and Emerson phonograph companies had been delayed until the big patent suit could be settled. Our business was piling up at a terrific rate and we were making contracts for the production of 50-cent records on a scale equal to the combined output of Victor and Columbia. The business was demanding an increasing amount of working capital, and we had to depend largely upon the banks.

With matters in this state, parties approached us with the intention of purchasing control. The prospective buyers had made much money during the war and were ready and eager. We stated that we would not consider selling unless the price offered Emerson and me were paid also for all the outstanding stock. The price meant a million dollars to Emerson and a million dollars to myself. The preliminary negotiations resulted in an agreement to pay that price, and gave us time to consider whether or not we would sell.

It looked like a lot of money for a piece of business that we had developed within four years. But we were absorbing a large slice of the record industry and preparing to dominate it. We had contracted for a production of 300,000 of the 10-inch, 50-cent records per day. And there was more at stake than the cash that we could take out. We were desirous of seeing the company develop into something that we could be proud of. We decided to refuse the offer and go on with the company's development. I have made a good many mistakes in my life, but this was one of the worst.

I do not know all the influences that subsequently were at work to weaken the company's position. The management which had succeeded my retirement was not equal to handling a rapidly growing business on a limited amount of working capital, even though the latter was augmented by the profits which were rolling up. Many of the contracts undertaken with artists and new manufacturers of records were of doubtful advisability.

Then came the Federal Reserve liquidation of 1920. Banks that had been giving the company liberal credit seemed to want all their money at once; the Emerson Co. was put into the hands of a receiver. I was myself a creditor to no small extent—the company not having liquidated all of the notes I held.

The other companies were faring little better. The Columbia Graphophone Co. a little later failed, with obligations running over $20,000,000. Still later, the radio industry, and the new competition that our patent decision had let loose, made great inroads upon the Victor Co., in spite of the fact that its stock had sold well above $1,000 a share and that it had an enormous surplus. Its business shrunk to unbelievably small proportions before it was able to readjust itself and meet radio and other competition by an improvement of its product.

This is simply a statement of facts which, I agree, appear to reflect upon my judgment. As a publisher and a stock market analyst I should not have gone further into the phonograph business than to raise the original working capital of the Emerson Co. I should not have identified myself with the enterprise so closely that its failure could injure me.

* * *

For some years past the number of failures among New York Stock Exchange firms had been the subject of criticism; but now, what with the post-war speculation, what with the public's far greater participation in stock market operations, these failures became an increasing menace.

The Stock Exchange had made an attempt to remedy the evil through a "police committee," known as the Committee on Business Conduct. It supervised, in a desultory way, the actions of members.

As the *Magazine of Wall Street* at this time had a circulation equal to all the other financial publications combined, we were in closer touch with a larger number of people dealing in the stock market and investing their money in bonds and stocks than any other organization. Hundreds of subscribers would write us whenever a Stock Exchange firm failed and inquire if some action could not be taken to prevent these calamities. It was bad enough (they wrote) to subject their money to the natural risks of the stock market without having to run the additional chance of their brokers' failures.

The *Magazine* started to call the attention of the Stock Exchange authorities to the necessity of measures for the protection of the public. The first editorial appeared in our issue of April 21, 1919. I pointed to the vast partici-

1923. *Floor of the New York Stock Exchange Showing Entrance to the New Building. On the Right and Left Are the Telephones Which Connect with the Brokers' Offices*

pation of the public in the security market, especially since it had begun liquidating its Liberty Bonds. I inquired what the New York Stock Exchange was going to do to insure the safety of the funds thus placed in the hands of brokerage houses.

My suggestion was that expert accountants, permanently and exclusively employed by the Committee on Business Conduct, audit periodically the books of every Stock Exchange member doing a commission business for the public. There seemed no reason why such a precaution should not be taken. Banks, trust companies, insurance companies were examined regularly by federal or state authorities.

Hundreds of millions of the public's money were entrusted every year to New York Stock Exchange houses and their correspondents with no effective supervision of their financial strength or of their methods of conducting business. No matter what capital or resources a firm might have, failure was possible—from bad management, from carrying stocks on thin margins, from unsound promotions, speculation by partners, defalcations by employees, and so on. By proper auditing, all but a small percentage of these failures could be avoided.

Of course, I wrote, many objections would be raised by members doing business on an unsound basis, but it might be well to examine first the books of those who protested most loudly.

Possibly a form of mutual insurance could be worked out, providing a fund to aid firms unexpectedly weakened through no fault of their own. Thus would be tided over, without failure, many houses which would eventually be put back on their feet or liquidated. This suggested insurance plan required the raising of a fund by direct assessment of members, or by a slight addition to the fee paid on the clearing of each hundred shares. Commission rates charged by members to clients had recently been raised; a clearing house fee of, say, 50 cents per 100 shares would not be felt by the brokers. Indemnity bonds might also be secured, with premiums payable out of this fund.

In all this I was not pleading for the public alone. In many failures of preceding years, members of the Stock Exchange had also been hit.

Members of the Stock Exchange, friends and subscribers, with whom I discussed the matter, believed my campaign a hopeless one. The Stock Exchange "would do nothing about it." I kept hammering away with editorials which, I knew, would enlist the aid of many subscribers who were also clients of brokerage houses throughout the country. Pressure would thus be brought to bear upon the Stock Exchange till it took steps to insure the public better protection.

That is what happened. So many letters were written to the Stock Exchange, not only from clients but from brokers themselves, in New York and different parts of the country, that the Governing Committee at last began to take up the matter seriously.

The principal objection to the insurance plan, President Cromwell of the Stock Exchange explained to me, was that many houses were not only members of the New York Stock Exchange but also held seats on the New York Cotton Exchange, the Chicago Board of Trade and other such institutions, with their capital employed in various branches of the business. Failures might occur through dealings other than stock transactions; it would be unfair to ask Stock Exchange members to amass an insurance fund which might be used to make good failures incurred not in stock trading, but in other commodities.

Although I had been assured that something would be done, it was not until 1922 that President Cromwell, addressing a meeting of the members of the Exchange and their partners, said: "The Governors of the New York Stock Exchange are now about to put into effect a plan for closer supervision by the Stock Exchange itself of the business methods of its own members. The Exchange will require, from its members doing a margin business, at periods as frequent as twice a year, the answering of a questionnaire which will cover all the points necessary to disclose their condition. This questionnaire, which has been developed after close study, has been found practicable and will constitute a reliable index of a firm's status."

From that day, the supervision by the Committee on Business Conduct has continuously become more thorough, and the questionnaires more frequent. A close check is now kept upon the operations of all the houses, not only through their periodical statements but by continued investigations. The result has been a constantly decreasing number of failures. In 1926 there was none. In 1927, one. In 1928, one.

* * *

One evening I attended the annual dinner of the Rocky Mountain Club, of which I was a member. After Colonel W. B. Thompson, John Hays Hammond and others had finished their addresses and Coleman DuPont had stopped firing off his six-shooter as a warning to the boys to quiet down so he could announce the next vaudeville number, the party began to break up.

One of the guests, a young fellow somewhat known about Wall Street as a speculator and promoter who had put through a few deals, said to me: "I am coming in to see you in a couple of days. Got something I believe will be interesting, and you can make some money out of it."

In a day or two he came in and described a proposition on which he was working, and which required the raising of $150,000 within a week. He said to me: "If you will help me raise this money I will make you a million dollars in sixty days."

And the strange part of it is that *he did!*

Lots of people had come to me with plans, schemes and promotions that were always made to look plausible. I didn't know whether he really had a good thing or not. But almost any man will be attracted by the offer of a million—even though as a matter of principle not believing such a thing possible. Even if impossible, it *might* happen! Once out of a thousand times, say! Or something like that.

It was his affair; he was handling it all by himself. He had an option on certain patents involving a process which, if successful, should be a tremendous money-maker in a wide field. Not only that; the enterprise was especially timely because it belonged to a class lately much in the public eye, and out of the stocks of which large profits had been recently made. He had all his papers in shape, and was in a position to raise part of the money, but not all. Unless he could raise it all, he would fall down on the deal. That is why he had come to me with his rather staggering offer.

I was not required to pass upon the engineering, patent, manufacturing or marketing end of the business. All I had to do was to raise part of $150,000. I investigated to

1923. *Annunciator Board on the Wall of the Stock Exchange*
Each broker has a number, and when it appears he is expected to report or send a page to his telephone.

see if the enterprise and the people identified with it had any substance, then determined to go ahead, putting my name at the top of the syndicate subscription list for a round amount. I told a few of my friends about it; they also subscribed for round amounts. Some others heard it from them, and in a day or so we had the $150,000. I had done my part; the rest was up to him. I awaited developments.

He took the money I had raised, paid it over to the party with whom he had agreed to purchase the patent rights, organized the company, brought out the stock, and sold it to the public at a figure which netted somewhere between 50 and 75 per cent profit to the underwriters. We of the subscription list had our money back, and this profit, and the company was launched.

Another branch of the enterprise now called for underwriting. To the amount of $300,000, I believe. I took a piece. Those who had gone in before, other of my friends, and a lot of Stock Exchange houses began piling in their subscription checks. By this time the market price of the first corporation shares had more than doubled, and everyone was eager to get in on this one. Those who did arrive before the door slammed were required to give options on their underwriting at a price that would yield them 75 per cent profit on the amounts they subscribed.

I didn't even know at what price the stock was going to be offered to the public, nor just how it was going to be handled, nor any of the plans for supporting the market after it was once opened. In fact, I was much in the dark about most matters.

Well, the day of the big party arrived. The stock was so heavily oversubscribed that my young friend who was running the deal disposed of all the underwriting stock, all the rest of the treasury stock, and, as protection to the market after it was opened, went short of 15,000 shares of stock more than there was in existence. This gave him a buying power for the support of the market, as is customary in such undertakings.

That afternoon we got together, and figured out that the promotion profits on this deal on that day totaled $4,000,000, of which my share was $1,333,333. That was a little over the million he had agreed to make for me in sixty days.

And I wasn't making any demands on that day for I knew it would take a little time to adjust the market, see how much stock was going to come back, and get things lined up on the commercial side. The financial end had necessarily preceded the business end. However, no such extraordinary results had been expected by anyone. It was simply a case of the public going after it hook, line and sinker, and the amount realized from the sale of all this stock was far more than was necessary properly to supply the company with working capital.

Things went along for a while and I was still kept in the dark as to how the stock was being handled, where my promoting friend stood, where I stood, how much stock had to be taken back, and, most important, when we were going to cut the pie. He put me off with evasions and excuses; he wouldn't tell yet just how he was coming out and I would have to wait.

I had planned a long trip which would keep me away from New York for some months, and didn't like the association nor the lack of frankness, nor the attempts at postponing the consummation of the matter. And the longer I was put off, the less I liked it. So I went to the young fellow one day, said I was going away, that I did not want the thing hanging fire so that it had to be handled by telegraph or mail, and that while I did not know how much was coming to me because he had not given me a statement, in spite of my insistence, I would take the million dollars he had promised me and call it quits.

Upon his refusal, I offered to accept $750,000, then $500,000, and finally, divining that I was going to be trimmed, I offered to settle for $250,000.

He refused to pay me this amount, which was one-fifth of my share of the profit, and one-fourth of what he had agreed to pay me. I then could easily have busted up the whole show, owing to certain peculiar circumstances. I could, for instance, have sold short 10,000 shares of the stock, and, by methods familiar to me, broken down the price so as to make several hundred thousand dollars out of it on the short side. I knew that if I did sell short he would not dare to try to run me in; to do so he would have to put the price of all the stock up to a point at which the public, which had taken it all off his hands, would sell it back to him at a profit to themselves and at a tremendous loss to him. Instead of being in danger of being cornered myself, I would have him in a box. I could have done this, or taken the matter into court and dished up a nice mess.

I decided to do nothing of the kind. I had made some money in the underwriting and some more trading in the stock; I was more anxious to get away on my trip than to stay here and fight it out.

The reader will ask: Didn't you have a contract with him? If some one offered to make you a million for doing a little piece of business like that would you believe him? I hadn't really believed him. I simply took a chance that

I would get something out of it. I did get something; more than he did, in fact.

The paternity of the baby was laid to me. It was not mine. I merely helped buy its swaddling clothes.

So that's the story of another million I made but didn't get.

* * *

What had happened in the Southern Pacific campaign had given me new proof of the difficulties which had arisen in this business of giving advice through the *Trend Letter.* I estimated now that the market effect of a definite campaign concentrated on a single stock resulted in the buying or selling of from 100,000 to 200,000 shares. This was too large a proportion of the total transactions, which then rarely ran over 1,000,000 shares in a single day, with an average total of daily sales around half a million.

It was evident that the largest interests in Wall Street were finding me much in their way. I was mussing up a lot of their deals. Their operations were comparatively easy to read on the tape; I was making them work for my subscribers. The Southern Pacific episode, for instance, would force Standard Oil to pay for their control of the oil properties many millions more than they had counted upon doing. It is not well for anyone in Wall Street to become too big if he is alone. My advices to clients were being increasingly interfered with—offset and nullified by operations on the opposite side of the market. When I would advise the purchase of certain stocks, these same issues would be hammered down immediately after my people had bought. It was as though I were in a clearing surrounded by thick woods from which concealed giants were shooting at me. I was not willing to risk trades without the protection of stop orders, having followed this practice for seven years with great success. I was restricting greatly the number of subscribers to the *Trend Letter* but I could not teach these to keep the advices to themselves.

Specialists on the New York Stock Exchange in those days readily exposed their buying and selling orders to large traders on the floor and to important operators and pools whenever they found it to their advantage. If I took a position, say, on the long side of certain stocks, some of these would be more amenable to manipulation than others. More followers would flock after my advice in these issues—say, Steel, General Motors, American Sugar, especially in the public eye at the moment—than in the other issues. Contrary to my warnings, subscribers would not only bid up at the opening the stocks they wanted to buy, but would enter their stop orders for 3 points below as soon as they knew what prices they had paid. The specialists then called the attention of a few big operators to these accumulated stop orders and attempts would be made to force the stocks down to our stop levels. If they were successful, then my subscribers became sellers on stop and the pirates would cover shorts. The latter would then bid up prices a few points and take their profits. Having first gone short, say, of Sugar, at 110, they could cover their shorts and go long at 107, which was my stop price; then boost Sugar to 110 again and make 5 or 6 points out of the operation.

In order to foil this maneuvering, I adopted a new method of advising my subscribers. I now gave them the technical position of individual stocks, and the range of from 1 to 3 points in which these stocks were showing accumulation or distribution. Instead of concentrating on

10 stocks, I issued technical indications on several principal groups, and stated the position of perhaps 30 or 40 stocks scattered among those groups. I ceased to give definite stops, but advised subscribers to limit their risks to 3, 4 or 5 points, according to the character of the stock traded in. This avoided the simultaneous buying and selling which had given trouble and got away from the grouping of stop orders. The subscribers' operations were now so well scattered that the sensation of being shot at by the big fellows gradually passed away.

When the market was in a generally bullish position, I would withdraw all selling advices, and vice versa. Operations conducted in this new way showed profits in February ranging from 12 to 22 points on several leading stocks and from 3 to 8 points on a still larger group.

By the end of May of that year I decided to discontinue the *Trend Letter,* though its subscription list was full and was supplemented by a waiting list. Its patrons included important people, some of the largest traders, and a number of banking and brokerage houses in the United States and abroad (these were served by cable). On the list were not a few of our original subscribers of 1911.

In the seven and a half years of its existence, the *Letter* had made many millions of dollars in profits for subscribers. How much more for the public through the passing on of its advices by brokerage houses and other individuals no one can estimate. I thought this was a good time to close down and take a vacation.

Subscribers were offered the cash value of their unexpired subscription, or the equivalent in our other service, "The Investment Letter," which gave the technical position of the general market and pointed to certain investment opportunities from time to time.

I had planned a two months' trip to the Canadian Rockies, Alaska and California. It was to be my first long vacation in nearly twenty years. The others had never been longer than two weeks, often had been only of a few days, and there had been periods of three or four years without any at all.

* * *

1920 ORGANIZING THE STAFF

THE TEN TRENDS

A YEAR after discontinuing the *Trend Letter* I organized the advisory end of the business on a more comprehensive scale.

The character of the market had radically changed since the war. Where, before, a few leading industries dominated, and a limited number of stocks could be used to force the market one way or the other, there were now many industries and many additional stocks with diverse and often contradictory movements. This made the business of advising much more difficult and called for much more machinery and interpretive talent.

I had been judging the market almost entirely by its own action, as shown on the tape of the stock ticker; but in this new, developing market I found I must consider other qualifying factors.

My purpose was to supply a limited number of people, to be known as Associate Members, with information and judgment for investment and speculation. This was to be based (as in the *Trend Letter*) on the action of the market and of individual stocks, but would also take into account money, credit and investment conditions, and whatever other economic factors were necessary. Through a broad survey of these elements, and the examination of the fields of industry in order to single out those enterprises which gave the most promise of greatest growth, through the selection then of the best securities in those, the operations of Associate Members, I believed, could be made highly profitable.

The staff required for such work would cost me, I estimated, from $200,000 to $250,000 a year. I was justified in assuming only a part of such an expense, and sought the cooperation of a number of people who dealt in considerable amounts of stocks.

I then founded the Richard D. Wyckoff Analytical Staff, Inc., of which I was sole owner.

The annual fee for this Service was fixed at $1,000 for each Associate Member.

The announcement was made in the *Magazine of Wall Street.* The response was gratifying and the Analytical Staff began business.

It was soon found that a part of the Associate Members were interested strictly in the investment branch, and a part in long pull speculative investments (some in both). The service, therefore, was split into two services at $500 a year each. The Trend Trading Service met the needs of those who wished to speculate, and the Analytical Staff Service the demands of those who wished to invest for profit, taking advantage of the principal swings of the market.

Members and subscribers handled their own funds with their own brokers, placing their orders themselves, as they received our advices. Our function was purely advisory. Many clients asked us to handle their funds. We never did this under any circumstances.

We added another Service later—The Investors' Advisory Board. This furnished investment counsel to those who desired to place the bulk of their money in investments principally for income. We were now able to meet the requirements of everyone.

* * *

With the further expansion of the stock market during the nineteen twenties, when several hundred additional stocks were listed, it became necessary to define in greater detail the numerous trends constantly operating in the stock market and in the prices of individual stocks. Summing these after eliminating the least important, I found that there were Ten Vital Trends operating simultaneously. These divided themselves into three groups: Corporate, industrial, and technical.

Under the Corporate heading were four subdivisions: (1) trend toward financial strength or weakness; (2) trend of management; (3) trend of earning power and dividends; (4) trend toward or away from leadership in the industry.

The Industrial Trends were (1) the trend of the industry represented by a group of stocks; (2) the trend of business conditions in general.

The Technical Trends were four; these related to the various market movements: (1) the trend of the long swing of the market; (2) the intermediate swing; (3) the short or daily swings; (4) the trend of manipulation.

Viewing a stock from all these standpoints, we were able to estimate its possibilities. When we found a corporation which was not only financially strong but whose management was so successful that it was beginning to dominate its industry, showing steady increases in earning power and promise of increased dividends, we knew that here was a likely candidate. But if we examined a corporation whose business was deteriorating with a slump in prospect in the particular industry to which it belonged, then we knew that the technical factors did or probably would show weakness because the trend of manipulation would be toward a lower level.

From this brief outline the reader will realize what an exceedingly difficult task the forecasting of the stock market has become. And how seldom the average man, untrained in the business of trading and investing, is qualified to select his securities, or decide the time to buy and sell them.

* * *

1921 LIVERMORE AND HIS METHODS

HIS OFFICE LAYOUT—SELLING SHORT—BASIS OF TRADING—TAKING A POSITION—ANTICIPATED PROFITS—FORCING THE MARKET—KILLING THE BUCKET SHOPS

I MET Jesse L. Livermore for the first time about in 1917, in the lobby of the Hotel Breakers, in Palm Beach. It was just after he had cleaned up a lot of money on a big line of Steel. A few days before, he had visited Jacksonville, and by wire from a broker's office there had asked Harriman & Co. the amount of the credit balance he had with them. Their answer was that his equity with them was something over a million dollars. There were rumors that he had since lost all of this and more, in the recent break in the cotton market, but he told me that he hadn't lost over $250,000 in cotton.

In June, 1921, I called to see Livermore on a certain matter and found him in a rather communicative mood. After the object of my visit had been accomplished, he began to talk of the market. Gradually he disclosed some of his trading methods.

He had a private suite at that time in Harriman & Co.'s office. His board room was equipped with a high, long silicate board with prices of about thirty active stocks, as well as cotton and grain options. Each was given an entire column so that transactions in it could be entered one under the other in a long string.

Three tickers—stock, cotton and grain—faced the board

so that he could stand behind them and read all three tapes by moving only a step or two.

There was a compartment containing telephones and a small private office with a desk, a ticker and a small settee.

I asked him if he had been doing much that day.

"No," he replied. "I have only dealt in five hundred shares. I don't do half the trading people credit me with. At times when I am buying or selling my line, or changing my position, I am quite active. But you can bear this in mind: Whenever you see that I am selling a big line and the traders say I am short, I am doing it for some one else, not for myself.

"I sell short," he continued, "only in a very limited way —perhaps a few thousand shares of a single stock, and never more than five per cent of the capital stock outstanding, because I never want to be squeezed on the short side. But when I go long I take all I can find. For example, Studebaker; last year it was kicking around below forty. I saw that they were trying to grab all the stock at that level, so I took on a wad of it myself. You remember a while ago Studebaker sold above ninety. Well, I just let them have it all at once."

"Evidently it discouraged the pool for the time being," I said. The stock had broken badly after it touched the high point.

"You used to do a lot in Steel, don't you trade in that any more?" I asked him.

"I don't trade in Steel nowadays because I don't care for the market in the stock. I like the fast movers, such as Crucible, Baldwin, Mexican Petroleum, and stocks of that class; they give me more action. No, I don't use stop orders, but if I think a trade is wrong, I close it out.

"My principal method is to study the effect of present and probable future conditions on the earning power of the various companies engaged in different lines of industry. Anticipation of coming events is the whole thing. When I have my mind made up about this, I wait for the psychological moment. I do not deal promiscuously; instead, I decide how much I will trade in, and how much money I will risk on that trade, and then I buy or sell the whole quantity at once."

"I understood you used to trade on a scale up or down," I remarked.

"I used to sell a quantity of, say, five thousand shares at the rate of a thousand at the market and a thousand each point down, but I found this was a mistake, for it got me short at an average of two and a half points below the level where I started to sell, whereas if I waited until the psychological moment I would be in a much better position by selling it all at once. If I am going short I wait until, some day, the traders are urgently covering shorts, and when the market seems to hesitate and then stop, then I give them the whole bunch as near as possible to what I believe to be the top figure.

"I do not trade as actively as I once did," he went on. "I wait until conditions prove that I am right or until my intuition tells me I am wrong. Very often I am wrong. When that happens I change my position by getting out altogether, or sometimes I reverse and take the other side of the market. My judgment gets me in, but my intuition gets me out. I learned much from an old Quaker who said that his brain figured out the moves, but his backside—his patience—got him the money.

"I never go into a trade unless I see at least ten points

profit," he continued, "because I can't take on a line and get a decent run out of short swings. After a trade is once made and has run several points in my favor, I forget about it to a certain extent, and let it ride until I feel it is time to close it out.

"The whole game is in anticipating future business conditions—say, six months or a year from now—and the thing for anyone to do if he wants to be successful in the stock market is to study these indications of the future and their probable effect on the various industries, and on the prospective earning power of the companies in those fields."

Then he went into a review of conditions prevailing at the time: the outlook for money; the new laws affecting the credit of the farmers, affecting in turn the market for grain; and why money would not come back from the West in the fall in the same volume as heretofore.

"All this talk about the Steel industry operating at thirty per cent is pure bunk," said he; "they are not doing over sixteen per cent according to my information. These bullish interviews given out by big men are unfortunately for the purpose of deceiving the public. One of the leaders in the Steel industry has been talking bullishly for eighteen months. No doubt he will be right in time. But every time he gives out an interview, I notice that it is followed by a certain amount of liquidation of Steel common, which looks as though it came from good sources."

"I have had a lot of success pyramiding *with* the market at times," I remarked. "As you know from the tape, frequently a stock gets into a position where a quick move of ten or fifteen points in a certain direction seems inevitable. You can judge it by the power, speed and volume behind the move, and with little risk in comparison with the profit you can get out of it, there is big money to be made that way."

"Yes," he said, "I have often done that, too, but in the long run I have had greater success taking all of my position at once. I make it a practice to locate the danger point and then buy or sell as close to it as I can. If the danger materializes, I take my loss and close the trade, especially when I am short. On that side of the market, I never like to be caught with a line that is too big for me to handle. I have learned a lot from the experiences of big operators who in the past were induced to overload and were thereby caught in a trap."

"In all these eighteen or twenty years you've been trading you certainly have gained a lot of valuable experience," I commented; "for some years you traded in the bucket shops, didn't you?"

"Yes, I had ten years' experience in bucket shops before I began trading in regular brokerage houses. One of the reasons why this form of speculating was valuable to me was because it practically forced me to trade with a stop. I had to put up only two points margin in a bucket shop, and of course if it went against me one and three-quarters I was wiped out of that trade. But it was good training for me because it limited my risk and got me in the habit of letting my profits run. The bucket shop is a great school for traders. It's much more difficult to learn in a regular brokerage office. I believe that when the present coterie of big traders who received their original training in the bucket shops no longer make their big plays in the market, the Stock Exchange is going to feel

1923. *The New York Stock Exchange after the Addition Was Completed*

it. Wall Street needs big traders who make markets and take important positions."

"How about forcing a stock the way you want it to go?"

"I do not try to force the market my way," he continued. "I want the public, the pools and the big insiders to make the moves, especially in the big active stocks, so that by accurately observing their moves and their purposes, I can operate without producing any artificial appearance in the market by my own dealings. In that way I have them working for me and I can go right along with them until I see signs of their cleaning up, which is the signal for me to do likewise."

"What do you think of my publication, the *Magazine of Wall Street?*"

"I like it and read it often."

"Have you any suggestions as to how I can make it more valuable to the public?"

"If I were running your magazine I would print articles showing the public the facts about various industries and the companies whose securities are listed on the Stock Exchange. And I would not let any big men contribute any of their deceptive interviews. I would study conditions in all the industries and especially banking conditions, and I would make definite forecasts as to the tendencies in these various fields of activity as well as in the money markets, so that the public would be informed as to what they should prepare for in the future, and on which securities they will make the most money by buying and selling. The whole game down here in Wall Street appears to be deceiving the public. And if you will help the public to that extent I believe they will appreciate it."

"That's just what I'm trying to do—help the public," said I as we shook hands.

* * *

Long before my time there were bucket shops in Wall Street. Also swindling games of all kinds. During the early 'nineties the Stock Exchange had a tough fight to keep its ticker quotations from reaching the bucket shops; once, as I have shown, it stopped its ticker service altogether for several days in an effort to curb the bucketeers.

Many of these bucket shops were large and powerful. They had branch offices, correspondents, and private wire systems all over the country. They extracted scores of millions from the public every year.

For a long time it had been evident that the bucket shop plague could not be eradicated by the methods then pursued. Laws were passed, offices raided and indictments found, but few heads of illegitimate concerns were ever really punished, and in few cases was any appreciable amount of the public's money returned. It was all spent or hidden away long before the police wagons arrived. The methods used were as effective as blowing peas against a battleship.

I believed that an appeal to the public through a complete exposure of the inner workings of the system would stop its patronage of these outfits; that the bucket shops would then fail and vamoose. If I could find a man who understood and could describe the inside of the bucket shop system, I would run a series of articles in the *Magazine of Wall Street* which would blow up the bucket shop powder barrel.

We finally found such a man. He had worked in bucket shops and was willing to tell the truth about them. I had Ralph Rushmore, who was then the *Magazine's* managing editor, call on the officials of the Stock Exchange to see what cooperation we could get from them. Rushmore's memo which I have before me is as follows:

The Stock Exchange would go the limit to help us put it across.

With your OK I'm going to tell McMahon to go as far as he can on this thing. He and I are going to get personal statements by Stock Exchange authorities; we're going to work up that "inside the bucket shop" idea that you wanted. I'm going to have the series *oozing* human interest.

You told me to outline our plans to you before going ahead. Here is the outline and I am now waiting for word from you.

Rushmore.

I told him to go ahead. A little later McMahon's report came in.

New York, October 16, 1921.

Mr. Rushmore:

This will detail my activities to date in the bucketeer mission.

Mr. Jason Westerfield is Chairman of the Committee on library and publicity of the Stock Exchange. Mr. Martin introduced me to him as the man whose cooperation and help would be invaluable. I told Mr. Westerfield of our proposed campaign against bucketeers. He introduced me to Mr. Green, another officer of the Stock Exchange who has the bucketeer data and who will place it at my disposal and assist me in all ways possible.

Now I want to lay before you something that Mr. Westerfield urged. He says that while the bucketeers have slain their thousands, the stock swindlers have slain their hundreds of thousands. That the victims of bucketeers are men of some sophistication—that the victims of the stock swindlers are the substantial, conservative citizenry of the country.

A year or so ago, Westerfield, with the sanction of the

other officers of the Stock Exchange, attempted a nation-wide crusade against stock and promotion swindlers. He appointed a commitee of which Myron T. Herrick was Chairman. He secured the promise of active cooperation of the Capital Issues Committee, of which Charles S. Hamlin was chairman. In the course of time, it was found that the expense of a campaign such as they wanted would be too great. Furthermore, that whenever the Stock Exchange was active in promoting a real reform, it was found that there were always some who attributed sinister motives to it. The matter was dropped.

Now Mr. Westerfield has scrap books a foot high containing clippings and recitals and circumstances which would make wonderful reading for subscribers of the *Magazine of Wall Street.*

Here is the point. I will practically quote Westerfield: "The *Magazine of Wall Street* is a high-minded financial magazine, especially intended for the ordinary investor. To that extent it is a popular journal. A series of articles lasting over a year, well written, containing human interest, strong and convincing, directed against the menace of stock and promotion swindling, would be the best work that it could do."

I gleaned this: If the *Magazine of Wall Street* goes after this sort of thing in earnest, and continues it, the Stock Exchange will see that the circulation is doubled at least in a few months. If the *Magazine* should do this, the Stock Exchange people would go to any extreme to help, even to the spending of real dollars.

My suggestion is that we start with our bucketeer articles and continue with the tirade against stock swindlers. You would be surprised at the data Westerfield has in his possession. What articles I could write! What stories I could tell!

Both Westerfield and Green have assured me that there have been so many flashes in the pan, that a serious and thoroughgoing campaign of the sort would command a cheerful and substantial cooperation of not only the Stock Exchange, but of National Chambers of Commerce, Congress, and of banks as well.

McMahon.

The first of the articles appeared in the *Magazine of Wall Street* on November 12, 1921. It referred to bucket shop failures that had recently occurred and showed that bucketing and swindling methods were flourishing in Wall Street as never before.

The article quoted the boast of one of the "cappers" in a local bucket shop. He had induced certain people to deposit over $150,000 with his house, not one cent of which they had recovered. As he expressed it: "When I get them, I clean them." His commission was 10 per cent of what he brought in; for every dollar "brought in" was immediately considered by the bucket shop as profit.

There was a difference between the old-style bucket shop, with its two-point-margin method, and the bucket shop 1920 style. The modern shop got hold of people with substantial amounts of money and swindled them by means of alleged information, discretionary accounts and actual transactions (frequently executed on the New York Stock Exchange through dummies). The bucket shop might even execute their orders to buy through one house, and then through other firms, sell the same quantity of these stocks short. District Attorneys are not clairvoyants. They could not know the names of all the dummies whose transactions were not even recorded on the B. S. books. If the bucketeer found things too hot, he "failed." Then he started another outfit just around the corner, under another name.

This article contained the following statement:

> The New York Stock Exchange has battled weakly and ineffectually against the bucket shop evil for many years. . . . Attempts to close the bucket shops by shutting off the quotations and depriving them of tickers were ineffectual because

the bucket shops by means of special wires to other cities were able to pick up the quotations there. The Stock Exchange would not allow the Western Union to transmit continuous quotations over their wires except by those houses approved by the Exchange, but this was gotten around by means of leased telephone wires and the quotations were transmitted vocally.

The bucketeer employing modern methods, the article said, got hold of a client, preferably in another city, ascertained how much money he had, induced him to put up more and more by reporting purchase for him of this or that stock at 3 or 4 points below the market and announcing that he "already had a profit" of $2,000 or $3,000, etc. When the amount of margin that could be extracted from the victim had about reached the limit, he was "sent to the cleaner"; in other words, he was put into a fictitious transaction that cleaned him out. Often, in fact, he was left in debt to the bucket shop.

This article, and the succeeding ones appearing on November 26, December 10, December 24, were picked up by other newspapers and publications, particularly by the New York *Herald*. This paper ran a series of front page stories based on our facts. There was much elaboration, also much talk of the "*Herald's* anti-bucket shop campaign." Newspapers and magazines throughout the country were crowded with anti-bucket shop stories—all from one original source. This was the very thing and the only thing that would do the trick: publicity; taking the public into the slaughter house and showing them the works.

Three days after the second of our articles appeared on November 26, bucket shops all over the Street began to fail. The public had been told in detail how the fleecing process was carried on. Anyone approached by the

1923. *Wall Street, Showing J. P. Morgan's Building and New York Stock Exchange*

crooks (operating under the guise of stock brokers) was now able to recognize them by their methods. If some of his money was already in their possession he promptly made an attempt to draw it out. This—although, of course, these concerns did not give anyone his money back—resulted in what amounted to a raid by the public. Bucket shops blew up all over the Street with loud reports.

We went ahead with the series. We gave more details of bucket shop technique. Of the long distance telephone game, for example. In this the easy mark in Atlanta or Tulsa, in any place far enough from New York, was called on the telephone with "confidential information" on which he could make a clean-up if he would hasten a few thousand margin by telegraphic transfer. Or if he would deposit his check in a bank of his own city to the credit of these philanthropists speaking with him from the other end.

We showed the bucketeer trading against his clients, making money out of the fluctuations without any risk to himself, knowing the client would never get his margin back. The bucket shop client might as well come to New York, we explained, tie his money up in a bundle, kiss it good-bye, and throw it into the bucket shop through the transom.

Long before the third article had appeared, the failures had spread to members of the Consolidated Stock Exchange. Twenty-two firms failed. In the several weeks following November 29, Mr. Cromwell, president of the New York Stock Exchange, issued a statement to the press, stating that only four of the twenty-two firms which had failed to a certain date had Stock Exchange tickers. However, as I have already shown, the bucket shops did not depend upon tickers.

George Horace Lorimer, editor of the *Saturday Evening Post,* then asked me to write three articles for him on the subject.

So "Bucket Shops and How to Avoid Them" appeared in the *Saturday Evening Post* during April, 1922. No one after reading these articles could fail to recognize a bucket shop by its earmarks, nor be ignorant of the danger of dealing with them. I traced the development of bucket shops from the time when orders in grain were executed in units of 1,000 bushels, or "by the bucket," down to the two-point-margin houses, already described. The eventual shifting into the partial payment scheme was shown. And how the war, leading 20,000,000 people to buy Liberty Bonds to the extent of billions of dollars—had furnished soft pickings for crooks, confidence men and bucketeers. These had eased their victims into fake oil stocks and on into stock trading, where they had completed the thorough fleecing.

By the time the conversion of Liberty Bonds had reached its full development (the articles continued) bucket shops had evolved into establishments occupying whole buildings, employing hundreds of clerks, working through branch offices in a dozen cities, using thousands of miles of leased private telephone wires. Their mailing departments were sending out market letters at the rate of 100,000 to 500,000 every week. They employed service men, statisticians, a traveling sales force, and had departments of newspaper publicity. Some of these bucket shops were larger than some of the biggest houses on the New York Stock Exchange.

Liabilities in recent New York failures had amounted

to $20,000,000, but this was only a fraction of what had been extracted from the American people every year.

Some of these houses were telephoning offers to buy as much as 1,000 shares of stock on a margin of $400. On such an account, a decline of as little as three-eighths of a dollar per share will wipe out the margin. Most of the bucketeers disdained to go after any prospective victim if he had less than $5,000.

After giving a full description of the inner workings of the bucket shops, I asked readers of the *Saturday Evening Post* whether they would entrust thousands of dollars to a complete stranger; a stranger who urged them to give him their money so that he might buy for them any kind of goods or property he fancied. They probably would not. Then why should they, or anyone, put dollars into invisible hands belonging to a voice heard over the telephone? The reader might be certain that he could not thus butt into the inner circles of Wall Street. He might be certain that the smooth-talking gentleman who represented that his firm did business for the greatest financiers, operated big pools, and so on, was not working in his interest but was merely trying to steal his money.

It had always been a mystery (so the articles said) why people speculating or investing did not use, in choosing their broker or banker, the care they displayed in establishing new business relations in their own lines—where transactions involved far less money. It was hard to understand why merchants and manufacturers, when they started to deal in stocks, threw their usual business methods to the winds. There was nothing about a brokerage house entitling it to more confidence than one gave to a commercial organization. People seemed to think that a broker buying stock for them was trusting them with his money. The reverse was true. The broker is the custodian of the client's money or of his securities. The client is almost never in actual debt to the broker, and then only through an accident or misunderstanding. The peculiar part of Wall Street business is that the first step involves putting some of one's capital into strange hands. This was scarcely true in any other line. It was worse than C. O. D. It was cash before you begin.

The articles continued to single out the earmarks by which bucket shops might be recognized—and avoided. Readers were warned against anyone who made frantic efforts, regardless of expense involved, to secure their business. Especially by long distance telephone and on unusually small margins compared with those required by legitimate houses. Representations that stocks already bought without one's authority had shown a profit, and requests for authority to trade for the client's account were other danger signs. But a clear test existed for those already in the bucketeers' clutches. Try to get your money out. If you don't get it, he's a bucketeer!

The New York State laws of the time were ineffective in bucket shopping and other forms of stock swindling. These were felonies, but no sentences were being imposed. There were indictments; but they were simply taken down and dusted off every few years.

Within two or three months after our campaign opened, it was evident that the best element in Wall Street was beginning to see that the bucket shops could be deprived of the New York Stock Exchange facilities which they indirectly had been using.

Other reforms within the Exchange itself were soon to result.

1925. *Jesse L. Livermore*

President Cromwell issued the following statement: "The time has come," he said, "when the members of the Stock Exchange must collectively assure themselves of the condition of one another's affairs. I stand absolutely for such a regular examination of the condition of Stock Exchange firms. There are certain facts which we must know about these firms who carry stocks on margin for the public. We must know the relation between their free capital and their commitments. We must know the obligations which they have entailed and which may be carried in the banks, and which might, due to the calling of loans, suddenly bring them into a condition of insolvency. We must know the character of 'numbered' accounts, so that the Stock Exchange can be assured that no members have sold for their own account the stocks that they should be carrying for customers."

Albany and Washington also woke up. The Martin Law of New York State, passed during the previous year, had been ineffective because the bucket shop lobby had pulled most of its teeth. The defects in the law were remedied. Within a year or two the Attorney General at Albany, through his deputy, appointed in New York, had been given powers that enabled him to close up the swindling concerns.

Finally, such pressure was brought to bear upon the Consolidated Stock Exchange that it virtually was obliged to suspend operations. Later its building at the corner of Broad and Beaver streets was sold.

One day, after the building was demolished, my managing editor and I were walking by there and we observed a deep excavation that had been made, preparatory to the erection of a new office building.

"The *Magazine of Wall Street* did more toward digging that hole than the contractors," I remarked.

"Yes," he replied, "and with all the vast increase in business that has come to the Stock Exchange as a result, not even a postal card of thanks has been received by us."

"You have the wrong idea about that," said I; "the important point is not whether our work was appreciated, but that the job was well done."

* * *

1922 AN ODD LOT PLAN

LIVERMORE'S INTERVIEW—WHAT RASKOB SAID—GENERAL MOTORS AT THE LOW—ODD LOT EXECUTIONS—PRESIDENT CROMWELL'S REPLY

IN A summer number, the *Magazine* reported an interesting interview with Jesse L. Livermore in which he advised the public to drop their wartime reasoning and to adjust themselves to post-war conditions. Money was then 3 or 4 per cent, and many high-grade stocks were earning two or three times their dividend rate in spite of the 1920-21 depression. He called attention to the comparatively low prices of stocks like Delaware and Hudson, Northwest, Great Northern Pfd., and stated that in former years it had not been unusual to see these stocks selling on a 5 per cent basis. They were now yielding 7 to 8 per cent.

Having covered all his short stocks at about the low point of the previous depression, he had taken the long side, and was openly bullish. His judgment was correct, as the market later demonstrated.

He called attention to improving prospects in certain industries while others, such as the railroads, were still lagging. Also he showed why one should select the strongest industries for his bullish operations, leaving the weaker ones until they showed more signs of improvement.

* * *

All those who have been in Wall Street for several years remember the financial disaster which overtook Mr. Durant in 1922, when, with a fortune estimated at over $100,000,000, he attempted to support the tenfold increased capital stock of General Motors and saw his millions melt away in the decline to 8⅛. It was at this point that John J. Raskob induced the DuPonts to secure control of the company and to begin the development which, within the next several years, resulted in the most spectacular success and the largest earnings ever realized by any corporation whose stock was listed.

Mr. Raskob was quietly but confidently optimistic when I called on him one day. At that time General Motors was selling under $9 a share. He told me just what the company was doing, showed me some of its latest reports, and expressed that form of optimism without enthusiasm which was characteristic of him. I told him I had been out to Detroit and talked with some of the leading production executives, and as it seemed probable that the result of the company's activities should have a favorable effect upon the stock, I was going to tell my people to buy it.

In the next issue of the *Magazine of Wall Street* this advice appeared.

* * *

My relations with Seymour L. Cromwell, president of the New York Stock Exchange, were friendly. I had frequent occasion to call upon him. One day I mentioned the fact that the execution of odd lot orders seemed to me a subject that required the attention of the proper committee, and that I had in mind a suggestion I would like to submit to him. Mr. Cromwell expressed his appreciation of any suggestions I might make. Accordingly

I addressed to him an open letter which was reprinted in the *Magazine of Wall Street* in June of that year.

My letter contained a plea for the odd lot trader and investor which related to the method of handling the increasing amount of this class of business which was flowing into the Stock Exchange. The letter expressed a hope that my suggestions would not be regarded as presumptuous; it was impossible that I, a non-member, should be better acquainted with the inside workings of the Exchange's machinery than its own members and committees. But it had occurred to me that an outside view, even if it did not touch the vital spot at the outset, might lead to improvements that would be of mutual advantage to the Exchange and its patrons.

It seemed to me, the letter went on, that the increased amount of odd lot business, which formerly went to the bucket shops but which now was executed on the Exchange, required that this class of business should be catered to more than ever before; that the odd lot buyers and sellers should be given the actual market advantage over the large traders and investors if this were possible. The small trader had always been under the handicap of a fractional difference between odd lots and hundred-share lots. Of late it appeared by actual test that several minutes more were required for the execution of a small lot than in former years.

The delay appeared to be in the transmission of orders and reports from the brokers' telephone booths on the floor of the Exchange to the odd lots dealers in the respective crowds and back again. Pneumatic tubes were being used—a method slow and cumbersome.

My suggestion was that engineers should at once be employed to work out a plan under which the whole odd lot machinery of the Exchange could be transferred from the main floor to another room—possibly to a room underneath the main floor. Special telephones could then run from the brokerage houses to that room; the specialists in odd lot trading or their clerks could be seated down there at desks. They must be kept in instant touch with their markets on the main floor, but there were various means by which this might be done. (I had in mind an electrical device somewhat like the one which was tested in brokerage houses later to supplant the old chalk or ticket quotation boards. Or the posts on the floor might be so altered as to accommodate a boy or two inside a round, elevated desk at the top of each post, so that a continual run of quotations could be supplied by telephone to the odd lot room.)

Reminding Mr. Cromwell that I was not submitting a plan, but making a suggestion, I believed that the problem so far as the mechanical devices, etc., were concerned, did not offer any unsurmountable difficulties. Should it be possible for the Exchange to work out such a plan in detail, I believed that the execution of odd lots would become a matter of five to thirty seconds in elapsed time instead of five to ten minutes, as at present.

Mr. Cromwell's reply to my letter was as follows:

NEW YORK STOCK EXCHANGE
President's Office

September 13, 1922.

Richard D. Wyckoff, Esq., Editor,
The Magazine of Wall Street,
New York, N. Y.

Dear Mr. Wyckoff:

I have discussed with the Committee to which you refer the matter of the suggestions in regard to odd lots. My personal

1927. *Floor of the New York Curb Market, Showing Telephone Desks in the Rear*

opinion is that all orders, whether in fractions or in full lots, must be executed on the Floor of the Stock Exchange, and this seems to me an insuperable obstacle to the method you suggest.

I hear that during my absence you brought before the Committee of Arrangements a further suggestion in the matter, and I believe that they still have it under consideration.

I trust that you will have a successful holiday, and hope to see you on your return.

Very truly yours,
SEYMOUR L. CROMWELL,
President.

I had, in fact, made another suggestion directly to the Committee at one of the hearings they gave me. This was that a trust company be formed for the clearance and financing of odd lots.

Stock Exchange brokers were finding more and more of their capital tied up in fractional lots. The trust company would receive and deliver the balances of odd lots which brokers had coming in to them or going out, thus releasing this capital. The trust company would hold these small lots as collateral and would advance a fair proportion of their market value to the broker.

1923 THE MAGAZINE ARRIVES

OTTO H. KAHN'S OPINION

CALLING at Kuhn, Loeb & Co.'s office one day upon some business I had to take up with Otto H. Kahn, he expressed quite an interest in the character of work the *Magazine of Wall Street* was doing.

"Your magazine is becoming an increasingly important factor," said Mr. Kahn.

The *Magazine* was now sixteen years old, and it was yielding for the first time—this may surprise people—a profit of its own. Money coming from the advisory end of the business had been poured into it for twelve years. The publication might have gone out of the red sooner. Perhaps too much was expended in building up the organization, or in circularization practices which many regarded as wasteful: however, it had taken all those years to put the *Magazine* on a paying basis, exclusive of money received from the advisory services.

Some people consider the stock market a highly speculative proposition. They should try the publishing business.

And the *Magazine's* final financial success was not due to the knowledge, experience, ability or wisdom of any one person. It came from the combined efforts of a large number of people—the organization included well over a hundred. Each played his or her part; some more important than others, but all important to a certain degree.

1924 LIVERMORE AND THE "INTERESTS"

A BEAR POOL—STAMPEDING THE PUBLIC—PUTTING ON THE KIBOSH—OUR GAIN; HIS LOSS—LIVERMORE'S COMEBACK—QUICK RESULTS IN TEXAS LAND TRUST

WE HEAR and read much about large operators in Wall Street gunning for each other. It cannot be denied that they follow this practice. Here is one instance:

In February I went to Palm Beach. As I arrived at Hotel Breakers, Jesse L. Livermore was the first man I met.

"Hello," said I, "I thought you were going to spend this winter in Miami."

"No, I didn't like it down there so I came back here."

We discussed the market for a few minutes and went our respective ways.

He was trading in Hutton's office at The Breakers. The local impression was that he was running the market in American Can and other stocks for the big fellows in New York; and that he was bullish on the market. It didn't seem reasonable to me that the leading financiers would turn the market over to an individual operator at a winter resort fifteen hundred miles from Broadway, with wires likely to be down for hours at a time during bad winter storms.

Then, in Munds & Winslow's office I met a friend who said to me: "Livermore is slipping out of all his stocks.

He's been selling for three days. He thinks it's better to be out of the market for the next week or so."

At the time it was not clear from the action of the market, or from the news, why he should assume such a position. The oil investigation was under way and every day the papers were printing disclosures, but there was nothing in this of primary importance, although it had a sentimental effect.

Then one night as I was going into Bradley's Casino after dinner, I saw Livermore outside one of the private rooms apparently calling certain men together and counting noses. He took them inside and closed the door. "I guess he's forming a new pool," I thought. And as he was out of the market himself, I would have made a bet such a pool would be on the bear side.

The next morning my broker called me up from one of the local offices and said: "There is something very bearish coming out; people who are close to Livermore are selling out all their stocks. Hutton's manager is tipping everyone off. We are loaded with selling orders at the opening. I don't know what it's all about but evidently he's got something up his sleeve. The story is all over Palm Beach."

The opening was weak and there was much evidence of liquidation. The character of the market had completely changed. Stocks were slumping and the air was charged with rumors, all centering around Livermore. A story was going the rounds that he was about to issue a bearish statement.

I sat in Munds & Winslow's office watching the market decline, and along in the morning Livermore hopped out of his car, came into the office, rushed up to the desk near the telegraph operator and said to the manager: "Here, put this over the wire quick as you can." It was a message containing the reputed bear statement.

When this was flashed over the wire and the gist of it appeared on the news ticker a further break took place.

Close analysis of the statement showed that he had nothing particularly new and that there was no real substance or foundation to the bearish attitude he had taken and the raid he seemed to be engineering. Newspapers in New York and elsewhere criticized him for pulling a one-man raid on a stock market that was going along nicely until he mussed it up.

A day or two later I took a train to New York. Upon my arrival, I told certain people who were "in the know" of what I had seen in Palm Beach. I asked what they thought of it. The general opinion was that Livermore was giving himself entirely too much importance, that he was running so many stocks in the market he thought he was the whole thing. It was a case of the tail wagging the dog. "Something was going to happen to him."

In Wall Street parlance this meant that Livermore was about to be given enough rope with which to hang himself. This was done, although I don't know now who donated the rope. About the end of May, the market had a very bearish appearance, but under cover of the unfavorable news and the bear raids by traders, I detected accumulation and put my people long of stocks. No sooner had the word got around the Street: "Wyckoff is bullish; his people are buying," than Livermore issued a statement to the newspapers, stating that in his opinion it was dangerous for anyone to buy at that time.

"Bankers," he said, "would be inviting disaster were

they to attempt to advance prices under prevailing conditions," and so on in like tenor.

We were thus lined up on opposite sides of the market. I hadn't seen him nor asked him what he was so bearish about. We read out of the same book—the tape—but it looked to me as though he had made the wrong interpretation. Time would tell. I recalled the ominous prediction that "something was going to happen to him," but did not know that his days of leadership were so near over for the time being.

The market steadily advanced until around the first of August, when I advised my subscribers to close out their long trades and take the liberal profits which had accrued. Meanwhile rumors about Livermore were flitting through the Street. It was said he was heavily short of the market and was holding his position. I asked how much money he had had to start this play and was told that he had begun with several millions. Soon after, it was reported in Wall Street that Livermore had been forced to cover his shorts and that the final figures left him in debt.

About the third week in July, in an interview which appeared in the New York *World,* Livermore denied that he had suffered serious losses. He stated that he had not been in the stock market for a fortnight, that he had been active only in the grain market. He pointed to the advantages of trading in grain, which was then having wide moves. Incidentally, he charged that the wires leading from his private office in upper Fifth Avenue to the offices of several brokerage houses had been tapped and that much information of a valuable and confidential nature had leaked into hostile ears. All this seemed to bear out the signs that somebody was out to get him.

Reading Wall Street events as they unrolled at the time, I can only assume that this is what happened: On his return from Florida, big people engaged him to handle bear pools. This caused him to believe that the "interests" were trying to unload their securities in anticipation of a lower market. And that was possibly the trap set for him. He doubtless became extremely bearish on his own account and backed his opinion with large personal commitments. I assume this because, left to himself, he could have interpreted the market action only one way—bullish. But in this case he (who knew better than anyone in Wall Street how to read what he saw on the tape) allowed his judgment to be biased by those who engaged his services. The tape was telling me, was telling him, the same thing. "Buy, buy, buy," it was saying. I did what the tape told me, and he did the opposite.

However, true to his former record, he soon recouped his losses. Getting short of 2-dollar wheat he began pyramiding on the bear side, and on the break to below $1.40 he corralled more millions and built himself a new $500,000 house at Great Neck.

Since the Florida episode, however, he, up to the autumn of 1929, kept himself less in the public eye. Perhaps he had interfered too much with the workings of the machinery; or there were "powers" who wished to show him that he was not "running the market." Possibly he has since become more adept at concealing his operations.

Livermore has made, and can make more millions out of small bank accounts than any operator since Jim Keene. Keene rarely ventured the bulk of his fortune in a single play, but Livermore does not hesitate to do so. Supreme confidence in his own judgment, and his ability to come back lead him to take risks that would appall most operators.[1, 2]

* * *

About at the time I came to Wall Street, the Texas-Pacific land trust was organized to take over the trusteeship of some three and a half million acres along the line of the Texas & Pacific Railway, granted at the time the road was built.

Against the land holdings trust certificates were issued to the amount of $10,370,000 par value. The trustees were authorized to sell, lease or exploit the land for the benefit of the certificate holders.

In the late 'nineties these certificates sold at from 5 to 8. Ten years later, they were selling in the 60s. The value of the unsold acreage was increasing and the proceeds were used to buy in and cancel the trust certificates. It was a long-pull proposition in which the fellows who stayed in longest were likely to get the greatest benefit.

I had not thought of this for a long time, until, as we were discussing Texas & Pacific Railway in an editorial

[1] As this book goes to press, the panic of 1929 is underway, with Livermore again very active on the bear side. It is his kind of a market —one in which an overloaded public is obliged to liquidate. He has publicly denied that he is operating for a bear pool and disclaims market leadership. As an individual operator, he is evidently taking full advantage of the fact, as proven in the past, that in bear markets, prices decline more rapidly than they advance in bull markets and that big money is quickly made by those who know how to detect the turning points, and how to pyramid profits on the way down. This should be his greatest coup.

[2] The volume of trading during the day's session on Thursday October 24, 1929 was the greatest ever recorded: 12,900,000 shares on the New York Stock Exchange, and 6,300,000 on the Curb—a total of 19,200,000 in one day. It was exceeded a few days later: 16,400,000 on the Stock Exchange and 7,100,000 on the Curb, Tuesday October 29th. This was nearly one-half as many shares as were dealt in during the entire year 1888.

meeting, the name of the Land Trust suddenly popped into my head. I said to one of my statisticians: "Please look up that Texas & Pacific Land Trust. There have been no transactions in it for a long time. Let me know how it stands."

Watching the tape next day, I noticed a transaction in it at 190. Some one else was having my hunch. I bought some at 195 in case anything should happen. Within an hour or two my man told me that the certificates were in a splendid position to have a move. I did not do a thing to make the stock more active, but activity started, either because my statistician told other folks what he had told me or because of its appearance on the tape after such a long, dull spell. The stock began to hop 10 and 20 points at a time.

On the second day after I bought, the certificates touched 325. Some one called up my broker and offered me $10,000 per hundred shares for a three month's option at 325 on what I had bought at 195.

I did not sell the option. Instead, I sent a man to Texas to get the latest facts on the Trust's position and prospects. From what he dug up there, I decided to hang on to the stock. I eventually sold it at something over 400.

There was a sequel to this incident. Texas Land Trust Certificates reacted to around 300 later. I called in my managing editor and said: "I would like to see this Texas Land Trust owned and controlled by the subscribers to the *Magazine of Wall Street.* There are now outstanding only about 20,000 shares. A few shares each, bought by a few thousand subscribers, would do the trick. I am sure the new owners would realize a big profit eventually."

We discussed the plan, but finally decided it to be impracticable. We could not advise certain subscribers and not the others. If we advised all, the rush to buy would force the price up 200 to 400 points a share. The floating supply was small; there would be few offerings on the way up; the sudden attempt to purchase would bring in a following which would carry the market away from our own people. We decided not to act.

While the final chapter of these certificates has not been written and while at present I have no opinion whatever on them and am not advising either their purchase or sale, it is fair to record that not long after this meeting the certificates sold at above 4,000, which was nearly ten times what I had realized for mine.

I hadn't been at all clever. I should have held on. Each hundred shares could have been sold for over $400,000. Five hundred shares would have been worth $2,000,000.

* * *

1925 THOUGHTS OF A MAGNATE

LUNCH WITH MR. KAHN—NO FUN IN INVESTMENT BANKING

As I was seated in the lounge of the *Majestic,* on my way back from Europe, a young man stepped up to me and said: "Mr. Wyckoff, I am Mr. Otto H. Kahn's secretary. Mr. Kahn has just learned that you are on board and would like to have you take lunch with him tomorrow."

Accepting the invitation, I found Mr. Kahn in his suite, very busy with the final draft of a statement prepared for release to the press upon his arrival in New York. He handed me a copy, gave me a rough idea of its nature and purpose, and said: "Will you please read this over and give me your professional opinion of it."

After I had complied with his request we went into the dining room and were seated with two of his friends, one of them a partner in a Stock Exchange house.

The talk, begun on the news that the heirs of Hugo Stinnes of Germany had just arranged a loan of $10,000,000, soon veered to the prospects of permanent peace in Europe, and the present position of the American holders of foreign bonds.

Before sailing from New York I had been rather bearishly inclined on the general market and none too optimistic on the European political situation; I now mentioned some of the disturbing reports I had gathered while visiting Vienna, Berlin and other European capitals. My host and his friends agreed that much had to be done before the possibility of another war was eliminated. No one disagreed with Mr. Kahn's suggestion that everyone should be willing to invest at least a part of his surplus funds in foreign bonds for the sake of helping the general situation in Europe.

The conversation then turned to the Union Pacific: how E. H. Harriman had taken that wreck of a railroad and made an outstanding success of it, both as a transportation plant and as a holding company for great blocks of other railroad investments.

"Yes," said Mr. Kahn, "Mr. Harriman put that company in such a strong position that nothing serious can ever happen to it."

But Kahn's most interesting observation had to do with the change in investment banking business that had occurred in recent years. Dillon, Read & Co. had just purchased Dodge Bros., giving their check for $146,000,000. "Clarence Dillon certainly stands in the front rank now," said Mr. Kahn. "Nothing is too big for him, and you've got to give him credit for his accomplishments."

"When Mr. Harriman was alive," Mr. Kahn went on, "there was romance and adventure in the business of underwriting securities. When he brought out a big issue (that is, big for those times) we never knew just how it would go; we were not sure that the public could absorb it. He did things in such a masterly way, his vision was so great and so broad, that often we could not fully agree with him as to the probable outcome. But nowadays there are a thousand investment bankers in the country. If they take an average of fifty thousand dollars each, a fifty million dollar issue is all sold before the ink is dry on the underwriting agreement. There is no fun in it at all!"

1926 GENERAL BREAKDOWN

TALK WITH PRESIDENT SLOAN—BUYING HEAVILY INTO A STOCK—DUMPING ON THE POOL—BIG POOL OPERATIONS—SUCKER POOLS—SECRET CODES—STAFF AMBITIONS—DESIRES AND REGRETS—PLANNING TO RETIRE—CLEANING HOUSE AT THE TOP—THEN THE BREAK—DECLINING HEALTH—CLOSING MY INTEREST IN THE MAGAZINE—BEDRIDDEN

During the World War I had bought ten acres of land in Great Neck, Long Island, where I built a twenty-six room country house. The land was delightfully situated about a thousand feet from Little Neck Bay, with many splendid estates all about.

A few years later, Snug Harbor, the estate across the road, was purchased by Alfred T. Sloan, Jr., president of the General Motors Corporation. I strolled over there to call, one Saturday afternoon. Mr. Sloan is tall in body, big in ideas, broad of vision, yet mild-mannered, genial and unassuming to a degree that would lead no one to suspect him of being the head of one of the world's greatest corporations.

We talked of Great Neck, of its advantages for residence, the attractions of its neighborhood, its convenience to New York.

I asked him if he played golf and he replied that he did not have time to play.

"You see," he went on, "I am traveling just about two weeks out of every four. Half my time is on the road, to keep in touch with the heads of all our units throughout the country. You may think this strange, but all I do is visit, consult and make suggestions. I never give an order. Some one has to be up in the conning tower, taking a broad view of the enterprise and that falls to me."

"There seems to be no limit to your company's expansion," I remarked.

"No," said Mr. Sloan. "Our business has grown so large and our available cash surplus so ample that from now on, instead of starting new units, wherever we see a promising field we will enter it by purchasing an existing company. We feel it is better to take a going concern; we get under way more quickly." [1]

Then he told me of some of the developments in motor trucks and their future application. I do not feel at liberty to repeat this, though some of it has begun to materialize.

* * *

With the large following of our several Services, we were at times an important market factor. The combined buying power of subscribers ran into large figures. When a number of factors combined to put a stock in an exceptionally strong position, we put everybody—subscribers to all the services—in it. When this could be done while accumulation was nearing completion and it looked as though we would not have long to wait for the marking-up period, we would unbelt and "play it across the board," as the saying is.

In one case of this kind our subscribers were able to

[1] This policy has since been followed in several fields, here and abroad.

accumulate about one-sixth of the outstanding stock of a certain company. Had we intended them to hold this for permanent investment, I could have secured their proxies and the election of myself, or some representative, on the company's board of directors. But what we were after was the cream of a manipulative move which we knew, from the action of the stock, that insiders were attempting.

The stock started up with little resistance. The pool and our followers had most of the floating supply. All we wanted the manipulators to do was to put it up higher.

The rise continued for about fifteen points. Then the action of stock indicated that the pool was getting ready to unload. I figured this would happen within two or three days. Just before the close, one afternoon, the price was rushed up on large volume in a way that characteristically precedes the dumping process, which, it seemed probable, would begin at the opening the next morning.

Next day there was front page publicity in the newspapers, a high and wide opening with large volume. I sent out "Sell" telegrams to all of our Service subscribers. They succeeded in unloading within a range of from 1 to 3 points of the top, cleaning up 15 to 18 points and several hundred thousand dollars in the aggregate. The stock did not reach those high prices again for many months. We had succeeded in selling on the beautiful market the manipulators had made for us. It was a long while before the pool got out of its own stock.

* * *

Many people have asked me about the inside operations of what is known as the "big banking pool." While there is no such permanent or regular organization, there is a form of joint operation by the largest interests in the Street which acts as a sort of flywheel in keeping the market steady, especially at critical times.

The "interests" in this big banking pool change according to market conditions, the size of contemplated operation, the necessities of the market and the objectives to be attained. When a large amount of securities is accumulated to avoid a disastrous break which might disturb investment confidence, the participants take up and carry their allotted share of the total amount purchased. They unload these holdings when the danger is past and conditions are more favorable.

Then there are the largest of the pools in certain stocks. Morgan ran a big pool in the big Steel markets of 1907 to 1909. In the panic of 1907 this pool gave an unlimited order to buy Steel common, which was then selling as low as 21⅞. There is reason to believe that it took on 500,000 shares. The turning point occurred then and there. Two years later the pool made a tremendous market in United States Steel, and forced the price, although the dividend rate had then only been restored in part, to 94⅞, at which point the tape said that the pool was getting out. The profit on this operation was probably upward of $25,000,000, but this is nothing to what the inside pool in General Motors has made in recent years.

There are, of course, pool operations of various sizes and grades of importance not only among the banking houses but made up of brokers, their clients, and certain large outside operators. Some of the biggest participators in pools are often the right-hand men of the big banking and corporation executives. Place one of those executives on the witness stand and he will probably deny ever taking part in a pool. Examine the private ledgers

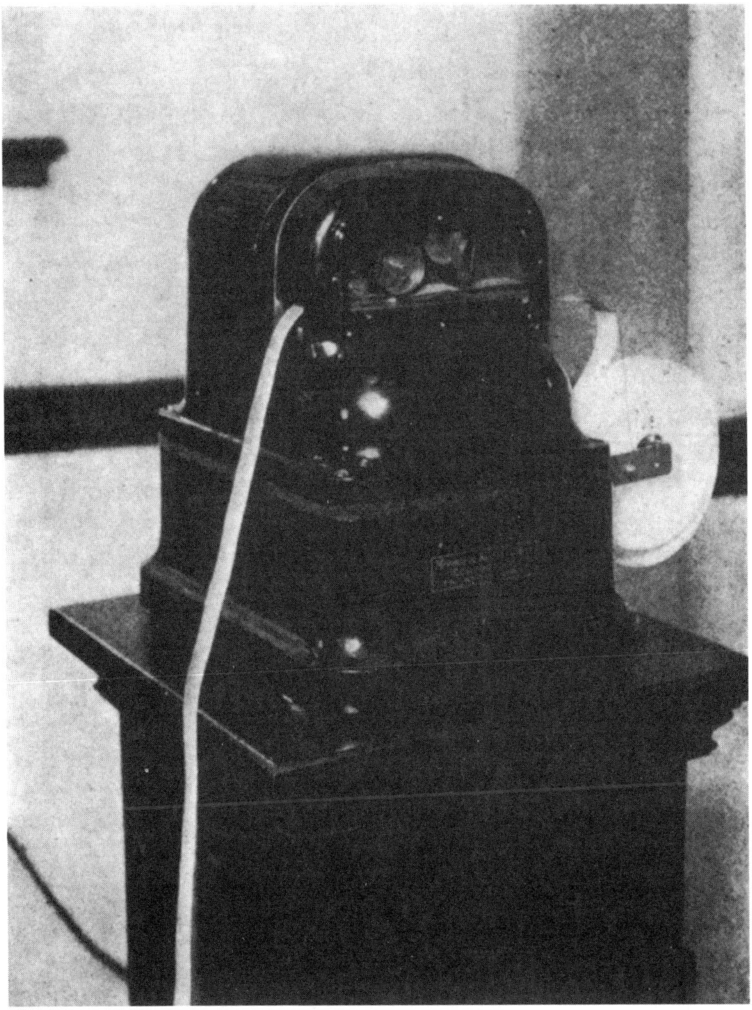

1928. *The New Stock Ticker Which Will Report a Larger Number of Transactions in a Given Time*

and bank books of his Man Friday, however, and you will find that this salaried assistant has been up to his neck in transactions altogether out of proportion to his resources.

These pools and syndicates are a big cause of market fluctuations. They are of all sizes and styles; it may be said that there is at least one pool operating in every stock on the list. Often there are several; there may be many in a single stock. They range from pools holding a few thousand shares to pools with hundreds of thousands of shares. They are usually managed either by one man or a small group.

Participation in a pool does not insure profits. Even pools made up of insiders and of their close associates frequently misjudge a situation and suffer losses. Insiders are often bad judges of the securities of which they are supposed to know everything; they know their company's affairs, but do not understand the stock market. If this be true of the insider, one can understand the handicaps of the outsider.

The greatest danger to the outsider is of being landed in what is known as a "sucker pool."

One day I found one of my friends—a partner in a prominent banking house—all worked up over the bullish possibilities in a certain low-priced tobacco stock. He was organizing a pool in it; had all his traders participating and was getting out a bullish circular. He said the stock would double in value in the next few months. I asked him what was the basis of his prediction. The facts he gave me in answer were not convincing. Tobacco companies do not double their earnings overnight. The thing didn't smell good.

Not long after that this stock shrunk to just half its

value. My naïve friend had been used to do a piece of dirty work. A tobacco man wanted to sell 50,000 shares of this stock. He could not find a market for such a quantity at anything around prevailing prices. By inducing my friend to form the pool, he created a market for the 50,000 shares several points above the figure at which the stock had been selling. Result: Clients and friends of the firm holding the bag, the big man holding the cash. When the price of the stock shrunk 50 per cent he was able to buy 100,000 shares with the money he had derived from the sale of the 50,000.

* * *

For many years there have been methods of transmitting secret advices by means of code letters and words printed in certain sections of daily newspapers. Formerly these advices were brief and simple, though quite effectively used among those who were "wise." They have since been greatly elaborated. If you have some knowledge of the subject, studying these signals, advices or forecasts, you can see that they emanate from the headquarters of important interests, and that they forecast the trend of the market in general, and certain stocks.

People may think this improbable; entirely too uncanny in this day of modern business procedure. But I know exactly what I am writing about!

However, I cannot advise anyone to search for this "Open Sesame." There never was a secret code which could not be changed on short notice.

* * *

In our advisory work on the Staff and allied services, much as we strove, we failed now and then to a degree that was embarrassing to us and disappointing to our clients. We would have liked to be infallible in every bit of advice and every opinion we issued. In the very nature of things, we could not be.

We would have liked to distribute profits and losses among our clients so that none might have too much and none too little; we would have been happy to anticipate profits and put the best trades in the hands of those who had had unprofitable ventures. But as each transaction in the stock market is a step in the dark when it is made, and no living man can tell its outcome until it is completed, we could do no such thing.

In this business of guiding a large clientele, selecting good opportunities was not the hardest task. The really difficult thing was to ascertain the turning points in the market. If I had my choice of the one most desirable thing to know about the stock market, I would choose to know *when* rather than *why* or *which.* That is, I would rather know *when* to buy or sell than why I should do so, or which stock.

For many years I searched for one man who would do this better than I. I wanted the best man obtainable. I would have been glad to start him on a salary of $25,000 a year. But as I could not find him, the best I could do was to train others into the intricate task of calling the turns, and this was a course of training that required years.

Men could be found who expertly analyzed banking and corporate conditions; selected safe and promising investment or speculative issues. But the man who could sense the top of a bull market, or the bottom of a bad break, or the important turning points in the intermediate swings, that one was the most difficult of all to find.

My reason for wanting such a man must be plain to any reader who is in business or forms part of any important organization. The concern that depends upon one man for its principal executive work is in a comparatively weak position; for anything can happen to anybody; and if that one man is ill, dies, resigns, or goes on a vacation, the organization is greatly handicapped.

From 1923 on, I put the members of my organization through a series of tests to develop their independent judgment and to train them in getting along without me. Absences on trips about the country and to Europe were part of this program. The organization did well under the circumstances, but there were times when I had to hop on a train or steamer and come back in a hurry; at least I felt that I should. Most business men will know what I mean. We gain the impression, after running a business for many years, that no one can do it quite as well as ourselves.

I was beginning to plan to retire and I had so informed the Staff. Also that the sooner they took responsibility upon themselves the better I would like it. It was up to them to show me that they could run the business profitably to all concerned—especially to the clients.

About the latter part of February I was able to give them a striking demonstration in the art of getting full benefit from an important turning point. The market had been advancing for many months. It began to look tired. There was increasing evidence of inside and banking house distribution. We had been working on the bull side and our people had not only realized large profits on the way up, but were then long a full line of securities bought on our advice, and long many others which they had selected and bought in addition. At this

1792-1928. *Medallion Showing the Buttonwood Tree under Which Trading Began in Lower Wall Street and the Completed Stock Exchange Building in* 1922

point I called a meeting of the Staff and went over the situation as it appeared to me. We found enough elements in the situation; we decided it was time to unload all holdings. This was not only so that our clients would realize the large profits accrued; but so that their capital should be released and with it their buying power when the anticipated decline should bring stocks down to low levels.

The advices of the Wyckoff Analytical Staff and the Trend Trading Service went out: "Sell at the market."

We had hardly completed our selling, the last of which took place at the opening, Monday, March 1, when a panicky decline lasting three days carried prices down to an average level which wiped out a large percentage of the previous rise.

In order to make this a matter of record—for no other advisory organization, and, so far as we could learn, no important brokerage house, had sent out advices to their clients "to clean house" at the time—we issued the circular on the following page.

That was the kind of work we aimed to do; these were the results we strove to secure for our clients. If we could have accomplished this in every campaign, we would have been more delighted than our clients, for the real satisfaction a man derives from his work is not in the amount of money which it yields, but in the skill and efficiency with which he operates.

* * *

All through the years following the end of the war, and up to this time, I continued to write scores of editorials and articles for the *Magazine of Wall Street.* In addition to the series on Southern Pacific, and other

RECORD OF RESULTS
Semi-investment Service
RICHARD D. WYCKOFF ANALYTICAL STAFF, INC.

As a matter of record, we wish to report that we have accomplished for those of our Associate Members who have followed all of our advices for the entire ten months' period ending March 4, 1926.

Profits Actually Realized on 100 Share Trades..	$36,450
Losses Incurred On a Few Losing Trades.....	4,800
Net Profits Without Deducting Commissions, Tax or Interest	$31,650
Cost of this Service for a Full Year Equal to less than 2% of the Profit Realized, or..........	$500

But this is not the whole story. The rest of the facts are these:

Before the biggest break in years, which occurred between 2 and 3 P.M., Monday, March 1, our Associate Members, on our fast-wire advice, were out of all the stocks which we had definitely recommended and in which the above net profits were secured. They were also specifically advised (while the market was somewhat under the extreme high levels), to close out all the highly speculative and vulnerable securities which they had bought on their own judgment. We gave positive advice to sell these. We advised each subscriber which of his stocks to sell. This is the way our individual service operates.

Therefore, when the panicky breaks of March 1, 2, and 3 occurred, our Members were standing ready with the cash with which to repurchase the numerous great bargains that were then offered.

By 3 P.M. Thursday, March 4, these purchases, none of which was more than 48 hours old, showed profits ranging from one to seven points.

features which I worked up, my leading articles defined the position of the stock market and carried definite forecasts as to its probable direction. Usually Saturdays were devoted to this work but frequently the articles were dictated direct to the typewriter or the dictaphone in the office. Other days, from nine to five, I devoted to a study of the market and the problems of the business.

As the Managing Editor and his assistants became more thoroughly trained in editorial requirements and standards, my work with him was reduced to consultation, suggestion, criticism. I did not wait for the editorial meetings, but sent memos to him whenever ideas occurred to me; often no one but he knew of these. I was not looking for credit but for good results.

As time went on, the Market Outlook was, in the main, written by him, but the conclusions and forecasts therein were mine.

The question of my severing my relations with the *Magazine* came up. He said: "Mr. Wyckoff, I would be lost without you."

"Oh, I don't think so," said I. "No man is ever so indispensable that he cannot be replaced."

* * *

For some years my health had been giving increasing evidence of the strain under which I worked and lived. I had never been seriously ill since childhood, but few constitutions, even of iron, could have stood the continuous stress put on mine. Hard work is one thing: nervous work under tension is worse; and probably the worst of all is a combination of these, with emotional anxiety.

I now found it necessary to draw my association with

the *Magazine of Wall Street* to a close. The conditions which brought this about are of no concern to the reader; but they were of much concern to me and to my intimate friends. Because of personal considerations which for some years had been accumulating, I determined to make a great financial sacrifice, in order that I might immediately be relieved of certain responsibilities, factors and contacts. In May, 1926, I made an arrangement by which the corporation which owns the *Magazine of Wall Street,* by redeeming certain securities, might return to me a small part of the value I had created.

I did not sell my interest to anyone, nor to any group. Statements to the effect that I was "bought out" and that I had only "a small minority interest" were merely interested propaganda, made for purely personal reasons. I did not desire then and do not desire now to dignify these with a detailed reply.

The *Magazine* which I conceived, founded, fostered and edited for nineteen years was by that time strongly intrenched, with a large circulation, growing advertising patronage at rising rates. It had the esteem of the financial community. Its earnings were large; its liquid assets over half a million; its organization big, broad and efficient. Earnings gave strong promise of doubling and trebling within the next few years.

In the face of all this, my friends could not understand why I accepted, for my interest in the enterprise, an amount of money which represented about one-third of its actual value at the time and a still smaller fraction of the value it promised to have within two or three years. But there are times when greater satisfaction is to be obtained than that of holding out for additional money and going to law about it. Peace of mind is worth more than many dollars. Ideals founded on mere accumulation of money are built on shifting sands.

Having disposed of my interest in the *Magazine,* I began to plan my retirement from the advisory services. Being sole owner of the Richard D. Wyckoff Analytical Staff, Inc., I decided to take the principal executives into partnership by presenting them with nearly one-half of the capital stock, and arranging a trusteeship which would keep the controlling interest from getting out of their hands in case anything happened to me.

Early in June while dining at a club with friends, I began to feel ill. A physician was called; he found that I had had an attack of angina pectoris, which in plain language is the bursting of an artery in the heart. On the following morning the doctor sent me to my home in Great Neck, and there, for several days, it was an open question whether I would live or not.

The change in my condition from that of a highly charged and rapidly functioning business dynamo to a more or less wrecked and seemingly useless piece of machinery was demoralizing enough without the personal and business situation involved. I had been directing a large enterprise, a staff, many men; I now myself was being managed—by doctors and by nurses. Examinations; consultations; medicines; a wheel chair. Endless days and nights. Finally at the end of three months I was given permission to go downstairs; then to my place in the mountains—still in the care of a trained nurse.

1927 UP AND DOWN AGAIN

RECUPERATION—OVERWORK—ANOTHER ATTACK

ORDERED to a warm climate for the winter, I first went to Florida, then to California. It seemed impossible for me to stay in one place more than a week or so. Changing my location was the only form of activity in which I could indulge. My doctor wired: "Stop making so many one-night stands. Settle down somewhere and get some repose."

I did—for a few weeks.

The suddenness of my removal from the business had put a heavy burden on those to whom the management had fallen. They had had difficulties; numerous readjustments were needed. I returned to New York in the spring and undertook these. I gave several hours of concentrated effort every day for about a week—and then my physician was responding again to a hurry call. Seven times that afternoon he administered a hypodermic. I was carried away on a stretcher, out by the New Street door of the building, and into an ambulance. Once more I spent most of the summer in bed.

1928 CLOSING THE ACCOUNT

GAINING STRENGTH—WRITING THIS BOOK—A STROKE—CLOSING OUT STAFF HOLDINGS—OUT OF BUSINESS—PLANS ABANDONED AND PASSED ALONG—NEWSPAPER FINANCIAL PAGES—WALL STREET COLLEGE—COMPENSATION

ANOTHER winter in California, this time under conditions of better health and more strength—enough to write the greater part of this book within a period of two months.

When, the following spring, the doctor told me to stop taking medicine and to begin to play golf, I had visions of resuming my work in Wall Street. But no! I took a long automobile ride—and my right arm and leg became partially paralyzed. Diagnosis: A small cerebral hemorrhage.

"Give up all business," the specialist said. "Close out any interest you have. Give up every management or concern over any management. Lead the life of Riley. Go up north in the summer and go to Egypt in the winter. Don't do any work."

Another couple of summer months in bed. More doctors. More nursing. An emergency call early in the morning. Any little overexertion or lack of caution led to trouble.

I gradually withdrew from affairs. I sold my interest in the Wyckoff Analytical Staff to my associates who had worked in it with me. They formed a new company, which acquired full control. And so it came about that in December, at the end of forty years in Wall Street,[1] I found myself actually and completely out of business.

* * *

My problems in former years had been those of most men: to establish myself in business; develop an earning power which would yield a large surplus over living expenses; attain financial independence. Like the majority, I found my expenses increasing, doubling and trebling; but that side of the ledger seldom bothered me. Always I concentrated on methods of increasing my gross income. So long as this could be done, the rest was of no concern. A man may spend $50,000 a year in living expenses without being extravagant. This depends upon the relation between his expenses and the earnings of his business or profession, and his other income.

But in working out these problems, one generally disregards the factor of wear and tear on one's constitution; on machinery which cannot be fully replaced once damaged or broken. And there is the element of age; few of us take that into account.

Looking back at my career, I see clearly that I continued at high pressure for too many years, and when certain additional strains were loaded upon those already placed upon me by business, I could not withstand them without a break.

My physician tells me that diseases of the heart due to excessive business activity are increasing at an alarming rate and he suggests that I cannot do better than to in-

[1] As the Stock Exchange was first established in 1792, that institution was, in 1928, only 136 years old. Forty years, therefore, equals nearly one-third of its existence.

clude here a word of warning to those who might be afflicted with a passion for work, or who might be obliged or be tempted to overwork.

Business organizations, advertising and selling campaigns, putting over deals, marketing securities, fighting competition, gaining prestige, making money—these are not all there is in life. But with most of us, it takes some sort of shock, it would seem, to awaken us to the fact that we are not married to these things; that beyond a certain point they are not necessary in our lives. It is not until we extricate ourselves and gain distance, and time to consider, that we begin to see that they are only a few things out of the many that make life worth while.

* * *

Had my health permitted, however, I would have undertaken two enterprises I had long had in mind. These were:

(1) The establishment of a syndicate which would supply material for the financial pages of daily newspapers throughout the country.

(2) The foundation and financing of a college in Wall Street.

As to the first: Daily newspapers have done little to keep pace with the development of the stock and bond markets in the last decade. Newspapers of today give the public but little more in the way of real news, clear analysis and helpful information than they did ten years ago, considering the increased size of the markets. The vastly greater number of listed stock and bond issues; the increased volume of trading, combined with the enormous public participation, call for something newer, bigger, broader and entirely different from what is now regarded as a good financial page.

Morning and evening papers all over the country carry prices, volumes, quotations and statistics relating to the day's transactions, but show little or nothing of what is really going on in the market itself and little of practical value to those who desire to trade and invest intelligently.

There could be added to one principal daily paper in each important city (preferably an evening paper) from one to three pages of material so valuable that it would be sought by everyone interested in the stock or bond markets, or in banking, economics, finance and business. This additional material would bring in increased circulation and advertising; instead of being an expense, it would be a producer of revenue and would add greatly to the prestige of the publications carrying it.

The other piece of work that I contemplated, The Wall Street College, was an institution in the very heart of Wall Street—in one of the skyscrapers! It would have provided educational facilities to all who desired to learn the principles, machinery, methods, practices and technique of the vast operations centered in and about the Stock Exchange, including brokerage, trading and investment science, banking and corporate finance. Students and graduates of such an institution would become better clerks, brokers, customers' men, bond dealers, salesmen, traders, investors, bankers, bank clerks, financiers and business men.

It was not my intention to do this for profit.

Now, being unable to carry out these plans, I pass the suggestions along to my friends in the Street who may see merit therein.

Although it is impossible for me to be again active in Wall Street, I am fortunately not condemned to idleness. My health is now more completely restored than I ever had hoped it could be. I can now do a considerable amount of work, studying and writing.[1] I find great pleasure in these; also in literature and in travel.

I feel a good deal—after the grind of long years—like a boy let out of school.

Everything has its compensation. Following all the turmoil, what appeared at first to be a calamity was merely a forerunner of health, peace and contentment.

I believe I can now do the most important work of my life; that my best years are yet to come!

[1] Some of my friends have suggested that I undertake to teach say one hundred people the fine points of what experience has taught me so that they may be able to operate successfully in the stock market.

INDEX